ALLOCATIVE EFFICIENCY OF RICE FARMERS

About the Author

Nursadh Ali (*b*. 1963) is Lecturer (SG) in Economics who is also the Head of the Department in Jawaharlal Nehru College, Pasighat, Arunachal Pradesh. Dr. Ali obtained his higher education from the Visva-Bharati University, West Bengal. He did his Ph.D. in Agricultural Economics from the same University. He has been the visiting Fellow in Indiana University, Bloomington, USA (2001-02) with the Overseas Post Doctoral Fellowship on Environmental Economics of the World Bank. Dr. Ali has published a large number of research papers/articles on various economic issues in reputed academic journals. His field of research is sustainable development and natural resource management through institutional approach.

ALLOCATIVE EFFICIENCY OF RICE FARMERS

Study of West Bengal

Nursadh Ali

CONCEPT PUBLISHING COMPANY, NEW DELHI-110059

Cataloging in Publication Data—DK
Courtesy: D.K. Agencies (P) Ltd. <docinfo@dkagencies.com>

Ali, Nursadh, 1963-
Allocative efficiency of rice farmers : study of West Bengal / Nursadh Ali.
p. cm.
Study conducted in the Birbhum District, West Bengal, India.
Includes bibliographical references (p.)
Includes index.
ISBN 8180693465

1. Rice—Yields—India—Birbhum (District). 2. Rice—Technological innovations—India—Birbhum (District). 3. Agricultural productivity—India—Birbhum (District). I. Title.

DDC 633.180 954 14 22

ISBN 81–8069–346-5

First Published 2007

Published and Printed by
Ashok Kumar Mittal
Concept Publishing Company
A/15-16, Commercial Block, Mohan Garden
New Delhi (INDIA)

Phones : 25351460, 25351794
Fax : 091–11–25357103
Email : publishing@conceptpub.com

To My Parents

Preface

The so-called green revolution in Indian agriculture has been the central focus of debate and discussion for a long time. There is no doubt that in many parts of the country the improved agricultural technologies helped increasing the production and productivity of some major crops practiced by Indian farmers. In spite of this fact the rate of adoption of these superior technologies is not uniform with respect to crops as well as of locations. The issues of this field of study are related with respect to the adoption of new agricultural technologies and the problem faced by the farmers and their effects on the society and economy in developing countries. One facet of constraints encountered by the farmers in accepting the available improved technologies is the shortage of capital as most of the farmers of the country are small and marginal and hence economically poor. Does this prove that the rich big farmers are found to adopt the technologies to a larger extent? There are two distinct aspects of accepting the modern agricultural technologies—replacement of traditional technologies by the improved technologies and application of improved technologies as recommended. The first feature of this problem has been dealt widely by many scholars and some few others have also tried to mention the various reasons of the second problem in conventional way. In fact, Indian farmers are not found to be allocatively efficient and it requires measuring how far they are inefficient under certain other constraints besides the basic problems they face in adopting the new agricultural technologies. Various parts of the country may find different types of problems while meeting the local needs in addition to the other constraints. Therefore, exogenous constraints such as local needs and social goals which may impede in adopting the recommended technologies at its full rate are to be incorporated in the programming of efficient allocation. The present book has taken these issues into consideration while finding out the allocatively efficient combination of rice technologies in West Bengal. This volume has been written keeping in view the needs of the students at Master Level of agricultural economics besides to meet the needs of the researchers of this field.

The book has been divided into seven chapters. The first chapter deals with introduction that comprising the problem statement, appropriate technology, objectives and limitations of the study. Second chapter contains systematic presentation of a comprehensive review of literature relevant to the present study. Third chapter of the book is concerned with the theoretical framework, operationalization of different concepts used in the study and formulation of some hypotheses related with the present study. Agro-climatic discussion and general information about the study area have been presented in chapter four of the book. Chapter five deals with the methodological aspects of the study. Results and discussion of the present study have been presented in Chapter six of the book. Chapter seven contains the summary and conclusion of the study.

This book is the product of help and cooperation of many people and institutions. The Indian Council of Agricultural Research (ICAR), New Delhi gave me permission to use some of the data of the sponsored project entitled—"Field Level Constraints in Crop Production and Identification of Appropriate Technologies in Sub-humid Lateritic Belt of West Bengal", which was conducted in Palli Siksha Bhavan of Visva Bharati by Dr. K.M.B. Rahim as Principal Investigator. I have benefited immensely from many discussions and valuable inputs on draft manuscript from Dr. K.M.B. Rahim who supervised the work at Visva-Bharati, Prof. K. Sain who is regarded as an expert at BCKV, Nadia, Prof. Ashok Rudra and Prof. Amiya Gupta of Visva-Bharati, Dr. D. Dasgupta and Dr. S. Chakraborty of PSB, Visva-Bharati. I acknowledge my indebtedness to all of them. I remain grateful to Md. Mohiuddin, Manager, Agriculture Farm, PSB, Visva-Bharati, staff members of Mahammad Bazar Community Development Block and Adaptive Research Farm, Nalhati of Birbhum; for their support and cooperation by providing inputs of this study. I desire to express my heartiest thanks to Sri Santosh Basu and all the members of his family for their valuable suggesions, useful comments, moral encouragement and constant inspiration during the preparation of the manuscript.

I shall consider my efforts meaningful if my book is found useful by the readers and serves its intended purposes.

Santiniketan **Nursadh Ali**

Contents

List of Tables

1

Introduction

Introduction of modern agricultural technology during mid-sixties in Indian agriculture which has been termed as 'Green Revolution' is indeed extremely significant for the country's economy in general and rural economy in particular since this is one that single factor which has given the present shape of the country in spite of the fact of its limitations from multiple angles. Among the improved agricultural crops rice is considered as the most important produce in Indian agriculture and agricultural scientists have innovated many high yielding varieties (HYVs) of rice which are responsive to the inputs like irrigation, chemical fertilizers and pesticides. Every improved variety has been proved to have potential yield at some level (certainly much higher than the traditional varieties) subject to the use of the prescribed doses of inputs and these technologies are recommended in a package form. Since, agriculture now is viewed as an enterprise, the objective of the farmers should be to maximize the profit and that is possible if they are found to be efficient in allocation of their resources which requires selection of the best or optimal combination of outputs by means of the most efficient combination of inputs. Hence, achievement of maximum output depends on the application of all the inputs at prescribed levels. But, unfortunately Indian farmers are found to accept, in most cases, only a part of the available improved technologies for rice production. Because, in selecting of both the combinations, farming community may face a large number of problems or constraints. As a result, rice yield in the farmers' field may remain below the potential yield and consequently there may exist a significant yield gap of rice. The low yield and the consequent yield gap can be explained by the low rate of adoption of modern rice production technologies and divergence from the recommended doses of inputs, methods and practices.

On the one hand, the responsible factors which prevent farmers from the exploitation of full potential of the improved technologies may be socio-economic, infrastructure, agro-biological, managerial, and technological in nature. While, on the other, the available technologies might be inconsistent with the particular setting of farms which is a complex of economic, cultural and political considerations. The technologies prescribed may not be properly suited to the local resource endowment or counteract with the objectives of farmers' preferences or societies' demand. Hence, the yield gap can be narrowed down either by removing the constraints responsible for application of improved rice technologies at recommended level, or by identifying the appropriate technologies for rice production which is suitable for local resource endowments and consistent with local needs and social goals. So far the first solution is concerned many efforts have been made but the results are not satisfactory and here emphasis has been given to the second form of solution by looking for the appropriate combination of inputs and outputs. The appropriate technology (which is the precondition for allocative efficiency) is defined as the technology which is technically feasible, exactly consistent with the particular setting of the complex sector and does properly suit the resource endowment. Therefore, the profit maximization function must be constrained in finding the allocative efficiency of the farmers.

In view of the above background the present study is an attempt to measure the yield gap of different rice varieties practiced by the farmers and to determine the important factors with their relative contribution on yield gap of rice. It has also been emphasized to identify the constraints related to the adoption of improved rice technologies at its recommended levels and to identify the allocatively efficient set of technology (appropriate technology) for various categories of farmers in rice production.

India is a developing country in which agriculture provides the live supports to the majority of rural Indians and the development of the country is contingent upon on the advancement of this vital sector of the economy. And very rightly it was given topmost priority in First Five Year Plan after the independence of the country. Till mid-sixties, expansion of agriculture was the main concern of the planners and policy makers which turned to the intensive agricultural policy with the innovation of modern agricultural technologies. These modern technologies have been found to be more productive than the then existing local technologies though they are not considered as well spread and equally useful for all places and crops.

Agriculture occupies the most vital place in Indian economy since it is not only the main source of livelihood of the majority of the countrymen but also a tradition and the most common way of life. Agriculture has been enjoying since immemorial a place of pride in our economic and social life.

Problem Statement

However, Indian planners have been concerned with the basic problems of increasing agricultural production. The first step for intensifying cultivation was taken in 1959 with the introduction of Intensive Agricultural Development Programme (IADP) in seven districts in India. The IADP approach envisaged adoption of package of practices by participating farmers in terms of fertilizers, seeds, pesticides and use of improved implements for cultivation and intercultural operations.

In order to increase the output of land, the "New Strategy" for agricultural development, which was initiated in 1966, in essence called for the implementation of High Yielding Varieties Programme (HYVP) in all the districts selected under IADP and IAAP schemes. The strategy was concerned with higher productivity of crops per acre, but with multiple cropping. The HYVP has assumed "crucial importance" in the Planning Commission's agricultural development strategy. The Fourth Plan put the new strategy as follow: (i) to supply scientific techniques and knowledge of agricultural production at all stages, particularly in the fields; (ii) to select a few areas with assured rainfall and irrigation for concentrated application of package of practices based on improved varieties of seed concentrated application of package of practices based on improved varieties of seed responsive to heavy doses of fertilizers and availability of inputs and to fix special targets of production of foodgrains for each area.......

> No doubt, a considerable change in the method of cultivation has been noticed after the introduction of new agricultural strategy in Indian agriculture. The area, under HYV went up from 1.5 million hectares in 1960-61 to 43 million hectares in 1980-81, and it went up further to 59 million hectares in

1984-85. However, this is accounting only for less than 50 per cent of the total cultivated area of the country.

The use of pesticides and fertilizers in Indian agriculture shows a way in which Indian agriculture has been changing from a traditional to modern stage. The consumption of NPK (Nitrogen, Phosphate and Potash) increased from 2,93,000 tonnes in 1960-61 to 87,22,000 tonnes in 1985-86. In the same period pesticides consumption increased from 45,000 tonnes to 55,000 tonnes. It has been estimated that the productivity of foodgrains increased from 710 kgs. per hectare in 1960-61 to 1154 kgs. in 1984-85.

As a matter of fact, rice is the most important crop in Indian agriculture and emphasis was given to implement modern agricultural technology for rice cultivation under the new strategy of crop production. It is a staple food of Indian people, particularly the people of West Bengal. The yield per hectare of rice in India is abnormally low as compared to the developed countries. The low rate of rice productivity is explained as a fact of the practices of traditional method of production by Indian farmers.

However, the productivity of rice has not increased significantly as expected after the introduction of modern technology in agriculture. Whereas, in the next 10 years the country will require to almost double the annual agricultural production capacity. But there is very little scope for expanding the area under different crops. No doubts the availability of management responsive varieties of crops and economically viable technology have helped in increasing the rice production in some of the States but the production of rice has not yet reached the warranted level. There is still scope for increasing production by following multiple cropping and through proper use of improved agricultural technology. The benefits of improved technology have been demonstrated on farmers' field through National Demonstration and Operation Research Projects. One may notice an awesome gap between the average yields obtained on farmers' field under National Demonstration Projects and the existing crop yields obtained under identical condition by the farmers. Different studies, conducted on this issue, indicate that there is a significant gap between potential yield and actual yield in Indian agriculture. The actual production break through is yet to come about. All these indicate that if the gap is reduced, the production may be increased remarkably.

According to various studies, conducted by different persons, it is really a difficult task to identify the potential yield, and there arises such confusion when one talks about 'yield gap'. This confusion stems up from one fact that there is not a single yield gap but whole range of yield gaps or differences between actual and potential yield (Barker, 1978). When working on Indian farms Mukherjee (1977) defined yield gap as the difference between the highest yield on a farm or at the experiment station and the national average yield. One of the common accepted approaches is to compare the yields of experimental station or demonstration plots with considering as potential yield the actual yield (Mukherjee, 1977; Herdt and Wickman, 1975). Mukhopadhyay (1982) reported that difference between achievable production and actual production is the 'production gap' or 'yield gap'. According to Izum and Ranatunge (1974) there is a very big difference in yield per acre in Sri Lanka. Zia and others (1984) reported that in Pakistan there was a big yield gap between potential rice yields and the yields actually achieved by farmers.

There are sufficient rice production technologies in the laboratories, but it has been estimated that only a small percentage of innovated improved rice production technology is accepted by the Indian farmers. Since in the real life situation the farmers are not in a position to continue the use of all the technologies recommended, there is a technological gap causing yield gap.

Patil (1964) analyzed yield data of paddy found that there was no appreciable reason for low yield; this was mainly due to the failure of farmers to adopt improved practices recommended by the State Department of Agriculture. Davidson and Martin (1965) concluded that yield gap was the result of limited input investment by the farmers.

The important question is what factor kept farmers using the recommended inputs that would increase yield and profits? Several factors can influence the application of modern agricultural technology and consequently the yield gap. Study of these factors in their proper perspective is essential.

The constraints to increase yield were considered to be the constraints to the adoption of modern rice varieties and other components of modern rice technology such as chemical fertilizer, pesticides and weed control. These could include the characteristics of technology, farmers' resource constraints and various non-farm factors that prevent successful application of modern technology.

The factors preventing farmers from applying all the necessary inputs may be physical, agro-bio-logical, socio-cultural, technological, economic and infrastructural relating to supply, services, etc. The physical conditions prevailing on some farms may prevent the farmers from using the full potential of the modern rice technology. Among the physical factors, perhaps water availability, quality of soil and climate are the most important elements determining the high yield.

It is quite embarrassing to note that the last decade of the previous century Indian agriculture still suffers from lack of assured irrigation which is the key factor of modern technology. In India only 30.4 per cent cultivated land is irrigated. Practically the fate of agriculture of the rest 64 per cent of the cultivated land depends on the gamble of monsoon rainfall. Assured irrigation is one of the most important components of the modern improved technology package.

Agriculture of this predominantly rain fed tract suffers not only from water scarcity but also from the poor soil condition. The productivity of rice mostly depends upon the fertility of soil. Along with irrigation and soil productivity climate is also considered as another important factor in achieving the high rice yield.

Economic factors, perhaps, are the most important preventing the farmers in applying the full recommendation improved farm practices. In our country predominant small and marginal farmers suffer from the lack of capital whereas the modern agricultural practices are capital intensive. The lack of credit facility may also be considered as a cause of non-adoption of modern rice production technologies.

Supply of labour and wage rate is also considered as the cause of non-implementation of modern agricultural practices in its full package. Lacks of marketing facilities, price policy and high prices of agricultural inputs are assumed as economic factors responsible for non-adoption.

Lack of education, ignorance and ineffective service may also contribute the poor and limited expansion of new agricultural strategy. Indifferent attitudes of village officials, their limited involvement in the overall development exercise and lack of administrative will power may be considered as some other reasons which keep the new agricultural strategy away from the recipients. The problem thus, remains to create conditions conducive to universal acceptance of modern agricultural technologies in order to make it uniformly effective.

Thus, there may be a combination of reasons—physical, economic and social—that explains why farmers are not getting a high yield which is possible with modern improved technology.

The production gap of rice estimated under different studies is significant. In an annual report of IRRI (1981) it was reported that the largest contribution to yield gap of 2.89 tonnes per hectare was obtained with low level of fertilizer application followed by insect control and weed control. The Operation Research Project on Integrated Management of Rice Pest at Warrangal has indicated that the yield gap between the yields obtained by farmers and those under the project is primarily due to three factors, namely, inefficient use of fertilizers, weed control and insect-pest control. These practices contribute to this gap to the extent of 52, 23 and 25 per cent respectively. The National Council of Applied Economic Research (1979) reported a positive correlation between observed yield and observed level of fertilizer use. Tripathy (1977), reported that water management, disease and pest control were responsible for 50.63 per cent of yield gap in rice. Kuo *et al.* (1977) reported that fertilizer itself contributed 60 per cent of yield gap in Taiwan.

So it can be concluded that the alternative way out to meet the challenge of food shortage is to increase per hectare productivity of agricultural crops. In other words, the challenge of food shortage can be confronted successfully by achieving the "achievable yield potential" of the crops at farmers' field that is by minimizing "yield gap" at farmers' field. This yield gap at farmers' field is the resultant effect of field level constraints and non-adoption of improved package of practices. Henceforth, to minimize the yield gap it is quite essential to win over the field level constraints and non-adoption behaviour of the farmers. And consequently to confront the field level constraint and non-adoption behaviour of the farmers to attain higher per hectare yield, it is essential to identify the field level constraints and reasons for non-adoption and assessment of their relative contribution of yield gap.

Appropriate Technology

The technological gap or input gap and the consequent result of yield gap in rice implies that the available rice technologies may not be exactly consistent with the particular setting of farms which is a complex of economic, cultural and potential considerations and may not properly suit the local resource endowment.

According to Desai (1984) the slow rate of adoption of high yielding varieties in the Eastern India indicates that the correct rice technology has not yet been evolved for various parts of area.

Kuader (1984) views on agricultural technology development favouring the development of indigenous technology based on local skills and resources, and the kind of technology that fits more appropriately into the local circumstances.

Therefore, the appropriate technology is to be identified which is suitable and profitable to the Indian farmers, consistent with the local resource endowment, and which satisfy local needs and social goals.

Objectives of the Study

The general objective of the present study is to make constraint analysis of rice production and identification of appropriate technology for the rice farmers in Birbhum District of West Bengal State. However, the specific objectives of the study are:

(i) To estimate the gap between potential yield and actual farm yield of rice.
(ii) To identify the factors responsible for yield gap in rice production, and factors responsible for technological gap and their relative contribution therein.
(iii) To identify the field level constraints in the adoption of improved rice production technology at recommended level.
(iv) To identify the appropriate technologies for rice production over different size of farms.
(v) To implicate some policy measures based on the study.

Limitations of the Study

The present study, similar to other investigation of this nature suffers from limitations of time, funds, conveyance study area and sample. However, efforts have been made to making the study as objective and systematic as possible. The findings of the study are based on the information supplied by the respondent farmers. Hence, the objectivity would be limited to the extent the respondents gave the information honestly and sincerely.

2

Review of the Literature

A comprehensive review of literature is an important part of any scientific investigation. Such review in the related field supports the researcher to acquaint with the work done before and the findings obtained by such studies. Besides, it provides a basis for formulating a theoretical framework as well as an insight into the methods and procedures along with deriving hypotheses. Finally, it renders guide for the interpretation of findings. The present study aims at measuring the yield gap of rice, identifying constraints on rice production through the application of modern technology and identifying the appropriate technology for the rice farmers. The review of literature relevant to the investigation is being presented under the following heads:

Extent of yield gap and factors related to yield gap of rice.
Factors related to technological gap
Constraints in adoption of improved technologies for rice production
Appropriate technology

Extent of Yield Gap of Rice and Factors Related to It

Different types of yield gaps depending upon the differential approaches of comparisons have been found in the literature. Efforts have been made by many scientists to define "Yield Gap", estimate farmer's level of yield of rice and to calculate the yield gap along with the identification of factors responsible with it.

Swaminathan (1977) defines three types of gaps which account for the untapped yield reservoir in Indian agriculture. According to him, the gap between yield possible on theoretical considerations and the best yield so far achieved can be referred to as Gap-I, which can also be called 'Research Gap'. Gap-II which can be referred to as 'Research-*cum*-Management Gap' is the gap between the best yield obtained in a research farm and the yield obtained by a good farmer. The difference between the best average yield realized by a farmer in a state and state average yield has been termed as Gap-III. This may also be called as 'Extension Gap'.

According to Gomez, K.A. (1979), there are two kinds of yield gap. The first one is the difference between the experimental station yield and potential farm yield which is called as 'Yield Gap-I'. The main contributing factors of yield gap-I are non-transferable technology and environmental differences. The second type of yield gap (Yield Gap-II) is the difference between potential farm yield and actual farm yield. Both biological and socio-economic constraints are responsible for Yield Gap-II.

Sen and Das (1983) reported that the yield gaps are of three types. The gap between the yields of research farm and demonstration farm, the gap between the yield of demonstration farm and average yield of the district, and the gap between the yield of demonstration farm and the average yield of small farmers' field.

Mukherjee (1977) defined the yield gap as the ratio between the potential yield as found in the national demonstration in a given State and the average State yield. When the gap ratio is low, farmers' competence is high and *vice versa.*

Matiramani and others (1979) estimated that the average rice yields in Balaghat (M.P.) were nine quintals per hectare, against the potential yield of 45 quintals per ha. under scientific production system and good crop management.

Fale, J.B. and others (1985) found that the gap between yields on experimental stations and those obtained on National Demonstration Plots, i.e. potential yields on farmers' field, is quite narrow (2 quintals/ha. or 3.83%). However, the gap between potential yield and actual yield on farmers' fields is very wide (27 quintal/ha. or 52%).

Desai, D.K. (1984) measured that the average per ha. yield of rice in Eastern India (1972-81) was 1010 kg, compared to the all India level of 1200 kg.

Haque, M.Z. (1977) found that the average yield over all farms in Bangladesh was about 1.6 t/ha. in the boro season. In the Aush season the yield gap ranged from zero to 0.5 t/ha. In case of Aman, the gap varied between 0.9 t/ha. and 1.6 t/ha.

Hidajat Nataatmadja and others (1977) reported that in the main experiment in the wet season of Indonesia the high input level produced an average yield of 5.4 t/ha. In contrast, yields averaged only 3.6 t/ha. with stimulated farmers' input level. So the estimated yield gap of rice was 1.8 t/ha.

Widodo, Nasrullah and others (1977) found that the yield gap of rice in Yogyakarta, Indonesia was greater in dry season (1.2 t/ha.) than in the wet season (0.4 t/ha).

Tripathy (1977) reported about 31 quintals per hectare yield gap in case of rice in wet season due to technological and environmental factors.

Gomez, K.A. (1977) estimated that the average farm yields in Philippines was 4.5 t/ha. in the dry season and 3.8 t/ha. in the wet season. The yield gaps were 2.0 t/ha. in the dry season and 1.7 t/ha. in the wet season.

De Datta, S.K and others (1977) revealed that in the 1977 wet season, the Philippines farmers' yield varied from 2.4 t/ha. to 6.0 t/ha. averaging 4.0 t/ha. With high dose of inputs, yield ranged from 3.2 t/ha. to 6.9 t/ha. averaging 5.3 t/ha. The average yield gap was 1.3 t/ha. It was also observed that yields at the farmers' level of inputs were more variable during the 1977 dry season. They ranged from 3.2 t/ha. to 8.6 t/ha. and averaged 4.8 t/ha. The highest farmers' yield was recorded on a farm ranged from 4.7 t/ha. to 8.9 t/ha. and averaged 7.0 t/ha. The overall yield gap was 2.2 t/ha.

Kamphol Adulavidhaya and others (1977) calculated that the potential rice yields based on experimental station's results in Thailand were at least 5 t/ha. But actual average yields obtained by farmers were less than 2 t/ha. This indicates a yield gap of about 3 t/ha.

Studies in International Rice Research Institute (1977 and 1978) suggested that environmental factors are important in explaining the gap between yield potentials of the modern rice technology and their average farm yields.

Herdt and Mandac (1980) pointed out that in wet season environmental parameters and a combination of weather related factors, and insects and diseases were responsible for some 80 per cent of the yield gap, whereas in dry season non-managed factors for 40-50 per cent of the yield difference.

Annual report of ICRISAT (1982) reported that more than 50 per cent of the gap (in terms of Rs./ha.) and lack of capital was found the most important single constraints responsible for the gap particularly on small farm.

Annual Report of CRRI (1980) observed that fertilizers contributed most of the yield gap followed by insect control and weed control. The mean contribution of these factors are being 0.95 t/ha., 0.79 t/ha. and 0.35 t/ha. respectively. At all locations the contribution of fertilizers and insect control were found significant. The next year Annual Report of CRRI (1981) reported that the average yield gap was 2.89 t/ha. and the individual contribution of fertilizer, insect control and weed control were highly significant.

Factors Related to Technology Gap

The economically profitable aspects of agricultural research which can be applied in increasing production are known as improved agricultural technology. The technologies suitable for the farmers of a particular situation are recommended in the form of package of practices. There may be various reasons for which the farmers might have not been able to adopt all the recommendations made in the package of practices. That is, there is a technological gap or input gap in Indian agriculture and consequently yield gap.

Technological gap in the present context refers to the proportion of the gap between the adoption of practices and the practices recommended which is expressed in percentage.

Similarly, yield gap of rice is defined as the proportion of the gap in the rice production and potential production, expressed in percentage.

In literature a number of studies have been conducted regarding yield gap and it was found that technological gap is the cause of yield gap. The following studies support the argument.

Rai (1985) reported that the average level of adoption of the monitory inputs (like fertilizer use, weed control, insect control, disease control and irrigation) was 32.7 per cent.

Yadava and Gangwar (1980) reported that the reason for the yield gap of rice in Bihar was the only partial adoption of new rice technology.

Marothia (1983) observed in Raipur Block in M.P. that yield gap is due to the application of low levels of production inputs, which is below potential package of recommendation.

Some studies on the factors related to technological gap which are equally responsible for yield gap of rice are furnished below:

Age of Farmer

A study conducted by Dube (1961) in Berala (M.P.) reported that the old farmers adopted more improved seed, fertilizer and manure than younger farmers which indicated an association between the age of farmers and degree of adoption of modern technology.

Kivlin and others (1971) found that age of the farmer was not related with adoption, similarly, Sinha and Kolte (1974) reported that there was no relationship between age and adoption behaviour of farmers in any of the age groups.

Caste

Singh and Singh (1970) in their study on multivariate analysis of adoption behaviour of farmers reported that caste was significantly correlated with adoption of recommended practices.

Roy and others (1968) observed that the farmers' caste status was positively and significantly related to the level of adoption of modern practices.

Jha and Shaktawat (1972) in their study about adoption behaviour of farmers could not find any significant relationship between caste and adoption behaviour.

Family Size

Roy and others (1968) and Biswas (1978) found that the family size was significantly related with the adoption of improved practices, indicating that the farmers with larger family size adopted more practices which led to the small yield gap.

Diez Patier (1980) reported that the size of the family was positively associated with the adoption of modern farm practices.

Education

Dhaliwal (1983) in his study of some important factors affecting the adoption of few selected agricultural practices found that the level of education of the farmers' family had a close association with the adoption of improved technology.

Similarly, Diez Patier (1980) also found that the level of education of the farmer was positively associated with the adoption of modern farm practices.

Singh and Singh (1970) while discussing multiple regression analysis comprising nine socio-psychological variables, reported that the educational status of the family was positively and significantly related with the adoption behaviour of the farmers. The partial correlation coefficient indicated that out of 18 independent variables, educational status of the family and economic motivation were the two variables significantly contributing in predicting the adoption behaviour of the farmer.

Waghmare and Waghmare (1985) on the findings of the correlation analysis showed that the technological gap decreases with the increase in education status, firm size, economic status, social participation and technological knowledge.

Tiwari (1983) and Singh (1984) showed that the educational level of the farm respondents was significantly and negatively correlated with the extent of technological gap.

There was a continuous increase in the adoption of innovations as the educational level of the farmer increased as found by Yadava (1964); Wilkening (1952); Reddy (1962); Rakshi (1962); Tripathy (1963); Sinha (1963); Tiwari (1964); Verma (1964); Sriballav (1964); Rati Ram (1964); Dasgupta (1965); Pandey (1967); Singh (1967); Gupta (1968); Katiyar (1968); Subedar (1968); Reddy and Kivlin (1968); Dev and Sharma (1968); Singh (1969); Muthayya (1971); Ernest (1973); Murthy and Singh (1974); Ranno Ray (1982); Rawal (1981); and Singh (1982).

Jetly (1977) and Basabramanian (1980) reported positive and significant association between adoption of rice technology and family educational status.

Economic Status

Roy and others (1968) in their study on agricultural innovations among Indian farmers pointed out that the farmers who were better-off economically were also progressive in adopting modern farm practices.

Dhaliwal (1963) in his study of some important factors affecting the adoption of some selected agricultural practices reported that economic status of the farmer was significantly and positively related with the adoption of improved technology.

Reddy (1962); Tiwari (1964); Yadava (1964); Verma (1964); Rati Ram (1964); Singh (1965); Radhasyam (1965); Jaiswal (1965); Das (1967); Prasad (1967) and Singh (1968) also reported positive association between economic status of farmers and adoption of agricultural innovations.

Farm Size

Hunumantha Rao (1966) found that the size of the holding significantly affects productivity, management and supervisory bottlenecks arise comparatively at lower level of farm size.

Sagar (1983) reported that productivity of rice had a positive and significant relationship with the farm size.

Waghmare and Waghmare (1985) revealed that the three factors namely, farm size, social participation, knowledge level all together contributed 35.66 per cent of variation in technological gap.

Sharma (1969) and Saini (1971) reported that productivity decreases with the increase in holding size and it accounted for largest variation in productivity at all India level.

Fragmentation Index

Reddy (1981) stated that tiny plots of less than one acre account for 42 per cent of our operational holdings. It is estimated that 10 per cent of our cultivable land is unproductive due to this particular problem alone.

Status of Land Ownership

Sagar (1983), while doing path analysis, revealed that status of land ownership had positive and substantial direct affect on the yield of crops.

Irrigation Index

Bhardwaj (1974) stated that irrigation can raise the productivity of land in three ways—by making possible multiple cropping, by increasing the yield per unit cost and by making possible the production of more lucrative crops.

Sagar (1983) observed positive and substantial direct and indirect effects of irrigation index in influencing the productivity of crops of the farmers.

Tripathy (1977) estimated technological gap in adoption of new rice technology in Coastal Orissa and reported that the highest mean technological gap was in water management in case of all the three categories (low, moderate and high group) of adoption.

Tiwari (1983) when conducting an investigation on technological gaps observed that majority of the farmers had gap in water management (63.16 per cent).

Singh (1984) reported 30 per cent technological gap in water management for rice cultivation. Similarly, Shandilya (1985) found 69.89 per cent technological gap in case of irrigation for rice cultivation.

Rauf (1984) estimated 36.87 per cent adoption gap in water management in case of contact farmers and in case of non-contact farmers the gap was 55.62 per cent.

Cropping Intensity

Sagar (1983) observed that cropping intensity was positively and significantly correlated with farmers' productivity of crops.

Level of Use of Organic Manure

Jadon (1973) reported that about two-fifth of the adopters had applied farm-yard manure to the crops as per recommendation.

Padheria and Patel (1975) showed that only about one-fifth of the adopters used compost manure as per recommendation in the *bajra* and paddy crops.

Level of Use of Fertilizer

The National Council of Applied Economic Research (1977) while evaluating the impact of Indo-German Fertilizer Education Project in West Bengal, found a positive correlation between observed yields and observed level of fertilizer use.

Rauf (1984) reported 33.4 per cent adoption gap in fertilizer use in case of contact farmers and in case of non-contact farmers the gap was 49.25 per cent.

Singh (1984) showed that the farmers had highest technological gap in fertilizer management (89.92 per cent).

Shandilya (1983) found that 60.02 per cent of technological gap in fertilizer management for HYV rice cultivation.

Sagar (1983) found positive and substantial direct and indirect effect of the level of fertilizer use in influencing the farmers' productivity of crops.

Zia and other (1984) revealed that fertilizer alone has about 50 per cent contribution in yield increase.

Abilay and others (1984) reported that farmers' yields rose as fertilizer use increased.

Haque and others (1970) observed that fertilizer use was the biggest contributing factors in yield gap.

De and Bangarava (1986) stated that technological gap was mainly because of the production factors like fertilizer; herbicides and agro-chemicals were not only costly in relation to the return but also because of the technological know-how were still deficient on recommended level of fertilizer use.

Level of Use of Pesticides

Programme Evaluation Organization in their report (1968) on HYV Programme for kharif 1967 showed that more than one-third of the area under high yielding rice varieties as covered by both preventive and curative measures. A quarter of the selected participants took preventive measures while curative measures were taken by 46 per cent. The successive report of the same organization (1969) pointed out that preventive plant protection measures were taken by 51.27 per cent of the participants cultivating high yielding varieties of rice.

Pandya (1981) reported that favourable pest experience regarding use of insecticides, fungicides, etc., possessing favourable attitude, positive value orientation, progressive personality trials, high level of aspiration and achievement motivation, favoured adoption of plant protection measures.

Tiwari (1983) found highest technological gap in pest control (65.79 per cent).

Rauf (1984) found that the adoption gap in weed control measures, disease control measures and pest control measures among the contact farmers were 74 per cent, 80.82 per cent and 89.31 per cent respectively. Among the non-contact farmers these gaps were, weed control 78.03 per cent, disease control 89.9 per cent and pest control 91.27 per cent.

Shandilya (1985) reported that the highest technological gap (85.14 per cent) for rice cultivation was associated with plant protection measures.

Singh (1984) observed that 56.69 per cent mean technological gap in the adoption of the total package of practices of rice cultivation. He further reported that mean technological gap of plant protection measures was 54.15 per cent and weed control with a mean gap of 47.75 per cent.

Waghmare and Waghmare (1985) calculated that lack of plant protection chemicals was one of the main impediments of speedy transfer of this technology.

Social Participation

Roy and others (1968) observed that holding office in some organization, and the combination of membership and holding office were positively and significantly related to adoption of farm practices.

Singh (1979) observed that farmers' social participation was positively and significantly related to adoption of chemical fertilizer.

Past attitudes (Reddy, 1962; Lionberger, 1960; Reddy and Kurlin, 1968; and Ernest, 1968) revealed a positive association between farmers' social participation and the level of adoption of innovation and, hence it was expected that social participation of marginal farmers would be positively related with farming situation and adoption of new agricultural technology.

Waghmare and Waghmare (1985) concluded that social participation and knowledge level contributed a significant variation in technological gap.

Extension Contact

Wilkening (1952), Bose (1961), Sawhney (1961) and Dhaliwal and Sohal (1965) reported that low adoption of improved farm practices was due to less contact with extension agency. Yadava and Gangwar (1980) pointed out that it was very much essential to strengthen the extension agency to promote the adoption of improved technology.

Adhikari and Patel (1987) observed that extension contact had no direct correlation with the technology utilization but was highly correlated with farmers' knowledge, which in turn was found to be associated with the utilization of technology.

Low adoption of improved farm practices was due to less contact with extension agency as reported by Dhaliwal and Soha (1965); Bordoloi (1978); and Rawal (1980).

Mass Media Sources of Information and Personal Communication

Information communication is an important accelerator in the process of transfer of technology from the research to the ultimate users—the farmers.

Sinha (1978) found that the use of mass media and personal cosmopolite sources of information was positively and significantly associated with the adoption behaviour of the farmers.

The Directorate of Extension, Ministry of Agriculture, Government of India (1982) realized that it would be necessary to make increasing use of the mass media to convey the agricultural extension messages to the farmers.

Sagar (1983) reported that utilization of mass media had positive and significant relationship with productivity of crops of the small, medium and pooled samples of farmers.

Dhaliwal (1983); Deshmukh and Bajaj (1981) reported that number of information sources used was positively and significantly associated with adoption.

Singh (1979), in his study on appraisal of some selected variables in farm adoption research, found that a number of communication sources and channels used was positively correlated with the degree of adoption. The larger the number of sources used by farmers, the higher was his adoption index.

Sharma and Gaur (1987) reported that for creating awareness of the practices, radio was found most effective sources but at other adoption stages, village level workers were preferred.

Participation in Training Programme

Singh (1968), while analyzing farmers training programme in Bihar concluded that in spite of various limitations the training imparted to farmers proved useful in affecting changes in knowledge, attitude and adoption behaviour of farmers with respect to improved methods in farming.

Index of Outstanding Credit

Ray Chowdhury (1975) concluded that it was essential to make a very intensive derive on an area basis in different districts through the lead banks in co-ordination with the State Governments and manufacturers in meeting the credit needs of the farmers which play a very important role in the adoption of improved farm technology.

Sen (1984) pointed out that the programme for achieving higher productivity and output calls for a marked increase in the volume of both production and investment credit, with a large share going to the weaker sections and the backward areas.

Constraints in Adoption of Improved Rice Technology

As a matter of fact, farmers do not accept the whole recommended package of practices for rice cultivation, which might be due to some constraints hindering the farmers from implementing these practices *in toto*. Therefore, discussion on constraints of transfer of technology is undoubtedly very much important. Analysis of constraints may provide some way out from the present obstacle position.

Studies conducted in India and abroad, relating to the constraints which may impede the adoption of improved rice technology by farmers, are classified into the following categories—socio-economic, technological, infrastructural and administrative and management.

Socio-Economic Constraints

Socio-economic constraints include farm power, cost of inputs, cost and returns of enterprises, credit and capital, tradition and attitudes, knowledge, input availability, risk, etc.

Singh (1981) reported that lack of knowledge was an important problem in fertilizer use. The study of Adhikari and Patel (1980) investigated the direct and indirect effects of various socio-psychological characteristics on the pattern of utilization of recommended technologies in rice cultivation. It was found that age, education, size of holding, family size, years of experience in farming and availability of irrigation facilities had little effect to the use of improved paddy cultivation technology. He also found that extension contact had no direct correlation with technology utilization, but was highly correlated to farmers' knowledge, which in turn was found to be associated with the association of technology.

Sinha and Sinha (1980) found that lack of knowledge of improved method of cultivation (77.10 per cent) was the important reason for non-adoption of high yielding crop varieties.

Ballav and Prasad (1985) observed that farmers' knowledge about different innovations bears significant negative relationship with gap in technology. In other words, greater the technical knowledge about the information lesser is the gap at field level.

De and Bangarava (1986) stated that the technological gap was mainly because of the production factors like fertilizers, herbicides and agro-chemicals were very expensive in relation to return and also because of the technical know-how was still deficient on the part of the farmers.

Hofer and Strangland (1958), Rogers (1962), Rai (1967), Singh (1968) and Somasundaram and Singh (1978) found that the level of knowledge of farmers regarding the improved practices was a crucial factor affecting the adoption of improved practices. It was also supported by Bhaskaran and Praveena (1982).

Kalirajan and Chand (1985) reported that the level of formal education of farmers was not a significant factor, but that farmers' non-formal education was a significant influence in adoption of new technology.

Widodo and others (1978) found that irrigation was not a constraint to farm yield, but technical knowledge and input availability were the main constraints.

Prejudices and negative attitude towards improved practices were important factors associated with low level of adoption—as observed by Narayan (1965) and Singh (1968).

According to Singh (1974) lack of marketing facilities was an important factor associated with the non-adoption of improved practices.

Lack of timely supports of production requisites to the farmers was a major obstacle to the adoption of improved agricultural practices. This was postulated by Choudhury (1967), Programme Evaluation Organization (1967), Rai (1967), Jaiswal and Singh (1968), Sinha and Bhasin (1968), Singh (1974), Behera and Sahoo (1975) and Sinha (1977).

A study conducted by Gupta and Kurkute (1979) in some villages of Hooghly district of West Bengal, revealed that lack of assured irrigation facilities, non-availability of credit and inputs, tenancy conditions and unsuitability of HYV paddy for sowing in the rainy season were the major constraints on the adoption of new technology.

Dutta and Gogoi (1973) studies that (i) lack of irrigation was a major constraints in the way of fuller utilization of fertilizer; (ii) lack of availability of inputs in time and insufficient quantities was another important constraints; and (iii) better credit supervision was emphasized to reduce division of loans to non-intended purpose.

Salunkhe (1976) pointed out unavailability of fertilizer and adulteration of fertilizer as the important problems faced by small farmers in adopting improved farm practices.

Mallick (1976) reported that non-availability of quality seeds, fertilizers and pesticides as the constraints of small and marginal farmers' agricultural development.

Adgaonkar (1978) found that non-availability of inputs like seeds, fertilizers, pesticides, lack of credit and technical information were the important problems faced by the new land holders.

The study conducted by Programme Evaluation Organization (1979) revealed that non-availability of the needed inputs at the right time was a cause for misutilization of input loans.

Waghmare and Waghmare (1985) also pointed out the constraints in transfer of technology as lack of standard agencies for quality seeds and their high cost, non-availability of finance in time.

Agarwal (1967) stated that technology transfer was in a direction opposite that of the traditional hierarchy of caste.

Parthasarathi (1969) and Kulshreshtha (1978) found tenancy as one of the main constraints in bringing improvement in agriculture.

Various Field Workshops organized by UNDP/FAO (1977) while identifying problems of the disadvantaged small farmers and peasants produced facts on: (a) local problems for early action; (b) long term problems of general applicability; and (c) trends responsible for aggravating these problems. (a) and (b) above refer to such problems as:

(i) Smallness (or absence) of holding and security over them,
(ii) Limited or non-availability of irrigation,
(iii) Monoculture,
(iv) Lack of subsidiary enterprises,
(v) Limited institutional credit, chemicals and protective inputs,
(vi) Unfavourable marketing system and prices,
(vii) Incapacity of existing institution,
(viii) Little share in the control and operation of rural institution, and
(ix) Extension and training methods aimed at more resourceful and responsible individual.

A seminar on 'Transfer of Technology' at Osmania University (1979) identified that:

(i) Customs and traditions act as constraints to modernization of agriculture through technology,
(ii) Subsistence agriculture resulted in freezing skills through a rigid caste structure,
(iii) In pockets where technology transfer was effective, commercialization of agriculture (both crops and livestocks) brought prosperity of the innovators, and
(iv) Technology became a handmade of a few caste group in power (the rural rich).

Socio-economic status had positive and significant relationship with the adoption behaviour of the farmers Wilkening (1952); Dhaliwal (1963); Murthy and Singh (1974); Tiwari (1964); Yadava (1964); Verma (1964); Rati Ram (1964); Singh (1965); Radhasyam (1965); Jaiswal (1965); Das (1967); Prasad (1967); Singh (1968); Rauf (1984); Singh (1984); Singh (1985); Kleynhens and Lyne (1986); Das Gupta and Chowdhury (1987).

Wilkening (1953) reported that family factors were positively related to adoption of farm practices.

Hoffer and Strangland (1958) found that the farmers who were conservative in their outlook failed to adopt new practices.

Freeman and Asadi (1983) concluded that the main effect of adoption of improved technologies was seemed to be severely constrained by highly unequal distribution of social power.

Misiko (1977), and Sinha and Sinha (1980) observed that non-availability of technical guidance was an important factor responsible for non-adoption of these technologies.

Tiwari (1983) reported negative correlation between knowledge and adoption of improved farm practices.

The finding of Chand (1986) with respect to knowledge and adoption revealed that the majority of the respondents had medium level of knowledge of adoption.

Koch (1987) found that there was a strong positive relationship between knowledge and adoption.

Verma (1964) reported that there was a positive and significant relationship between knowledge and their adoption behaviour.

Roy Chowdhury (1975) pointed out that it was essential to make a very intensive derive on an area basis in different districts through the lead banks in coordination with the stable Government and manufacturers in meeting the credit needs of the farmers which played a very important role in the adoption of improved farm technology.

Sen (1984) reported that the programme for achieving high productivity and output called for marked increase in the volume of both production and investment credit, with a large share going in the weaker sections and backward areas.

Singh and Jha (1971) in their study of farms of Rural Delhi observed that inadequate capital was a great bottleneck in full exploitation of the potential productivity. Inadequacy of available resources and capital scarcity was more acutely felt by the progressive farmers.

Saini (1972) stated that with the absence of additional capital availability the shift from adoption level of technology did not offer much scope for increasing the farm returns on irrigated farm; on irrigated farms in the absence of additional capital availability the shift from accepted to recommended level of technology led to decrease in farm returns.

Waghmare and Waghmare (1985) reported that lack of standard agencies for quality seed and their cost and availability of finance were the main constraints in transfer of technology.

Roy (1960), Singh (1961) and Rai (1967) reported that the high initial cost of agricultural innovation was an obstacle to adoption of improved agricultural practices.

Radhasyam (1965) and Prasad (1967) pointed out that high cost and lack of money were the reasons, expressed by majority of non-adopters of fertilizer. It was further stated that 56 per cent of the non-adopters of improved implements did not adopt them due to poor draft animals.

Prasad (1967) reported that 42.2 per cent of the non-adopters of improved seeds did not adopt it due to high cost.

Dubey (1968) reported higher cost of pesticides, herbicide and equipments, untimely supply of pesticides, small and fragmented holdings were the main reasons for non-adoption of pesticides and herbicides as reported by more than 50 per cent of the non-adopters.

Nair (1969) found that high cost of fertilizer was an important problem faced by farmers in adopting modern rice practices.

Marothia (1983) in his study in Raipur Block (M.P.) found that high cost of inputs, financial limitations, risks of crop failures and inadequate supportive input facilities were found to be responsible for the slow adoption of paddy technology.

Chidambaram (1977) argued that new and modern implements, and machinery involved high cost and as a result small and marginal farmers could not introduce these due to lack of credit.

Marothia (1985) reported that the most important factors contributed in the yield gap were high price of fertilizer, small size of holding, lack of capital, low price of farm price, lack of technical knowledge, non-availability of recommended seeds and fertilizers, lack of communication facilities, non-availability of credit, soil problems and the protective nature of irrigation.

Waghmare and Waghmare (1985), in constraints analysis of lab to land programme observed that high cost of fertilizer, lack of plant protection chemical and high cost of chemicals, lack of regular number of irrigation, high labour wages, non-availability of labour in time were the main impediments in speedy transfer of technology to the field.

Sen and Sharma (1986) opined that the production inputs were beyond the reach of about 80 per cent paddy growers in Kurukshetra district of Haryana State as the cost of these inputs were exorbitant.

Raheja and Singh (1981); Jaiswal and Roy (1968) reported that high cost of inputs was main reason for non-adoption.

Veerasamy and Bahadur (1979) revealed that small farmers had medium economic motivation in adoption of improved rice technology.

Rao (1969) revealed two main constraints limiting productivity: (a) low market demand and low price for the produce, and (b) difficulty in adjusting the crop in existing cropping pattern.

Yojiro and Rattan (1970) concluded that extremely wide differences in agricultural productivity had been traced to three categories: (a) resource endowment, (b) technology as embodied in field or working capital, and (c) human capital.

Singh (1974) stated that one of the reasons for rejection of farm technology was labour scarcity. Moreover, high labour wages make the cost of production high.

Sharma and Nair (1974) stated that the important problem related to the cultivation of high yielding varieties was low price for the produce.

Division of Rural Survey of RBI (1975) identified the defects in the distribution system of input from their survey of SFDA in 13 districts. These defects were: (a) inadequate sales point, (b) a multiplicity of retail depots for seeds, fertilizers and pesticides managed by private dealers, Government and co-operatives, (c) uncoordinated and untimely supply of inputs, (d) adulteration of fertilizers, (e) weak extension services, and (f) inadequate godown facilities.

Garg and others, Mishra and others, and Singh and others (1976) opined that exorbitant rise in the price of production inputs adversely affected the level of their use and the productivity of agricultural commodities.

Non-availability of loan, cumbersome procedural formalities associated with concession of loans, delay in sanctioning loans and disbursement of loan amounts and inadequate credit were often mentioned as constraints of small and marginal farmers by Athavale (1973), Ali and Barthakur (1973), Singh and Goswami (1974),

Radhakrishna Menon and Dorai Swamy (1975), Mallick (1976), Radhakrishna Menon and Knight (1976), and Singh and others (1976).

Bhilegaonkar (1976) reported that medium and small farmers perceived inadequate finance to match the cost of production as second important problem.

Chaddha (1978) making a comprehensive study of the farm size productivity relationship during pre and post green revolution period in Punjab pointed out that "capital-labour ratio" to be the main explanatory factor of farm size productivity relation to the new production technology just as the "land-labour ratio" did under the traditional technology.

Mehra (1968) observed that profitability, compatibility, feasibility and cost were considered very important attributes influencing adoption of improved practices.

Chavan (1979) pointed out that the adopter farmers of HYV programme faced some problems viz., product price unremunerative, adulteration on hybrid and high yielding varieties of seeds, high cost of seeds, higher labour charges, unavailability of improved seeds, lack of timely technical guidance, insufficient irrigation, susceptibility of the hybrid and HYV crops to pest and disease and insufficient finance.

According to Gee-Clough and Paterson (1985) in some cases, inappropriate price policies for rice had effectively made it impossible for the small farmers to finance any improvement in production.

Gomez and others (1979) concluded that reasons for low yield may include cost of inputs, lack of knowledge about improved technology, lack of credit, poor irrigation system, non-availability of inputs and traditional beliefs.

Ranjan and Binswanger (1979) pointed out that low level of national research experiment was itself an important socio-economic constraint.

The study of Gangadharan (1980) called for increased involvement of credit institutions in promoting much greater fertilizer use for raising farm output and income.

Sen (1984) stated that farmers had too little credit for investment and efficient use of their labour; they also lacked adequate facilities for development of skills. He also pointed out that the law of succession had contributed to continuous subdivision and fragmentation of holdings. The heavy, erratic and uneven seasonal pattern of rainfall created soil erosion problems, constraining agricultural development.

Sen and Purandare (1985) pointed out that the technologies and practices under different sectors might be technically quite sound but could not be adopted by the clients unless they generally observed deficiencies such as lack of material inputs, financial constraints, inadequate supply of service facilities etc., were met with. These were especially true in case of economically and socially backward people who were the majority of the targeted population.

Urff (1985) observed that the sources of yield discrepancies were price relation, land ownership or tenancy, risks associated with production and selling, technical know-how, social background and availability of materials.

Lack of capital was an important barrier for not making use of improved agricultural practices. This was found by Saxena (1965), Basram and Gapner (1968), Behara and Sahoo (1975), and Sinha (1977).

Singh (1981) found lack of finance and high price of inputs, as some of the important problems in fertilizer use.

Choudhury (1973) reported that small farmers perceived lack of money as the most important problem along with high price, non-availability of fertilizer and inadequate knowledge of its use.

Patel (1976) considered low and instable farm income, low level of education and low investment capacity as the constraints faced by the small and marginal farmers.

Singh (1961), Sahay (1961), Jaiswal and Singh (1968) were of the opinion that poverty of farmers was a factor responsible for low level of adoption of improved agricultural practices.

Khalon and Singh (1981) reported that labour turned out to be a severe constraint to the adoption of intensive system of farming recommended by research investigations.

Murthy and Singh (1974) in their study concluded that farmers' socio-economic status, family income, education, farm size, degree of commercialization of the farm, perception of the economic system, value orientation and proneness of change, were found to be constraints to the adoption of modern technology.

Quasem and Hossain (1979) from their study on Bangladesh observed that the predominance of small farmers in Bangladesh and the crop sharing system might not act as constraints to agricultural growth through expansion of these modern inputs, provided credit was made available to poor cultivators on favourable terms.

Ryan and Gross (1950), and Roy and others (1968) reported that farmers, with higher income and who were better off economically, intended to adopt improved practices.

Fliegel (1957) and Copp (1957) found that high farm income was associated with high farm practice adoption level.

Dube (1958); Bose and Vishnoi (1960); and Reddy (1962) found that economic condition or financial position of the farmers always played dominant role in the acceptance of an innovation.

Low income of the farmers is one of the main handicaps in farmers' response to improved farm practices as observed by Fliegel (1960); Sahay (1960); Parthasarathi (1975); and Patel (1965).

Singh (1968) while highlighting the importance of economic factors in adoption of new agricultural technologies stated that when a farm was confronted with a stimulus (like HYV seed), the probability of its adoption, among other things, was influenced by a credit system, that was the source of credit, types and terms of loans, and consequences of defaulting of loans.

Myrdal (1968); Singh (1969) and Nair (1969) found a positive and significant relationship of credit orientation of farmers with their adoption behaviour.

Singh and Singh (1968) and Misiko reported that timely availability of credit was positively associated with the adoption behaviour of the farmers.

Roy Choudhury (1975) showed that credit needs of the farmers played a very important role in the adoption of improved farm technologies.

Ranno Ray (1980) reported that farmers' attitude towards credit institutions, credit utilization index, credit repayment behaviour, economic performance index, credit repayment behaviour, economic performance index per acre were found to have significant influence on their adoption behaviour.

Roumasset (1976) reported that risk involved in rice production was positively and significantly associated with the level of adoption of modern rice technology for small and marginal farmers.

Jaiswal (1965); Singh (1966), Supe (1969), Singh (1971), Ernest (1973), Ramachandran (1974), Singh (1974), Bhilegaonkar (1976),

Singh (1977), and Bhaskaran and Praveen (1982) have concluded that risk orientation was positively related to the adoption behaviour of the farmers.

Technological Constraints

Constraints in relation to ecological factors, water management, farm machinery, production inputs, pest and diseases, and research and extension in the transfer of technology, etc., have been included in the presentation of review of literature under the category of agricultural constraints.

Basrur (1949) recommended that successful operation of tractors by private individuals of technical assistants, spare parts, training, oil and lubricants etc., were removed.

Nead (1954) put forth the difficulties in the introduction of mechanization in agriculture. She stated that the introduction of mechanized tools was confronted by an obstacle in small size of holdings. In some areas, it was uneconomic to introduce mechanization because human labour was cheaper.

National Demonstration Report (1966) stated the reasons for low yield and failure of modern varieties of rice to be diseases and pests, late transplanting, deep planting, poor water management, scarcity of fertilizers, strong winds at the time of flowering and shortage of water at maturity, etc.

Nair (1969) observed constraints in cultivation of HYV of rice in Kerala as:

(i) High incidence of pest and diseases;
(ii) Lack of assured irrigation;
(iii) High cost of inputs;
(iv) Low price for the produce;
(v) Untimely supply of fertilizer;
(vi) Shortage and high wages of labourers at the peak period;
(vii) Less straw yields;
(viii) Non-availability of easy credit;
(ix) Lack of co-ordination between official agencies; and
(x) Poor infrastructure.

Sharma and Nair (1974) stated that the important problems related to the cultivation of high yielding varieties of rice, in order of importance were, high incidence of pests and diseases, lack of assured irrigation and high inputs prices.

Programme Evaluation Organization (1969) in their report of "HYV of Rice in Kharif 1968" pointed out the following constraints:

(i) Attack of pest and diseases;
(ii) Marketing problem;
(iii) Untimely supply of fertilizer;
(iv) Non-availability of plant protection chemicals;
(v) Lack of irrigation;
(vi) Problem of easy and adequate credit;
(vii) Labour shortage; and
(viii) Higher cost of cultivation.

Gupta (1969) reported less fodder and inferior taste of grains were the main problems mentioned by farmers participating in HYV programme for IR-8 in Saharanpur district of U.P.

Barker and Pal (1979) revealed environmental constraints as the most important factor limiting on increase in rice production in Eastern India.

Nair (1969) in his study of HYV programme in Kerela observed that only 40 per cent of the farmers adopted the recommended seed rate of rice.

Pal (1975) in his study on HYV programme of rice in Cuttack district of Orissa reported that most of the farmers did not use the correct seed rate. In almost all cases he observed a higher seed rate than the recommended level.

Parthasarathi (1975) pointed out that organic manure had been virtually replaced by fertilizers in the delta well before 1965/1966 when the HYV programme had gone underway. He also reported that, although inorganic fertilizers accepted and widely used were inappropriate, farmers deferred considerably in the quantities applied and in their use of the three components viz., nitrogen, phosphorus and potassium.

Pal (1975) while studying adoption of HYVs in Cuttack district of Orissa stated that under delta condition recommended water management practices were extremely difficult to adopt. He further stated that not a single farmer in his sample could adopt the recommended water management practice faithfully.

Tripathy (1977) reported that water management was the most important casual factor (20.92 per cent) followed by disease and pest control (19.92 per cent) and nitrogen application (12.37 per cent). The ecological factor like temperature, soil, rainfall and sunshine intensity together contributed to the extent of 19.83 per cent of the yield gap.

Kahlon and Singh (1981) stated that most physical constraints were likely to be influenced directly or indirectly by a single factor i.e. water control and water management.

Reddy (1981) stated that three factors had a bearing in the adoption of new technology. Situational factors were the adverse climatic factors and unfavourable soil conditions which discourage farmers from the risk of adopting input intensive and costly technology. He also found that as a result of low diffusion of plant protection, farmers had to forego benefits of modern agricultural technology and endure heavy crop losses with new varieties.

Some of the technological constraints identified by Chand (1984) in Nepal were:

(i) Lack of knowledge about technology;
(ii) More water requirement;
(iii) Lack of irrigation facility;
(iv) Irregular rainfall;
(v) Inadequate field channel for delivery of water to field;
(vi) Unequal opportunity to get water;
(vii) Non-control over the unwanted quantity of water during monsoon;
(viii) Less water holding capacity of soil;
(ix) Lack of drainage facility;
(x) Occurrence of floods;
(xi) Lack of equipments and improved implements;
(xii) Preference of other crops;
(xiii) Neighbourers do not adopt (lack of demonstration effect); and
(xiv) Complicated process and lack of conviction.

Pal (1974) in his study observed that the major constraints to yield were related to difficulties in obtaining seeds, chemical fertilizer and production credit along with inadequate irrigation water and attack of insects, diseases and other pests.

Sen (1984) mentioned some technological constraints on water management, research and farm machinery. A sound infrastructure on irrigation and drainage, which could overcome the constraints posed by physical environments, had not been developed. Further, research efforts to develop a crop technology appropriate to physical environments of the eastern region in India had not been adequate. He also pointed out that inadequate bullock power available to the small and marginal farmers had added to the need for improved farm tools and implements.

According to Urff (1985) a major reason for yield divergence between crops was differential fertile sides with favourable climatic conditions and available production technology.

Matiramani (1979) argued that the main constraints of rice production in Balaghat of M.P. were the underlying topography of the fields and the use of poor quality of seeds.

Barker and Pal (1979) pointed out that physical environments, lack of suitable technology were the factors hindering the adoption of improved rice production technology in Eastern India. They concluded that yields could be raised by improving water control or by developing varieties of rice tolerant to the prevailing floods and droughts.

Lack of irrigation facilities was the major factor associated with low level of adoption of improved technologies. This conclusion was drawn by Roy (1960); Singh (1961); Radhasyam (1963); Prasad (1967); Programme Evaluation Organization (1967); Singh (1967); Choudhury (1967); Singh (1974); Jaiswal and Singh (1968); Singh and Singh (1968); Singh (1974); Behara and Sahoo (1975); Singh (1977); Parthasarathi (1977); Gupta and Kurkute (1978).

Choudhury (1980) concluded that chemical fertilizer was one of the most important constraints in rice production.

Sriballav (1964) observed that strong animals with a farmer led to greater adoption than poor animals.

Pal (1978) observed that the gap between yields in experimental plots was due to difference in soil-water conditions, management practices and input use.

Rogers (1972) reported that characteristics of a technology were themselves partially responsible for its adoption or non-adoption.

Mitra (1968); Jaiswal and Roy (1968); and Roy (1966) found that profitability, compatibility, complexity were considered as very important attributes influencing in adoption of improved practices.

Sethy (1978) found farm power efficiency of the farmers negatively and significantly associated with technological gap in the adoption of fertilizer.

Khalon and Singh (1981) stated that labour turned out to be a severe constraint to the adoption of intensive system of farming.

Kamphol (1977) concluded that inadequate fertilizer was the dominant constraint responsible for a gap of 0.5 tonne/ha. during the wet season and 1.5 tonnes/ha. during the dry season in Thailand. He also reported that insects and weeds reduced yield between 0.1 and 0.3 tonne/ha. and combination of inputs higher than that the farmers were using profitability increased yields by 0.3 to 1.0 tonne/ha.

Haque (1977) conducted a survey in Bangladesh and found that chemical fertilizer had a contribution of high percentage in yield gap of rice.

Datta (1977) in his study observed that the constraints of rice production in dry season were level of fertilizer used and management of fertilizer. But in wet season insect control was found as an important factor in rice production.

IRRI (1978) reported that in tropical Asia, rice yield had been low for many countries. Reasons for this low yields were warm day and night temperature, high humidity, low light intensity and poor rice varieties.

Adulavidhaya (1977) reported that in Thailand the average yield gap was about 1 tonne/ha. in the wet season and about 2 tonnes/ha. in the dry season. The main contribution to the gap was fertilizer, about 55 per cent in the wet season and 75 per cent in the dry season. In the wet season, 27 per cent of the gap was the result of inadequate weed control and 9 per cent was the result of inadequate insect control. In the dry season, 15 per cent was the result of inadequate weed control and 5 per cent was the result of inadequate insect control.

Datta and others (1977) found that the relative contribution of the inputs to the yield gap as insect control contributed about half, fertilizer about one-third, and weed control less than 10 per cent.

Infrastructural Constraints

The factors included under infrastructural constraints are supply of inputs, service and supports, and system of the farmers.

Planning, Research and Action Institute, U.P. (1968) revealed that the fragmentation of land holding was rendered sound cultivation impossible and small scattered plots were generally unfit for introduction of improved agricultural technologies.

Patel (1978) mentioned inadequate and untimely supply of inputs as constraints of modern agricultural practices.

Patel (1965) reported that lack of knowledge of agricultural activities, lesser contact with extension agents, lack of availability of seeds and fertilizers at local market, small size of holding and low income were the problems of small adopter farmers.

Prasad (1967); Nair (1969); Sawhney (1961); Reddy (1962); and Roy (1967) observed inadequate and untimely supply of inputs were the main reasons for non-adoption of new agricultural technologies.

Lack of timely supply of production requisites to the farmers was a major obstacle to the adaptation of improved agricultural practices as reported by Chowdhury (1979); Jaiswal and Singh (1968); Ernest (1973); Programme Evaluation Organization (1967); Rai (1967); Sinha and Singh (1968); Behara and Sahoo (1975); Sinha (1977); and Singh (1974).

Myrdal (1968) and Singh (1974) stated that lack of marketing facilities was an important factor associated with non-adoption of improved practices.

Tiwari (1983) reported that there was a significant and positive relationship between production facilities available to the farmers and their adoption behaviour.

Patel (1965) and Parthasarathi (1965) reported that the adoption of modern varieties was associated with the farm size.

Sengupta and Ghosh (1968) examined the trend of HYV programme for rice in Birbhum district of West Bengal and found that the biggest problem facing the cultivators in the adoption of HYV programme was the small size of farm.

Dubey (1968) observed that small and fragmented holdings were the main problems responsible for non-adoption of pesticides and herbicides.

Murthy and Singh (1974), and Ranno Ray (1980) reported that farm size was closely associated with non-adoption of improved farm practices.

Singh (1983) reported that size of holding had emerged as the most significantly associated variable with the level of farm mechanism.

Arya and Shah (1984) concluded that the non-adoption of farm technologies was due to high fragmentation and scattered holdings.

Adhikari and Patel (1987) pointed out that size of holding had little relation to the use of improved paddy cultivation technology by Nepalese farmers.

Reddy (1981) stated that three types of factors in the client system had a bearing in the adoption of new technology. Situational factors were the adverse climatic factors and unfavourable soil cultivation which discouraged farmers to adopt input-intensive and costly technology.

Risk orientation was reported as a crucial factor positively associated with adoption behaviour of the farmers by Jaiswal (1965); Singh (1966); Supe (1969); Singh (1971); Ernest (1973); Ramachandran (1974); Singh (1974); Bhilegaonker (1976); Singh (1977); Bhaskaran and Parveen (1982); Dasgupta (1980); and Ranno Ray (1980).

Singh (1984) found that risk preference was significantly and negatively associated with technological gap.

Ongkili and Quilkey (1986) reported that risk had attached an overwhelming concern among agricultural economists.

Huijsman (1987) reported that farmers' aversion of the risk taking had been suggested as one possible factor explaining the adoption.

Singh (1984) concluded that change proneness was significantly and negatively associated with technological gap in rice cultivation.

The Directorate of Economics and Statistics (1967) reported that farming experience and know-how, higher managerial ability and spirit of innovations of displaced persons and higher literacy were some of the factors associated with the inner district differences in levels and rates of change in agricultural output in Punjab.

Bose (1967) analyzed that agricultural situations in Orissa with special reference to rice cultivation and observed that lack of irrigation facilities, fertilizers, scientific knowledge of methods of cultivation, extension help and illiteracy were the main causes of low yield per acre and low growth rates in agriculture.

Directorate of Evaluation, U.P. (1967) and Programme Evaluation Organization (1968) reported that the main problem associated with growing high yielding varieties were lack of adequate irrigation facilities, inadequate supply of fertilizers and lack of finance. Similarly Dutta (1973) reported that lack of irrigation, lack of availability of inputs in time and lack of good credit facilities were the main constraints.

Rama Rao (1969), Hodgdon and Harpal Singh (1966) observed that non-adoption of small farmers in technology adoption was due to low access to infrastructural support than to low risk taking ability.

Programme Evaluation Organization (1968, 1968b and 1968c) observed that 19.72 per cent of the farmers mentioned untimely supply of fertilizers as one of the important problems. Other problems were lack of irrigation facilities (13.5 per cent) and inadequate supply of fertilizers (8.3 per cent). Further, in its report, they listed the following: shortage of credit (20.18 per cent), shortage of irrigation water (20.18 per cent), unavailability of fertilizers (17.91 per cent) and inadequate supply of fertilizers (17.91 per cent).

Chowdhury and Ojha (1969) and Nair (1969) reported that the main problems expressed by the farmers were non-availability of desired fertilizer, black marketing in the sale of fertilizer and insufficient credit facilities.

Singh and Srivastava (1970) reported that the main problems of small cultivators were lack of irrigation facilities and uncertainty about the availability of irrigation water.

Chowdhury (1973) reported that small farmers perceived lack of money as the most important problem in implementing full package of improved practices. The other problems in order of importance were high cost of fertilizers, non-availability of fertilizers in village, lack of adequate knowledge about fertilizers, use of fertilizers, deteriorating quality of land, adulteration in fertilizers, lack of transport facilities and supply of short weights of fertilizer bags.

Sharma and Nair (1974) stated that the important problem related to the cultivation of high yielding varieties was untimely supply of fertilizers.

Pandey (1974) stated in his study on "Development of Marginal Farmers and Agricultural Labourers", that there was hold of big farmers in the co-operative societies to have the benefit of inputs supply. He also reported that one third of the marginal farmers were not aware of the infrastructural facilities available for them.

Pal (1974) reported that the major constraints to yield were related to difficulties in obtaining seeds, chemicals, fertilizers, and production credit, inadequate irrigation water and attack of insects, diseases and other pests like rodents, etc.

Rajagopalan (1975) reported major economic constraints related to the distribution of land and irrigation water, lack of capital constraints related to farm size. Most serious constraint was inadequate supply of modern inputs followed by drainage and storage facility.

According to Izum and Ranatunga (1974) the current tenure arrangement was found to the main constraint on production of rice.

Grewal and Singh (1975) referred that small farmers were aware of the new technology of agricultural production but they needed adequate, assured and timely supply of crucial inputs to augment their agricultural production.

Herdt and Wickman (1975) reported that lack of water control was the single biggest yield constraint and was responsible for about 35 per cent of the difference between potential and actual yields. Seasonal factors such as available solar radiation accounted for another 20 per cent of the yield difference and economic factor including risk accounted for another 15 per cent of the difference. They also reported that lack of supply of inputs markers and infrastructure prevented the farmers from realizing the highest yield potential.

Patel (1976) considered low and unsuitable farm income, low level of education and investment capacity as the constraints of small and marginal farmers.

Asian Development Bank (1977), FAO (1978) had indicated that irrigation was a crucial component of the infrastructure for agricultural development in rice growing areas of Asia.

Haque and others (1978) found that most of the farmers had small size plots, and it was difficult for them to obtain sufficient capital for achieving high level of production.

Jaiswal and Arya (1981) indicated that the major problems of increasing the area under the high yielding varieties were the lack of inputs, particularly seeds, fertilizers, irrigation and pesticides. Supply of inputs necessitated proper distribution and transport all the way to the village.

Reddy (1981) stated that some Government policies on price structure of commodities acted as a matter of discourage for the adoption of improved technology. He concluded that the role of price incentives as a strong stimulus for agricultural production had been well established; especially pay-off technology was available to promote investment by farmers.

Joff (1980) carried out a study on Sierra Leone to identify the constraints in production system and possible strategies for change and development planning. He concluded that there was a need for better management and workable strategies to add dynamism to the diffusion adoption process.

Robertson (1981) revealed that technology did least harm in a society with a well developed infrastructure and adequate manpower and harmonized with ethos and culture of the society.

Monu (1981) from his study on the "Transfer of Technology to Small Farmers in Nigeria" observed that existing explanations of the gap between farming recommendations at the research institute and what actually took place on the farm were inadequate, placing undue emphasis on the farmers' socio-demographic characteristics and communication variables. More important that the farmers' socio-demographic characteristics were the characteristics of the technology itself and the institutional support was provided for its diffusion.

Gill (1982) observed that the marketing system had not been able to cope with the rate of increase of marketed surplus of farm produce and the dependence on labour for holding and cleaning had led to long market delays, leading to deterioration of crops.

Sagar (1983) concluded that fragmented land holding, lack of soil testing were important factors hindering higher productivity of crops.

Lakshminarayan and Rahim (1983) found that absence of a link between credit and marketing, pre-occupation of the bank officials with recovery of overdue loans and the consequent inability of these credit agencies to formulate meaningful agricultural development programme in their area of operation.

Chowdhury and Das Gupta (1983); Sengupta (1987) and Chowdhury (1988) reported that apart from few agro-biological constraints most of the important constraints centered on socio-economic and infrastructural dimensions.

Sen (1984) stated that low use of modern inputs like HYV seed and fertilizers was largely due to shortage in supply, substandard quality and poor input delivery system and power supply. Use of inputs and on-farm investments had suffered as flow of institutional credit was not adequate. Investment in basic infrastructure like roads, transport, marketing, cold storage facilities, rural godowns and processing facilities, etc., have been neglected.

Arya and Shah (1984), identifying the main constraints on the adoption of technology showed that due to high fragmentation and scattered holdings, farmers waste human as well as bullock labours in moving from one location to another distant location and they were unable to exploit locally available water resources for irrigation purposes. Moreover, valuable lands were wasted on boundaries.

Sen (1984) stated that farmers had too little capital for investment and efficient use of their labour. They also lacked from adequate facilities for development and skills. He also reported that the law of succession had contributed to continuous sub-division and fragmentation of holdings. The heavy erratic and uneven seasonal pattern of rainfall created soil erosion problems, constraining agricultural development.

Waghmare and Waghmare (1985) derived the constraints in transfer of technology as lack of standard agencies for quality seeds and their high cost, non-availability of finance in time.

Singh and Sharma (1986) stated that supplementary factors like electricity for running tubewells, diesel for engines and labour for farm operations were not only costly but also scarce. Marketing of their produce had been exploited by the traders and farmers had not been provided with technical guidance as to how to get rid of this exploitation.

Administrative and Management Constraints

The factors associated with effectiveness of administration in relation to agricultural development programmes are: lack of trained personnel

(Mishra, 1960; Yadava, 1960; Singh, 1961; Nejamuddin, 1964; and Singh, 1964); lack of training of non-officials associated with the administration in community development (Sharma, 1965); lack of co-operative spirit among the personnel (Mishra, 1960; Singh, 1961), lack of effective leadership (Nejamuddin, 1964); under pressure from superior officers to lower staff (Nejamuddin, 1966; Khosla, 1966); dual control on technical personnel (Singh, 1964); lack of co-ordiantion between different departments (Mishra, 1960; Singh, 1964; Singh, 1966); provision of inadequate budget and delay in allotment of budgets (Singh, 1964; Tewari, 1966).

Sharma (1965), while conducting study on organizations and working of Block Committee with special reference to non-official members, observed that the majority of the members had not been trained for their assignments nor intimated officially with their functions. He also observed that the various sub-committees were not functioning well and meetings were not held regularly due to loose administration of Block Development Committee.

Singh (1966) showed that poor co-ordination between canal irrigation department and officials of package programme adversely affected the agricultural development programme.

Tiwari (1966) pointed out that inadequate and untimely allotment of funds, slackness in executing the programme were the factors responsible for poor progress of agricultural development programme under Panchayati Raj.

Lokahanathan (1967) reported that the greatest bottleneck to economic progress in this country had been inefficient administration.

Chauhan (1968) found that lack of close supervision of Panchayat Samiti on the working of individual Panchayat and non-functioning of Gram Sabha were the two important factors responsible for the failure of village panchayat.

Chamber (1974) concluded that a highly authoritarian hierarchical organization was inappropriate for agricultural extension.

Ray (1976) pointed out that lack of farmers' organization as one of the critical factors affecting the development of small and marginal farmers.

Nattahai (1979) stated that management gap was not due to inefficiency of farmers' alone but research scientists and extension personnel had an equally important responsibility in this respect. He further stated that unless a management perspective was included in all these engaged in pursuit of achieving agricultural progress, the whole of their efforts would prove to be self-defeating.

Roy (1979) pointed out that the existing administrative organizations were not structured to cater to the specific needs of small farmers and guard against manipulation by the rural rich.

Muthey (1979) reviewed several constraints and finally emphasized the need for overhauling extension training and co-ordination.

Taylor (1980) concluded that the institutional weakness was one of the primary factors limiting the improved welfare of people in Asian small farms.

Rao and Prasad (1980) stressed the need for imparting managerial skill to the personnel for effective planning and implementation of the programme.

Jain and Chowdhury (1981) pointed out that a large portion of the officials engaged in development tasks had a more bureaucratic attitude, which hindered the progress of change and development.

Das Gupta and others (1981) from their study noted that some of the enterprises of Lab to Land Programme of Visva-Bharati, particularly sericulture and animal husbandry were affected due to lack of proper management on the part of the target groups.

Menon and Bhaskaran (1984) concluded that the lack of agricultural development should be made easier if the researchers, extension workers and farmers work together with management zeal i.e. by rationalizing their behaviour in their own sphere of activity.

Jaiswal and Veerabhadraiah (1985) reported that management services for small farmers combined with the development of participatory institution could help them break away from subsistence life and give them a chance to move into the modernizing agricultural works. Thus, according to them, providing management services was an extremely vital approach that warranted much more attention and resources.

Pandey and Singh (1985) identified 12 major constraints that did stand in the way of successful extension administration. These constraints were:

(i) Defective planning procedure,

(ii) Lesser degree of decentralization and over centralization in the extreme hierarchical administrative relationship,
(iii) Cause of lesser degree of decentralization which creates a serious block in speeding up the administrative efficiency,
(iv) Lack of proper direction and supervision,
(v) Lack of intra and inter co-ordination,
(vi) Difficulty of budget,
(vii) Delay due to unreasonable workload and placement of insufficient and unsuitable staff,
(viii) Delays caused by frequent and inconsiderable transfer of personnel at the criteria stage of work,
(ix) Lack of timely inspection and evaluation system,
(x) Rural administration,
(xi) Intentional delays, and
(xii) Delays and corruption committed for non-material gain.

Nanadapukar and Shetay (1985) stated that most of the farmers lacked information regarding the important management functions such as planning, organization, directing, co-ordinating, controlling. Similarly, most of them were not clear about the objectives of the farm planning and also were not giving due attention to preparing the farm plan rationally. They also suggested some solution to overcome these key problems in agri-business. These were:

(i) Motivating the extension workers to produce more literature in regional language,
(ii) Setting up a teaching research centres with AV aids and TV system,
(iii) Broadcasting success stories on AIR,
(iv) Feedback,
(v) Plan and stimulate the extension worker in planning,
(vi) Training the farmers in management,
(vii) Co-ordinating planning activities at block and district levels,
(viii) Training in management to extension workers, and
(ix) More emphasis on farm planning.

Das Gupta, Chowdhury and Sengupta (1985) and Sengupta (1987) identified some important aspects of management in the Lab to Land Programme. Such identified aspects were:

(i) Correct visualization of the programme,
(ii) Integration of the programme with the original research and extension programme of the implementing institutes through the Department of Extension Education,
(iii) In-built system of active involvement of scientists and technologists,
(iv) Administrative backing and support to the co-ordinators of the programme, and providing other additional infrastructural facilities,
(v) Co-ordinating the programme of other agencies working for rural development in the area,
(vi) Strengthening of support system, marketing and credit facilities, and
(vii) Evaluation/appraisal of such operational-programme both phasic and continuous types.

Appropriate Technology

Biggs (1976) in his study on Bangladesh stated that attention should be given to the question of the best mixture of different types of technologies—old and new in the implementation of agricultural development plan in Bangladesh. He also argued that national policy should be considered in selecting the technology.

Ahmed (1977) identifying appropriate rice production technology for Bangladesh revealed that the objectives of output and employment maximization could be reached by the use of HYV technology in conjunction with bullock power. He also pointed out that the use of tractors/power tillers could not be justified since it created unemployment and did not raise output. The use of HYV technology also led to increased labour utilization in slack periods and to the use of a higher proportion of hired wage labour which was important in Bangladesh in view of the large proportion of landless rural people.

According to Henry and others (1978) appropriate technology was identified as technology which promoted the increase of income for the poorest section of a community, the provision of a minimum level of goods and services for all people, and the growth of productive employment opportunity.

Tandon (1979) argued that production processes needed to be so designed as to utilize modern technology in the development of various activities at the local level with substantial employment potential involved.

Matiramani and others (1979) showed that the policy implications were that capital intensive production technology did not find easy adoption among a farming community—operating under scarce capital resource and low management ability. These must be set as alternative to allow for choice depending on resource base and managerial ability.

Thenes (1979) showed that the concept of appropriate technology for basic needs, rather than high yielding, profitable agricultural modernization was gaining ground. He also pointed out that both traditional and modern technology might be adapted to specific environments and situations.

There was hardly any need to emphasis that the improved farm technologies were available adequately, but the potential results were not generally achieved on the farmers' field. Kaliranjan's (1980) experience showed that the improved varieties failed to approach their experimental yield potential under field conditions and frequently achieved yields below or barely matching those of the existing local or improved varieties.

Abalu and Yayock (1980) pointed out that the low rates of adoption of improved farm technology observed did not necessarily reflect the innate of undesirable psychological characteristics of small farmers. Rather they probably reflected the inappropriateness of the technologies being recommended and the limited access most serious farmers have to these technologies.

Silier (1980) opined that the use of modern agricultural technologies remain generally limited in spite of their availability because of the unequal distribution of land, capital, etc.

The reasons, as mentioned by Hildebrand (1980) for the resistance on the part of the small farmers, to accepting change was not one of motivation but rather one of not having available technology which was appropriate from these farmers' own point of view.

The manual was prepared by Byerlee and others (1980) for the professional involvement in research on improving agricultural technologies for farmers. The main themes were that effective research on agricultural technology started and finished with the farmers.

Qram (1980) concluded that in order to counter the effects of land and water scarcities and the anticipated agricultural labour shortage of the future, a continuum of research will be required to find appropriate technologies designed to foster labour, capital and energy intensive production of high value crops and livestock in these areas.

Cernuda (1980) pointed out that in order to make best use of the limited resources and provide more employment opportunities, appropriate technology was required.

According to Skromme (1980) a technology was defined as appropriate when it closely met the specific existing needs of the intended user could be readily acquired, and effectively and profitably used to increase the quantity and/or quality of production.

Mansha (1980) argued for appropriate, dependable and easy to operate technologies with the purchasing power of small farmers and adequate in bringing them economic returns.

Anderson (1981) suggested that the technologies were to be tested in the three dimensions of (i) resource appropriateness, (ii) needs appropriateness, and (iii) goals appropriateness.

Rajagopalan (1981) pointed out that for sustain growth it would be necessary to build resource support and extension approaches relevant and appropriate to local conditions.

Flit (1981) argued that the necessity for developing countries to adopt technologies suited to their conditions and needs. This had resulted in confusion about the concept of appropriate technology. In his study the principal theories on this matter were examined and the error of equating adequate or appropriate technology with small, rural or intermediate technology was emphasized. The interaction between the level of technology used and the social, economic and political environments were underlined. It was suggested that the central theme of the debate should not be limited to the existence or lack of appropriate technologies, but should be concentrated on the steps carried out by a society to achieve its goals. Obviously appropriate handling of technology required social and economic development policies, national awareness of validity of these policies and an allocation of priorities for their achievement.

Pearson (1982) suggested that every successful project had six points in common. These are:

(i) an appropriate agricultural technologies was developed to meet that need,

(ii) an agricultural need was identified,
(iii) a prototype was developed to technological local manufacturers,
(iv) the product was field tested,
(v) the prototype was modified after trials, and
(vi) the product was extended to manufacturers and end users.

Timber (1982) examined the major roles played by technology choice, appropriate national price policies which provided incentives for bottom up development, and the adoption of practical and available innovations.

Morris (1983) discussed the most appropriate system of small holding mechanization which depended very much on local socio-economic factors. He found that in many Third World countries the use of animal power, or even simply of human power using improved hand implements were more attractive.

Mecormick and others (1984) discussed the need and availability of appropriate technology. The indirect role that non-agricultural technologies can play an increasing food production was found in their study.

Veda (1984) presented as a working hypothesis that the introduction of an appropriate technology could improve the rice production and the efficiency of rice farming of tropical Asia.

Desai (1984) reported that the slow rate of adoption of high yielding varieties in the Eastern India indicated that correct rice technology had not yet been evolved for various parts of the area.

Kuada (1984) viewed an agricultural technology development of indigenous technology based on local skill and resources, and the kind of technology that fitted more appropriately into the local circumstances.

The methodological aspect for identifying and evaluating appropriate new techniques for small farmers had been analyzed by Chapmam (1985).

Gee-Clough and Paterson (1985) had pleaded for selective emphasis on technology suitable for the typical small farm situation of scarce resources and limited access to information and inputs.

Rahim and Hazra (1991) while raising the question "how appropriate the appropriate technology (presently advocated) is", had tried to come up with a clear comprehension of the concept of appropriate technology as: "The technology which is technically feasible, and exactly consistent with the particular setting of the given sector which is a complex of economic, cultural and political considerations and does properly suit the local resource endowment. This concept of appropriate technology is indifferent to the genesis of the technology—traditional or improved, indigenous or imported."

The above studies related with the present investigation presented under review of literature led the author to conclude that in spite of the innovation of modern agricultural technologies for higher productivity, the yield per acre of rice in India remains at its low level as compared to that of other countries. It has also been pointed out that a difference between potential yield achievable at demonstration plot and the actual yield at farmers' field is very much in existence. No doubt, the yield gap of rice is caused due to the sub-optimal application of production inputs in rice fields by the farmers. That is, the yield gap is directly related with the technological gap. There must be some reasons which impeded the farmers from the application of recommended level of production inputs in their rice fields. These factors may be social, economical, infrastructural and administrative.

At the same time it can also be concluded that the factors responsible for non-adoption of improved rice technologies have been identified and recommended to remove these factors to increase the rice productivity. But fruitful results are yet to come. Therefore, it seems that the farmers do not adopt the modern rice technologies at full package in the present socio-economic and political set up. Therefore, when these factors have been found impossible to be removed without changing the institutional, social and economic framework of the country, the technology itself may be reformulated. In other words, farmers are unable to accept the available improved rice production technologies due to the inappropriateness with respect to their existing circumstances. Therefore, rice production technologies could be reformulated in such a way that these may be properly suit with the farmers' resource endowment at the existing socio-economic conditions and institutional framework.

3

Theoretical Framework

The conceptual framework of the study has been discussed in this chapter in order to provide a complete theoretical base for the empirical investigation and identification of relevant factors. Finally, a set of working hypotheses were developed for the study.

The review of literature presented in the previous chapter has helped to formulate the theoretical orientation for the present study. The present chapter has been divided into the following sections:

The conceptual framework of the study
The operationalization of the concepts
Derivation of hypotheses

Conceptual Framework of the Study

Conceptual framework, no doubt, is an integral part of any research work. Rogers and Sovening (1969) said that the development of a conceptual framework made a research more meaningful, for whatever in nature; an empirical investigation without theoretical basis became bogged down in masses of relevant data and at the same time ignored potentially fruitful objectives. For systematic discussion the present chapter has been further divided into:

Constraints, and
Appropriate technology.

Constraints

The Random House Dictionary of English Language gives the meaning of "constraint" as something that constraints; the condition of being constrained.

The Oxford English Dictionary defines the term "constraint" as to force a person to (into) a course of action, state, place, etc., to restrain within bounds; or to limit. In dynamics, constraint means to restrict the motion of (a body or particle) to a certain course.

The psychologists define constraint as "arrest by some cause, reason or principle, foreign to self" e.g. external constraint.

Pandya and Tiwari (1988) defined constraints as "those items of difficulties or problems faced by the individuals in adoption of...technology". Zinyama (1988) and Petharam (1989) called the problems and/or limitations as constraints. Waghmare and Pandit (1982) identified constraints in terms of "causes hindering... adoption of new technology".

In the present study it has been assumed that the farmers cannot use the optimum level of rice technologies in their fields which are available. The recipients of the modern technology of rice cultivation might be facing certain difficulties or hindrances in adopting the technology. These constraints are perceived by the rice producers.

The conceptual and theoretical basis for the selection of dependent and independent variables for the study are discussed below.

Technological Gap

One of the common features of Indian agriculture is that farmers do not apply all the necessary inputs/cultural practices for rice production at the recommended level. Jadon (1973) reported that about two-fifth of the adopters had applied farm yard manure ... as per recommendation. Padheria and Patel (1975) also found that only one-fifth of the adopters used compost manure as per recommendation.

In the present study "technological gap" has been conceptualized as the difference between the level of use of a particular input/practice for a specific rice variety in Adoptive Research Farm and the level of use of that particular input/practice for the variety in farmers' field. Technological gap can also be known as input gap. For this study technological gap and yield gap both have been considered dependent variables with separate sets of independent variables in different cases.

Yield Gap

Yield gap has been defined in various ways by different scientists depending upon the level of comparison.

Gomez (1977) developed a conceptual model to show the concepts of yield gaps. He divided the difference between the experimental station yield and actual farm yield (the yield gap) into two distinct parts by introducing an intermediate yield level representing the potential farm yield or yield obtained in farmers' field using the highest possible inputs combinations. The difference between experimental yield and potential farm yield has been defined as yield gap-I. The causes of yield gap-I are environmental differences between experimental stations and the actual rice farms, and some components of the technology that not transferable to the farmers' fields. The yield gap-II has been defined as the difference between that potential farm yield and the actual farm yield. The gap exists because farmers use inputs or cultural practices that result in lower yields than those possible on their farms. The present study is concerned with the yield gap-II.

Swamianthan (1977) defined three types of yield gap which account for the untapped yield reservoir in Indian agriculture. According to him, the gap between yield possible on theoretical considerations and the best yield so far achieved can be referred as yield gap-I, which may also be called as 'Research Gap'. Gap-II, which may be referred to as 'Research-*cum*-Management Gap', is the gap between the best yields obtained in a research farm and by a good farmer. He termed the yield gap-III as the difference between the best average yields realized by a farmer in a State and the State average yield. The gap-III is also called as 'Extension Gap'.

Barker (1977) defined the gap as the difference between the highest yield on a farm or at an experimental station and the average national yield.

According to Mukherjee (1977), the gap can be defined as the ratio between the potential yield as found in the demonstrations in the given state and the average State yield. He concluded that when the gap ratio is low (i.e., the state average yield approaches the yield of the demonstration plots), farmers' technical competence is high and *vice versa.*

Herdt and Wickham (1975) defined gap as the difference between the yield potential at the experimental station during the dry season in a good year and the average national yield.

Sen and Das (1983) found that yield gaps are of three types, the gap between research farm and demonstration farm, the gap between demonstration farm and the average yield of the district and the gap between demonstration and small farmers' field.

In the present study the difference between potential rice yield with the application of optimal package of practices in demonstration plot and actual farm yield has been conceptualized as the yield gap.

Explanatory study, review of literature, discussion with the agricultural scientists and with the progressive farmers, helped in identifying the factors related with yield gap and technological gap.

Amongst a large number of variables which may have theoretical relationship with the dependent variable, a manageable system of important variables that could be adapted to empirical measurement has been considered in this study. The independent variables considered having influence on yield gap and technological gap have been grouped as (a) biological factors responsible for yield gap, (b) general or situational variables related with technological gap, and (c) various kinds of constraints related with rice production.

(a) Biological Factors

The yield of rice depends directly upon the biological factors/cultural practices such as quality of seed, fertilizer, manuring, weeding, etc. In the present study yield gap has been considered as dependent variable, independent variables conceptualized as follows:

Seed Rate: It refers to the amount of seed (kg./ac.) of a particular rice variety required for proper sowing. The recommended dose of seed should be used for optimal production.

Seed Treatment: This is considered as one of the important practices for rice production. In the present study seed treatment refers whether the seeds of various rice varieties cultivated by farmers are treated with chemical or certified. Farmers are recommended to use certified seeds for higher production as the productivity of rice variety decreases if old and raw seeds are used in rice cultivation by the farmers.

Ploughing: It refers the frequency of times of tilling in a particular rice field in the crop season. It may be considered as an important cultural practice for high rice yield.

Method of Sowing: In the present study the method of sowing refers whether farmers do use the broad casting method or line transplantation for rice cultivation. Farmers should follow line transplantation for higher productivity.

Level of Use of Organic Manure: It indicates the amount of organic manure in cart per acre used in the farmers' rice fields. Organic manure involves the physical properties of the soil and increases the supply of availability of nutrients to the plants (Buckman and Brady, 1980).

Sagar (1983) found a positive and significant relationship between farmers' productivity of crops and their level of use of organic manure.

Level of Fertilizer Use: It refers to the amount of NPK (kg/ac) used by an individual farmer for a particular rice variety. Chemical fertilizer is one of the key inputs of increasing agricultural production and productivity. The National Council of Applied Economic Research (1970) while evaluating the impact of Indo-German Fertilizer Educational Project in West Bengal found a positive correlation between observed yields of the farmers and the observed level of fertilizer use.

Level of Use of Plant Protection Chemicals: It refers to the number of times applying pesticides in the farmers' rice farm. Multiple cropping with high yielding varieties and use of more fertilizer and irrigation water have made the rice varieties vulnerable to attack of diseases, insect pest etc. Unless the negative factors of production like insect pests, diseases, weeds, rodents, etc., are properly taken care of, the farmers are not likely to get a good harvest. The use of plant protection chemical in right amount at proper time is, therefore, necessary in getting high yield of rice varieties.

Weeding: This is one of the crucial cultural practices essential for rice production. In this study the number of times the farmers do apply this culture in rice fields has been considered.

(b) Situational Variables

The situation or the circumstances under which an individual receives a stimulus forms an important element in any theory of human action.

This element has been recognized by Pearson and Shils (1951) as they have stated that behaviour of any living organism is called action only when it is analyzed in terms of situation in which it occurs. In the present study technological gap may be the course of rice yield gap. The variables which assumed to be related with technological gap are conceptualized below:

Age of Farmer: Age refers to the number of years the respondent lived since birth at the time of interview to the nearest whole number. Farmers, younger in age likely to be progressive and may have less technological gap due to more adoption of recommended package of practices.

Caste of the Farmer: A caste system is one variety of society divided into a number of self-contained and completely segregated units (caste), mutual relation between which are ritually determined in a graded scale (Hutton, 1933). Caste still remains its pivotal position in the social structure of Indian villages. Studies by Ray and others (1968), Kumar (1976) have shown that the caste of the farmers have positive relationship with their adoption of practices.

Family Size: It refers to the number of members in the individual farmer's family. Generally up to a family of 5 members is regarded as a small size family and a family with more than 5 members as a large family size. A large size of family is more conducive in better management of farm and hence, may result in less technological gap.

Education: Education is the process of producing desired change in the behaviour of the people. It produces changes in the knowledge, skill, attitude and action. It widens their mental horizon by helping them to develop favourable outlook; correct perception and objective assessment. It also imparts an ability to substitute an obsolete practice with an improved one. Education gives a favourable disposition to the farmer to adopt new ideas.

Economic Status: Economic status refers to the position a farmer or his family occupies in comparison to others in respect of land, type of house, farm power and materials possession. It may be assumed that higher the economic status of an individual, the more favourable he would be disposed towards increasing production by adopting improved rice technologies at recommended level.

Social Participation: Social participation refers to the voluntary sharing in person and group to group relationship beyond the immediate household affairs (Hay, 1951). It shows the degree to which the farmers are involved in formal organizations as member or office bearer and regularity in their attendance to meetings.

Farm Size: Farm is a tract of land possessed by an individual farmer for the purpose of growing crops. Studies on adoption and diffusion have indicated that farm size, in most cases, is positively and significantly correlated to the adoption of improved farm practices (Singh and Sohal, 1967; Roy and others, 1968; Singh and Singh, 1970; Sinha, 1978 and Singh, 1979). Farm size is also an economic status in rural India.

In the present study the whole farm families have been classified into four categories on the basis of land holding. The farmers those who have farm size below 1 acre are category-I farmers. Category-II farmers' land holding ranged between 1 tc 2.5 acres. If the land holding is 2.5 to 5 acres, are classified as category-III farmers. Category-IV farmers' size holding is 5 or above 5 acres.

Status of Land Ownership: Land ownership status refers to if a farmer cultivates his own land or a land taken on lease as share cropper. It is presumed that the tenant farmers generally apply inputs at a lower dose in comparison to the land owner farmers

Irrigation Index: Irrigation index refers to the percentage of total area of a farm under irrigation. Assured irrigation is considered as a prerequisite for the adoption of improved rice technologies at recommended dose. The proportion of irrigated area to the total cropped area may as well indicate the level of adoption of improved farm practices.

Index of Outstanding Credit: It refers to the proportion of loans taken from different sources to the total cost of rice production. To meet the production cost, farmers borrow money from different various sources like nationalized bank, block agency, co-operative bank and money lenders. It is assumed that farmers who follow modern method of cultivation need more cash and subsequently repay the loan from the increased output.

Utilization of Mass Media: It indicates that how far the farmer is aware about the modern rice production technology through mass media. One of the major functions of mass media in India is to disseminate the improved farm technology. Implied in it is to motivate the farmers to adopt improved package of practices and thereby to reduce technological gap.

Sagar (1983) found that productivity of crops was positively and significantly correlated with the utilization of mass media of small, medium and pooled sample of farmers.

Utilization of Personal Cosmopolite Sources of Information: Cosmopolite sources of information are conceptualized as those from outside the social system being investigated (Rogers and Shoemaker, 1971). In developing countries, personal cosmopolite sources of information play an important role in inducing desirable change. Personal cosmopolite sources are important because they act as carriers of change provide face to face, word to mouth communication and motivate people to adopt new technology.

(c) Constraints Perceived by Farmers in Adoption of Modern Rice Practices at Recommended Level

There are a number of constraints faced by the farmers in the adoption of improved rice technologies at recommended level. Sen (1985) pointed out that the poor performance of agriculture in Eastern India is generally associated with physical, institutional, socio-economic and organizational environments which together determine agricultural growth. Farmers' choice and decision making in the production process are greatly constrained by factors which are beyond their control. It was opined that micro level studies will have to be carried out to identify constraints in the village and block levels.

In the present study constraints refer to items of difficulty perceived by the farmers in adopting the recommended technologies on rice production. The constraints are related to agro-biological, socio-cultural, technological, social, economical, infrastructural and relating to supply, services, etc.

Gomez (1987) shows that the above mentioned constraints which are the causes of yield gap can be divided into two broad categories. One is the biological constraints and other is the socio-economic.

Biological Constraints: The biological constraints include the factors such as quality of seed, weeding, fertilizer, soil fertility, diseases and insects etc. The biological explanation of yield gap shows that farmers' yield is higher if they use certified seeds, apply recommended level of fertilizers and plant protection chemicals and use the best cultural practices.

Socio-economic Constraints: The socio-economic constraints explain why farmers do not use the practices and inputs necessary to obtain potential yields. There are many factors retained the farmers in using such input combinations viz. costs and returns, lack of knowledge about improved rice technologies, lack of credit and capital, non-availability of inputs, lack of motivation, size of the farm, tenure status, traditional beliefs of cultivation etc.

Appropriate Technology

In the present study as it has been tried to identify the appropriate technologies of rice production for different size groups. Appropriate technology may be considered as one which is technically feasible, economically viable and socially desirable.

Pande (1984) pointed out that a development plan should incorporate organic methods of farming, recycling of nature and utilization of industrial by-products.

Premberton-Pigott (1987) argued that the labour intensive processes of production are not applicable, but viable at the micro-economic level. He concluded that once it has been established that the first priority is people and their employment, the correct type of machinery and tools, the tools and implementation model, the appropriate technology and appropriate social technology can be found.

According to Krech and Crutchfield (1984) "the selection of goals as well as means would depend on three criteria namely, (i) cultural norms and values; these act as a standard and provide criteria by which people visualize their goals, (ii) biological capacity—individual differs in their perceptual and cognitive capabilities which influence their goals, and (iii) accessibility in the physical and social environment—an individual will most likely orient his behaviour towards some goals attainable within his environment."

The term 'appropriate technology' is very cleverly used modifying the term like intermediate technology, labour intensive technology or low cost technology. Although practically it refers a combination of them.

In an over populated and energy scarce country like India appropriate technology is frequently viewed as labour intensive technology. Thomas (1974) stated that a necessary condition for compatibility is a choice of technique suiatable for the attainment of high employment in an unskilled labour surplus economy.

Bunting (1979) observed that the generation of yield maximizing technology was getting priority rather than more important problems of the farmers faced in the real life.

Amla (1979) said that the technology, supposed to be transferred should clearly establish its economic advantage.

According to Das (1981), development is the goal and the technology is the means. Appropriateness depends on the time and space to which the human beings belong.

Burraw (1981) found that the assumptions for the appropriate technology have changed over time. In the past, technology has been viewed as the product of a global evolutionary process so that the present technology is by definition better than older technology. Secondly, technological evolution is inherently technical-culturally neutral process leading towards more productive and efficient solution. Thirdly, institution like research institutes, university, laboratories and experimental stations are seemed as responsible for the variety of the innovation process. Fourthly, technological advancement in rural areas is essentially a process of dissemination of information from centralized institutions to ignorant rural people. Fifthly, increasing inequalities associated with new technologies (since it is aimed at increasing efficiency only) is unfortunate but unavoidable. And finally, failure of rural people to adopt this technology is usually attributed to a conservative, resistance to change and/or ineffective training of extension workers.

Rahim and Hazra (1991) have tried to come up with a clear comprehension of the concept of appropriate technology. According to them the technology is appropriate which is technically feasible, and exactly consistent with the particular setting of the given sector which is a complex of economic, cultural and political considerations and does properly suit the local resource endowment. The appropriate technology is indifferent to the genesis of the technology i.e. indigenous or imported, and nature i.e. traditional or improved.

The Operationalization of the Concepts

Actual Yield: It is the production of rice in quintal per acre of land in existing farm condition.

Potential Yield: It is the maximum amount of rice production in quintal per acre attained at the recommended level of input combination. The yield of the demonstration plot is termed as potential yield.

Yield Gap: In the present study "Yield Gap" has been conceptualized as the comparison of yield of a particular rice variety in the demonstration field (potential yield) and in the farmers' field (actual yield). In other words yield gap is the difference between potential yield and actual yield. Mathematically "Yield Gap" can be derived as

$$Yig = Yip - Yia$$

Where,
Yig = yield gap of the rice variety
Yip = potential yield of the variety
Yia = actual yield of the variety.

Technologies: In the present study technology is simply considered as the improved agricultural practices. In the term of operational research, the technologies have been considered as activities. If there is any change in any element of the input-output matrix of any activity then it has been considered as another technology.

Adoption of Technology: It implies that the application of the improved rice production practices in the farmers' field.

Technological Gap: "Technological gap" or "input gap", for the present study, has been conceptualized as the difference between the level of use of a particular input and/or practice for a particular rice variety in the demonstration plot (Recommended dose) and the level of use of that particular input/practice for that particular input and/or practice for that particular rice variety in farmers' field. In other words, the difference between recommended level of input/ cultural practice application and actual level of input/cultural practice application has been termed as "Technological Gap" or "Input Gap". Mathematically technological gap can be derived as:

$$Xjg = Xjr - Xja$$

Where,
Xjg = gap in the use of j input/practice for a particular rice variety

Xjr = level of use of j input/practice in demonstration plot i.e. recommended level for a particular variety

Xja = level of use of j input/practice in farmers' field for the variety.

Farm Plan: It means that plan which is unique for the farm, allocating its resources—natural, human, and capital as rationally as possible to satisfy given objective function subject to given constraints including predetermined social goals and local needs.

Cost of Cultivation: In the present study, the cost of cultivation of a crop enterprise has mainly been used in the comparative analysis among the crop enterprises. Hence cost A, excluding land revenue, cesses and other taxes, depreciation on implements farm buildings, has been considered in this study.

Cropping Pattern: It is the set of crops with specific varieties cultivated in the farm with the particular sequence in two crop seasons, viz. kharif and rabi.

Assets: It is that property which has a money value and ensured a monetary return in future. Thus cash is excluded from this head.

Contributory Factors: It refers to that factors of occurrence which ensures greater likelihood of influence of independent variables on the dependent variable(s).

Derivation of Hypotheses

On the basis of review of literature and theoretical framework coupled with authors experience and keeping in mind the objectives of the present study some working hypotheses related to this study were set up and the investigation was carried out to test these hypotheses.

Hypo. 1: Significant yield gap in rice production exists in the farmers' field.

Hypo. 2: There is a positive relationship between the overall yield gap and overall technological gap.

Hypo. 3: There is a relationship between yield gap of rice and the gaps in the application of inputs/cultural practices such as seed rate, seed treatment, method of sowing, ploughing, manuring, application of NPK fertilizers, weeding and application of plant protection chemicals etc.

Hypo. 4: A relationship between technological gap and situational factors such as age of the farmer, caste of the farmer, family size, education, economic status, social participation, farm size, irrigation index, index of outstanding credit, status of land ownership, utilization of mass media, utilization of cosmopolite sources of information and participation in training programme etc.

Hypo. 5: The constraints perceived by the farmers for non-adoption of modern rice technologies in its full recommended package might be social, economic, infrastructural and institutional in nature.

Hypo. 6: A technology might be appropriate irrespective of its genesis, i.e. improved or indigenous; and nature, i.e. improved or traditional.

4

Profile of the Study Area

This chapter is devoted to present a brief description of the study area. Knowledge of the general features of the area facilitates a proper understanding of the problem under study. Hence, an attempt has been made to present some relevant and significant features of the agro-economic situation of the study area. The present study has been carried out in the sub-humid lateritic belt of West Bengal. Though the sub-humid lateritic belt includes the districts of Birbhum, Bankura, Purlia, part of Midnapur and part of Burdwan, this study has been conducted in the Birbhum district which covers the central area of the belt.

A brief discussion related to agro-economic background of the study area has been given in the following paragraphs.

Location of the District

Birbhum, an important district of "Rarh Region" is situated in the Northern most part of Burdwan division of West Bengal. The district lies between 23°-32′-30″ and 24°-35′-00″ North Latitude and 88°-01′-40″ and 87°-05′-00″ East Longitude. In shape it looks like an isosceles triangle. The apex is situated at the northern extremity not far south of the point where the Ganges and the hills of the Santhal Parganas of Bihar begin to diverge while the river Ajoy forms the base of this triangle. Birbhum is bounded on the north and west by the Santhal Parganas, on the east by the districts of Murshidabad and Burdwan, and on the south by Burdwan from which it is separated by the Ajoy River.

The district of Birbhum comprises three Sub-Divisions, namely Bolpur, Rumpurhat and Suri Sadar. There are 19 Blocks and 19 Panchayat Samitis, 7 in Suri Sadar, 8 in Rampurhat and 4 in Bolpur

Sub-Division. There are 14 Police Stations, 6 towns and 169 Gram Panchayats in the district.

The district is spread over 4,514 sq.kms. A considerable area of the district is characterized by undulating topography. The rocks of Chhotanagpur Plateau have been extended into the western portion of the distict comprising Rajnagar, Khayrasole, Dubrajpur, Mahammad Bazar, Suri-I, Illampbazar, Rampurhat-I, Nalhati-I and Murarai-I Blocks.

Agro-climatic Situation

The Agro-climatic situation of the district is mainly influenced by the presence of a number of rivers, rivulets, dams, barrages and forests. Except in the monsoon season dry wheather normally prevails in this district round the year with variation of temperature 12.7°C to 28.3°C in winter and from 25.5°C to 39.4°C in summer on an average. The predominant soil types are old alluvium and red laterite. The alluvium soils are mostly of loamy, medium in organic matter and available phosphate, medium to high available potash. Soil is acidic, pH varies from 5.0 to 6.5. The red and lateritic soil are light textured, porous, gravel, poor in organic matter, available phosphate and bases, pH varies from 4.8 to 6.

Demography

The total population of the district according to 1991 census is 21,11,088 which is 3.85 per cent of the total population of the State. Out of the total population of the district 10,78,387 (50.06 per cent) are male, and 10,32,701 (49.02 per cent) are female. Total rural population of this district is 19,83,249 (91.72 per cent) and urban population is 6,24,521 (8.28 per cent). The Scheduled Caste population is 6,24,521 (29.79 per cent) and Scheduled Tribe population is 1,45,135 (6.96 per cent). The density of population of the district is 468 per sq.km. The literacy rate of the district is about 42 per cent. Recently the literacy rate may have been increased due to eradication of illiteracy drive by the State Government.

The total number of workers in this district according to 1981 census is 5,88,622 (28 per cent) out of whom 2,23,505 are cultivators and 2,25,930 are agricultural labourers. The percentage of workers engaged in agricultural sector is 76.35 per cent. The total number of marginal farmers is 84,473, small farmers are 28,151. The number of landless labourers are 2,70,981, the total number of bargadars are 81,280, number of pattaholders are 55,432, and big farmers are 15,530. The number farm families of land holding up to 1 ha. is 1,81,144 (66.1 per cent), 1 to 2 ha., is 62,472 (22.8 per cent), 2 to 4 ha., is 24,112 (8.8 per cent) and above 4 ha. is 6,302 (2.3 per cent) of total holding.

Land Utilization

As has been stated earlier, of the total geographical area of 4,514 sq. kms, the net sown area constitutes 3,30,418 ha. (72.42 per cent). The grossed cropped area is 5,31,463, that is 161 per cent is the cropping intensity. Area under non-agricultural use is 72,784 ha. Forests constitute 15,822 ha., barren and uncultivable land is 4,717 ha. The area of the current follows land is 1,545 ha. The area of high land situation is 1,02,000 ha., the medium land is 1,45,000 ha., and low land is 83,080 ha. The areas under flood prone and drought prone are 21,000 and 80,000 ha. respectively.

As regards the cropping pattern of the district, relevant data reveal that food crops dominate the cropping pattern of the district. The principal crops of the district are paddy, wheat, pulses, oilseeds, vegetables, sugarcane, potato, and jute. Amongst the paddy alone accounts 90 per cent of the net sown area in Kharif season. The high yielding varieties of rice are practiced both in kharif and boro seasons. The area under boro cultivation is increasing in recent times.

Irrigation plays crucial role in agricultural development. The various sources of irrigation of the districts are river lift irrigation, river valley project, deep tubewells, minor irrigation, small irrigation, shallow irrigation schemes and tank irrigation. There are two big irrigation projects—one is Mayurakshi River Project and second is the Hinglow Reservoir Scheme. The area under D.T.W. irrigation is 3,080 ha., the area under R.L.I. irrigation is 7,050 hectares, shallow tubewells supply irrigation to 42,820 hectares, 1,142 ha. land irrigated through dugwell. Tank irrigation provide to 84,900 ha. Canal is the main single source of irrigation, it includes 2,21,000 ha. The total gross area irrigated through S.I. Schemes and Boro Bundh is 850 ha.

Marketing Facility

The marketing infrastructure in the district is developed with 103 nos. of local markets and 14 nos. of whole sale markets to cater the needs of the people. Besides, there is one regulated market at Bolpur. Co-operative Thana Marketing Societies and Agro-Industries Service Centres also cater the needs of the farmers for their inputs, like seeds, fertilizer, pesticides, and implements. Moreover, there are 10 nos. of cold storages for storing of about 27,898 tonnes of tomato.

Communication and Transportation Facilities

Communication and transports are considered as the key factors for economic development. Trade and business largely depended upon these facilities. Most of the areas are connected by roads and railways throughout the length and breadth of the district. All the block headquarters, important urban areas and trade centres are connected with the district headquarters with *pucca* roads. Interior areas are also connected mostly with either Morrum or *Kachcha* roads. The state highways connect Bolpur, Suri, Rampurhat, Sainthia, Dubrajpur and Nalhati towns, G.T. Road and NH-34. As a result, quick communication and transport of agricultural commodities and consumers goods over different parts of the district, linking Calcutta and other adjoining district have been made possible.

Banking

As regards to financial institutions, the district is well served by nationalized and commercial banks, regional rural banks, co-operative banks, land development and co-operative societies.

It is hardly need to emphasize the importance of banking institutions for economic development. The farmers are provided different types of credit facilities for agricultural as well as non-agricultural purposes throughout the year. The banking network in the district of Birbhum is presented in the following table:

Table 4.1: No. of Bank Branches in Birbhum (as on 31.12.90)

Sl. No	*Bank*	*Urban*	*Semi-urban*	*Total*
1.	UCO Bank	20	08	28
2.	State Bank of India	19	07	26
3.	United Bank of India	07	06	13
4.	Allahabad Bank	08	06	14
5.	Union Bank of India	05	04	09
6.	Central Bank of India	05	02	07
7.	Syndicate Bank	03	—	03
8.	Canara Bank	02	—	02
9.	New Bank of India	01	—	01
10.	Indian Overseas Bank	01	—	01
11.	Mayurakshi Gramin Bank	60	05	65
12.	District Central Co-operative Bank Ltd.	—	—	14
13.	Land Development Bank Ltd.	—	—	03

Industry

Though agriculture is the main occupation of the people of the district, a sizeable proportion of total working population is engaged in industrial and business activities. The district is rich from minerals. The mineral products of the district consist of iron, coal, limestone, laterite, granite and sand stone. Extraction and manufacture of iron from its ore constituted at one time an industry of considerable importance. However, there are some coalmines in the district adjoining to the Ranigang coal fields.

The district also consist many small scale industries in town areas. Handloom is one of the famous cottage industries of the district. The total number of handloom in the district is 10,185. There is a sugar mill in Ahamedpur. Sainthia is one of the biggest business centres of the district. A big thermal power station is being constructed in Bakreshwar.

Mahammad Bazar Community Development Block

In the present study the Mahammad Bazar Community Development Block was selected on the basis of Crop Yield Index developed for the study.

This Block is situated in the western part of the district and outlined by Santhal Parganas in the west, Rampurhat Community

Development Block in the east, Sainthia Community Development Block in the south-east, and Suri Sadar in the south.

The area available for cultivation in the Block is 18.28 ('000) ha. and 100 per cent of the soil of this Block is predominantly Red and Lateritic type. Out of total cultivable land, 7 ('000) ha. in high land situation; 7 ('000) ha. is medium land situation and 4.35 ('000) ha. is in low land situation. 7 ('000) ha. land of this Block is drought prone. In kharif season 370 ha. of land receives irrigation through River Lift Irrigation, 86 ha. through Shallow Tubewell, 25 ha. receives irrigation from Dug Well, 1300 ha. through Tank and 5600 ha. through canal, and through S.I. Schemes and Boro Bundh 125 ha. land of this Block receives irrigation in kharif season. In Rabi and summer seasons 370 ha. of land of this block receives irrigation by River Lift Irrigation, 86 ha. by Shallow Tube Well, 25 ha. by Dug Well, 1300 ha. by Tank, 3700 ha. of land by Canal and 320 ha. of land receives irrigaton by S.I. Schemes and Boro Bundh.

The Mahammad Bazar Community Development Block comprise 152 mouzas. Out of 152 mouzas of the district 4 mouzas namely Kaijuli, Fullaipur, Tajpur and Raghunathpur were selected by random sampling method.

Mahammad Bazar Block is totally a rural area. Total population of this Block is 93,484 out of whom 47,713 are male and 45,771 are female. Literacy rate of male is 37.8 per cent and that of female is 20.2 per cent. According to 1981 Census Report, out of total population 13,213 (14.2 per cent) are agricultural labourers of whom 10,157 are male and 3,056 are female. The total percentage of backward population is 47.3 per cent. Percentage of Scheduled Caste population is 29.20 and 18 per cent belong in the Scheduled Tribe category.

5

Methodology

This chapter describes the methodological details of the study i.e. the sampling techniques, collection of data, empirical measurement of variables, and analytical procedures used for fulfilling different objectives of this study. Accordingly, the chapter has been divided into four main sections. The first section deals with sampling technique used to select sample farmers in the study area. The second section describes the types and sources of data, and methods of collection of data. The empirical measurement of variables has been presented in section three. The last section is devoted to specification of the analytical tools used to attain different objectives of the study.

Sampling Techniques

The present study has been conducted in the Birbhum district which falls into the sub-humid lateritic belt of West Bengal. Mahammad Bazar Block, one of the 14 Blocks of the district was selected on the basis of "Crop Yield Index". The selection criterion was to choose a block having crop yield index about 100 as 100 is the average of the district. The crop yield index of the Block was calculated to be 100.12. In the next stage random sampling technique was used to select four villages from the Block. In this way Kaijuli, Fullaipur, Tajpur and Raghunathpur were selected as the study villages. Finally, 100 farmers scattered in the four villages were selected on the basis of stratified random sampling of farmers with probability proportion to the farm size so that the sample can represent the actual proportion of all four strata of the farmers. The whole farm families have been divided into four categories—category-I, category-II, category-III and category-IV. Thus following a multistage stratified random sampling technique finally 100 farmers in total were selected. The distribution of sample farmers into different categories was as 14 farmers in category-I, 26 in category-II, 40 in category-III and 20 in category-IV. The farmers having land holding below 1 acre were considered as category-I, farmers having land between 1 to 2.5 acres were considered as category-II, 2.5 to 5 acres land as category-III farmers and above 5 acres land holding was considered as category-IV farmers.

Method of Field Data Collection

The relevant primary data pertaining to the present study were collected from the selected respondents during June 1988 to May 1989 with the help of specially designed pre-tested Farm Record Book and two structured schedules through cost accounting method and personal interview method respectively.

Schedule-I contains five parts. The first part contained items on certain socio-personal variables and some general information like age, tenancy, land holding, irrigation index etc. The second part contained the cropping pattern. Next part contained different types of constraints faced by the farmers, spread over four point scale. The fourth part of the schedule contained information related to yields of different rice varieties. The last part of the schedule contained reasons for non-adoption of improved farm technologies for rice production.

Schedule-II was prepared to identify technological gap for various rice varieties cultivated by the sample farmers in study area. The first part of this schedule contained technological information regarding seed, land preparation, method of sowing, farm yield manure, fertilizer, irrigation, weeding, plant protection measures etc. The second part of the schedule-II contained some general constraints of rice production perceived by farmers, spread over a four point scale. For this purpose 49 constraints were selected.

The Farm Record Book contained every activities performed by the sample farmers during the study period. The information related to agriculture, business and services. The detailed agricultural activities of the sample farmers performed every day were recorded in Farm Record Book. The required data for the present study were obtained from the Farm Record Book and schedules prepared for this study.

Secondary data related to this study were collected from different agricultural offices, blocks, etc. The data on available improved rice technologies were collected from the Adaptive Research Farms of Sriniketan and Nalhati and Experimental farm of the Institute of Agriculture, Visva-Bharati.

Empirical Measurement of Variables

In the present study the yield gap and technological gap were considered as dependent variables in different occasions. The selected independent variables were classified into three categories—biological factors, situational variables, and constraints of rice production. The number of biological factors, situational variables and constraints were 10, 13 and 49 respectively.

Dependent Variables

The overall yield gap and technological gap were considered as the dependent variables for the study.

Yield Gap of rice (variety-wise) has been defined as the proportion of gap in yield, to the potential yield, expressed in percentage. The overall rice yield gap of the farmer is the mean of the yield gaps for all the varieties practiced by the farmers in the same crop year.

Overall Rice Yield gap of the farmer can be computed using the following procedure.

Computation of Overall Yield Gap of Rice:

Farm	:	'X'
Village	:	Kaijuli
Block	:	Mahammad Bazar
Rice varieties practiced	:	IR-36, Assam, Kadamshal, Boro Ratna
District	:	Birbhum
Year	:	1989-90

Table 5.1: Computation of Overall Yield Gap

Sl. No	*Rice Variety*	*Percentage Yield Gap*
1.	IR-36	33.46
2.	Assam Aush	20.3
3.	Kadamshal	18.50
4.	Boro Ratna	12.22
	Total	84.50

Total number of rice varieties practiced by the farmer in the same crop year = 4.

Then, overall yield gap of rice of the farmer 'X'=84.50/ 4 = 21.12 per cent.

$$\text{Where, Percentage Yield Gap} = \frac{\text{Potential yield} - \text{Actual yield}}{\text{Potential yield}} \times 100$$

The following major rice varieties (HYV and local) cultivated by the sample farmers in the study area were selected for the study.

There were nine high yielding rice varieties and eleven local rice varieties practiced by the sample farmers in kharif season, and in boro season the number of high yielding rice varieties cultivated was only three. The kharif high yielding varieties were IR-36, IR-50, Ratna, Pankaj, Masuri, Sita, Panth-IV, IET-1444 and IET-5656 and Boro HYV were IR-36, IR-50, and Ratna. The local rice varieties practiced in kharif season were Assam Aush, Khajurchari, Gokulshal, Nagrashal, Kadamshal, Laghuşhal, Rajamanik, Radhashal, Sundarmukhi, Bhasamanik, and Hurkashal.

The production of rice depends upon the application of production inputs and practices. In the present study it was assumed that the level of yield of a rice variety is a function of seed rate, seed treatment, method of sowing, number of ploughing, organic manure, nitrogenous, phosthatic and potassic fertilizers, weeding, and plant protection. These ten practices were considered as independent variables. The gaps in the input/treatment application were assumed as independent variables in this case.

The overall technological gap of the farmer was also considered as the dependent variable. The overall technological gap is the mean of the technological gaps of different varieties cultivated by the farmers.

In this case, there were 13 independent variables which were expected to be related with the overall technological gap. These variables are age, caste, family size, farm size, education, economic status, social participation, irrigation index, index of outstanding credit, status of land ownership, utilization of mass media, utilization of personal cosmopolite sources of information, and participation in training programme.

The technological gap for practice of a particular rice variety was calculated as follows:

$$\text{Percentage gap in the use of seed rate of X variety} = \frac{(\text{Kg / ac recommended}) - (\text{Kg / ac applied})}{(\text{Kg / ac recommended})} \times 100$$

The technological gap for a particular rice variety cultivated by the farmer was calculated in the following way:

$$\text{Technological gap for IR-36 variety} = \frac{\text{Total gap for all practices of the variety}}{\text{Number of practices applied for the variety}}$$

The overall technological gap in respect of each farmer measured as shown below:

$$\text{Overall Technological Gap} = \frac{\text{Technological gap for the all varieties cultivated by the farmer}}{\text{Number of varieties cultivated by the farmer during the year}}$$

The overall technological gap for each farmer was computed to find the relationship between overall technological gap and overall yield gap of the farmer.

Computation of Overall Technological Gap: The following example is given to get a clear cut concept about the method of computation of overall technological gap.

Farmer	:	'Y'
Farm category	:	Category-II
Village	:	Fullaipur
Block	:	Mahammad Bazar
District	:	Birbhum
Year	:	1988-89

Table 5.2 for the computation of overall technological gap is presented.

Table 5.2: Computation of Overall Technological Gap

Sl. No.	*Practice*	*IR-50 Gap in %*	*Khajur-chari Gap in %*	*Kadam-shal Gap in %*	*Sita Gap in %*	*Boro IR-36 Gap in %*
1.	Seed rate	00.00	00.00	00.00	00.00	00.00
2.	Seed treatment	100.00	100.00	100.00	100.00	100.00
3.	Method of sowing	00.00	00.00	00.00	00.00	00.00
4.	Number of ploughing	20.00	00.00	40.00	20.00	00.00
5.	Use of FYM (cartload/ac.)	42.36	58.94	70.30	30.50	20.25
6.	Use of N fertilizer (Kg/ac)	46.72	82.43	85.92	55.36	30.32
7.	Use of P fertilizer (Kg/ac.)	80.82	90.45	90.20	85.40	72.12
8.	Use of K fertilizer (Kg/ac.)	80.82	90.45	90.20	85.40	72.12
9.	Weeding (No.)	50.00	50.00	50.00	50.00	00.00
10.	Plant Protection (No.)	50.00	100.00	100.00	100.00	50.00
	Total	470.72	572.27	606.62	526.66	344.81
	TG for the variety	47.07	57.22	60.66	52.66	34.48

$$\text{Overall technological gap of the farmer} = \frac{47.07+57.22+60.66+52.66+34.48}{5}$$

$$= \frac{251.89}{5} = 50.38 \text{ per cent}$$

Independent Variables

(a) Factors/treatments directly related to the yield level of rice

The factors/and treatments were considered to have direct effect on the production of different rice varieties. The method of measurement of these varieties has been discussed below.

Seed Rate (X_1): It is the amount of seed (Kg/ac.) used with respect to various rice varieties.

Seed Treatment (X_2): It was measured in terms of expenditure (Rs./ac.) incurred for getting the seeds of different varieties treated with recommended chemicals and methods.

Method of Sowing (X_3): Both the method of sowing viz. broad-casting and line sowing has been considered in this study.

Ploughing (X_4): The number of times of ploughing or tilling operations conducted for land preparation before sowing.

Level of Use of Organic Manure (X_5): The level of use of organic manure was measured in terms of cartload per acre applied in the actual field where rice varieties were grown.

Level of Nitrogenous Fertilizer Use (X_6): For this purpose different fertilizer used by a farmer for each rice variety and each plot recorded and the quantities in terms of nitrogenous fertilizer were computed. The unit of measurement was Kg./ac.

Level of Phosphoric Fertilizer Use (X_7): In this case also, like (X_6) different fertilizers used by a farmer for each rice variety and each plot recorded and the quantities of P-fertilizer was computed in Kg./ac.

Level of Potassium Fertilizer Use (X_8): The same procedure and method were used to compute K-fertilizer (Kg./ac.).

Level of Weeding (X_9): The number of times of weeding of a rice variety was considered as the level of weeding.

Level of Use of Plant Protection Chemicals (X_{10}): In the present study, plant protection chemicals included insecticides, fungicides, herbicides and rodenticides. The frequency of plant protection chemical application was noted for each variety.

(b) Factors Related to Technological Gap

Age of the Farmer (X_1): In the present study the number of years rounded up to the nearest whole number the respondent lived since birth at the time of interview.

Caste of the Farmer (X_2): The method of scoring for caste adopted by Haque (1981) given below was followed in the present study.

Sl. No.	*Caste Category*	*Score*
1.	Brahmin	5
2.	Kayastha	4
3.	Muslim	3
4.	Scheduled Caste	2
5.	Scheduled Tribe	1

Family Size of the Respondent (X_3): It refers to the number of members in the individual farmers' family. To quantify the family size, the actual number of members in the family was taken into consideration.

Farm Size (X_4): The actual area under cultivation of the respondent in acre was taken as a measure of farm size.

Level of Education of the Respondent (X_5): To quantify the educational status of the respondents, the scoring system followed by Pareek and Trivedi (1964) in their Socio-economic status scale-rural was used. The method of scoring was as follows:

Level of Education	*Scoring*
Illiterate	0
Can read only	1
Can read and write	2
Primary	3
Middle school	4
High school	5
Graduate	6

Family Economic Status (X_6): The economic status of the farmers was measured with the help of some components of the socio-economic status scale—rural developed by Pareek and Trivedi (1964). The scale consists of nine items—land, house, farm power and material possession were taken into consideration for measuring economic status.

Social Participation (X_7): It refers to the number of members of the farm family participating in social or political organizations. Operationally, it has been defined as the degree to which the respondents were involved in formal organization as members or office bearers and regularity in their attendance to meetings. The scoring of the items was as follows:

Items	Score
No membership	0
Membership in one organization	1
Membership in more than one organization	2
Office bearer in one organization	3
Office bearer in more than one organization	4
Distinctive features (M.L.A., M.P., etc.)	6

Attendance to meetings either as a member or as office bearer was considered important. Score for attending meetings 'regularly', 'occasionally' and 'never' were given as 3, 2, and 1 respectively. To obtain the final score of a respondent the scores given as a member or office bearer were multiplied with the scores given for attendance to meetings by virtue of his status as member or office bearer and added up (Lokhande, 1974).

Irrigation Index (X_8): Irrigation index has been operationally defined as the percentage of the total area irrigated and was calculated by the formula as follows:

$$\text{Irrigation Index} = \frac{\text{Total irrigated area in acre}}{\text{Size of holding in acre}} \times 100$$

Index of Outstanding Credit (X_9): It is the proportion of total amount of outstanding credit to the total credit received from various sources by the farmer for rice production during last 3 years, expressed in percentage. This index was calculated as follows:

$$\text{Index of Outstanding Credit} = \frac{\text{Total amount of credit outstanding}}{\text{Total amount of credit received from different sources in last three years}} \times 100$$

Status of Land Ownership (X_{10}): It was calculated by the formula as follows:

$$\text{Status of Land Ownership} = \frac{\text{Owned land cultivated in acre}}{\text{Total land cultivated in acre}} \times 100$$

For example, if a farmer cultivated 4 acres of land. Out of which he owned 1.5 acres, his status of land ownership would be

$$(1.5/4) \times 100 = 37.50 \text{ per cent.}$$

This method was followed by the National Council of Applied Economic Research (1974) and Fertilizer Association of India, Singh (1981), Sagar (1983), and Bora (1986).

Utilization of Mass Media (X_{11}): The mass media sources of information considered for the study were Radio, Television, Newspaper, Educational Film, Farm Publications, Demonstrations, Krishi Mela/Exhibition.

To measure the degree of utilization of mass media sources, each respondent was asked to indicate on a 4-point continuum as to how often he got information about improved farm practices from each of the sources. The scoring procedure for the responses was most often-3, often-2, sometimes-1, and never-0. The score of an individual respondent was obtained by adding the scores over different sources.

Utilization of Personal Sources of Information (X_{12}): The personal cosmopolite sources of information considered for the present study were lab to land personnel, Agricultural Extension Officer/Agricultural Development Officer, Village Level Workers/ Krishi Prajukti Sahayak, University Extension Personnel, Input Dealers, and progressive farmers of other villages.

To measure the degree of utilization of the personal cosmopolite sources of information, each respondent was asked to indicate on a 4-point continuum as to how often to get information about improved farm practices from each of the sources. The scoring procedure for the responses were most often-3, often-2, sometimes-1, and never-0. The score of an individual respondent was obtained by adding the scores over different sources.

Participation in Training Programme (X_{13}): In the present study participation of the farmers in any training programme for agricultural development was scored. The number of training programme attended by the farmers was scored.

(c) *Constraints Perceived by the Farmers in the Adoption of Improved Rice Package in Full Recommended Level*

Constraints refer to the item of difficulty perceived by the farmers in adopting the improved rice production practices at the level of recommendation. These may be agro-biological, socio-cultural, technological, social, economical, infrastructural, and relating to supply service, etc.

A number of constraint items perceived by the farmers were collected initially from available literature, scientists and experts of Agricultural Universities and Rice Research Institutions. These items were scrutinized and edited. Constraint items were finally retained in this study after completing the pre-testing of the schedule.

To measure the degree of constraints, the respondents were asked to indicate on a 4-point continuum the extent to which such constraint was perceived as hindering the adoption of improved package of practices for rice recommended to them. The scoring procedure was followed as very much-3, much-2, not so much-1, and not at all-0.

Analytical Procedures

There were large number of constraints items in addition to some situational variables related with technological gap and some biological factors/treatments responsible for yield gap. The total number of respondents was 100. The computer applications in calculating the results were essential due to huge data generated and method of analysis selected. The data were analyzed with the help of a number of appropriate computer packages at the Ganitra Sadan and Department of Agricultural Extension, Economics and Statistics, P.S.B., Visva-Bharati, Santiniketan. The statistical techniques employed in the various phases of the study were Multiple Correlation, Multiple Regression Analyses and Factor Analysis. One Operational Research Technique i.e. Linear Programming was also applied.

To fulfil the first objective of the study i.e. to measure the extent of yield gap of rice varieties, the tabular analysis had been made. This was done for examining the magnitude in terms of percentage and actual figures of yield gap of various rice varieties in kharif season as well as in boro season. These varieties were, IR-36, IR–50, Ratna, Pankaj, Masuri, Panth-IV, Sita, IET-1444, IET-5656 which are included in high yielding category and the local varieties were Assam Aush, Khajurchari, Gokulshal, Kadamshal, Nagrashal, Laghushal, Rajamanik, Bhasamanik, Sundarmukhi, Radhashal, and Hurkashal. In boro season also the yield gaps of IR-36, IR-50, and Ratna have been estimated using tabular method. The tabular analysis has also been applied to identify and to measure the extent of technological gap of each farmer in rice production.

Correlation Coefficient

It was expected that there was a positive and significant relationship between yield gap and technological gap of the respondents. That is, a high degree of association between yield gap of a rice variety of the farmers and respective technological gap was assumed. The correlation coefficients (r) of all the varieties cultivated by the sample farmers in kharif season and boro season were estimated to measure the degree of association between these two gaps.

The simple correlation coefficient matrices were formulated considering all the independent variables used for fitting different multiple regression equations (discussed below). The matrices were critically examined to find out if there was the existence of any multicollinearity problem among the independent variables.

Multiple Regression Analysis

The second objective of the study can be analyzed with the help of multiple regression method. There are two sub-objectives within it. In the first case the factors affecting the level of rice yield, it was hypothesized on the basis of the past studies of the similar nature and the preliminary observations made in the study area that the following factors/treatments might have significant effect on the yield of various types of rice varieties improved or local in either season—kharif or boro.

1. Seed rate,
2. Seed treatment,
3. Method of sowing,
4. Ploughing in rice field,
5. Manuring,
6. Application of N-fertilizer,
7. Application of P-fertilizer,
8. Application of K-fetilizer,
9. Weeding, and
10. Plant protection measures.

To quantify the relationship between these factors and the extent or magnitude of yield gap in respect to each rice variety the following form of regression equation was tried to the cross-section data.

$$Yi = a + b_{i1} X_{i1} + b_{i2}X_{i2} + \ldots\ldots\ldots\ldots\ldots + b_{i10}X_{i10}$$

Where,

i = a particular rice variety

Y_i = Yield gap of the variety

X_1 = Gap in the application of seed (Kg./ac.)

X_2 = Gap in the seed treatment

X_3 = Gap in method of sowing

X_4 = Gap in ploughing

X_5 = Gap in application of organic manure

X_6 = Gap in application of N-fertilizer

X_7 = Gap in application of P-fertilizer

X_8 = Gap in application of K-fertilizer

X_9 = Gap in weeding, and
X_{10} = Gap in application of plant protection measures
b_i = Regression co-efficient (i=1 to 10)
a = Intercept

For each variety separate regression function was tried to the set of data as and where possible. Moreover, in some cases regression function of the same type was constructed for pooled data also.

Besides, before estimating parameters of the above functions a correlation matrix was also computed to examine if there was any existence of multicollinearity among selected variables. Finally, the linear regression function was fitted following the least square technique.

The multiple regression models were also applied to measure the relationship between technological gap and some situational factors. In this case it was hypothesized on the basis of some past studies of the similar nature and the preliminary observations made in the study area that the overall technological gap of the farmer might have been affected by the factors such as:

Age of the farmer (X_1),
Caste of the farmer (X_2),
Family size of the respondent (X_3),
Farm size of the respondent (X_4),
Educational level of the respondent (X_5),
Economic status of the farm family (X_6),
Social participation of the farmer (X_7),
Index of irrigated land (X_8),
Index of outstanding credit (X_9),
Status of land ownership (X_{10}),
Utilization of mass media (X_{11}),
Utilization of cosmopolite sources of information (X_{12}), and
Participation in training programme (X_{13}).

To quantify the relationship between these factors and the extent of technological gap the following form of regression equation was formulated to the cross-section data.

$$Y = \alpha + \beta_1 X_1 + \beta_2 X_2 + \ldots\ldots\ldots\ldots + \beta_{13} X_{13}$$

Where,

Y = Technological gap

α, β = parameters

X_i (i = 1 ......13) = different independent variables as listed above.

Four regression equations of the same type for four farm categories were constructed. Besides, before estimating parameters of above functions a correlation matrix was also computed to examine the multicollinearity among selected variables.

Factor Analysis

The principal concern of factor analysis, according to Harman (1976) is the resolution of a set of variables linearly in terms of a small number of categories of 'factor'. This resolution can be accomplished by the analysis of correlation among the variables. A satisfactory solution will yield factors which convey all the essential information of the original set of variables. Thus, the chief aim is to attain scientific parsimony or economy of description.

The original variable X_j is represented by the following linear composite expressed in terms of the factors as follows:

$$X_j = \sum_{i=1}^{p} I_{jr} f_r$$

where p is the number of factors retained and f_r (r = 1, 2,......, p) represents common factors and I_{jr} are factor loadings of the original variable X_j on factor f_r.

The method of Principle Component Analysis was followed in the present study. The Principle Component Analysis extracts m-Eigen vectors (principle component axes) and corresponding m- Eigen values, (the variance measured along the eigen vector) from mXm symmetrical matrix of correlation. The Eigen vectors obtained from this Principle Component Analysis are all orthogonal (i.e. intercolumn correlations are near zero). The Eigen values account for all of the original data variances in decreasing order such that each has variance or Eigen value less than the previous ones. The total of the eigen values $\lambda_1 + \lambda_2 + \ldots\ldots\ldots\ldots\ldots + \lambda_m$ which is the same as the sum of variances constituting the diagonal or trace of the correlation matrix before transformation. The principle components are then converted into factors by multiplying each element of the principle components or eigen vectors (V) by the square-root of the corresponding eigen values ($\lambda^{1/2}.V$). Factors, thus, besides the direction also represent the variances.

The analysis calls for the selection of a minimum number of meaningful and useful factors, considering fewer in number ($p<m$) than the original variables which will account for most of the variances in the data set and therefore, convey the same information. Various criteria for selection of suitable factors are available. Kaiser (1958) and others have recommended retaining all those Eigen values which have values more than 1.

Next step is to remove the noise imposed by (m–p) unnecessary axes. To accomplish this p–orthogonal reference axes or factors are rotated about the origin to positions such that the variance of the loading from each variable into each factor axis is either extreme (± 1) or near zero. This maximization of the range of loadings was performed by using Kaiser's Varimax Criterion (1958). Scanning through each factor column for large absolute values in the varimax matrix will reveal a few variables with significantly high loading and many others with insignificant loadings. The column showing communality (Σh_j^2) is the total amount of variance of each variable retained in the factors, and is computed by summing the squares of the elements of the factors in each raw of the varimax matrix. Fairly high communality of each variable implies the appropriateness of the model adopted in the study. The last step involved meaningful interpretation of the factors.

In the present study 49 constraints perceived by the farmers were selected and asked to indicate the degree of constraint in four-point scale. Applying the method of factor analysis the most important constraints in the adoption of improved rice technologies at recommended dose were identified. The constraints were $X_1, X_2, X_3, \ldots\ldots\ldots\ldots\ldots X_{49}$.

Where,

X_{1og} = lack of ownership of land

X_2 = fragmentation of land holding

X_3 = lack of moisture retention capacity of land

X_4 = lack of irrigation facility

X_5 = high irrigation charges

X_6 = non-availability of irrigation at time
X_7 = occurrence of flood
X_8 = low rainfall
X_9 = drought
X_{10} = lack of capital
X_{11} = lack of easily available credit
X_{12} = lack of adequate credit
X_{13} = lack of timely credit
X_{14} = lack of statutory price of rice
X_{15} = lack of marketing facility
X_{16} = lack of market demand of rice
X_{17} = lack of transportation facilities
X_{18} = low market price of rice
X_{19} = non-availability of farm yard manure
X_{20} = non-availability of seed treatment chemicals
X_{21} = non-availability of fertilizer
X_{22} = non-availability of skilled farm workers
X_{23} = high labour wages
X_{24} = not profitable
X_{25} = lack of technical knowledge for field application
X_{26} = guided by the adoption of neighbours
X_{27} = less taste of produce
X_{28} = inadequate training
X_{29} = lack of advice and guidance
X_{30} = non-availability of HYV seeds
X_{31} = non-availability of plant protection chemicals
X_{32} = inadequate supply of HYV seeds
X_{33} = inadequate supply of fertilizer
X_{34} = inadequate supply of plant protection chemicals
X_{35} = non-availability of HYV seeds in time
X_{36} = non-availability of fertilizer in time
X_{37} = non-availability of plant protection chemical in time
X_{38} = non-availability of HYV seeds at fair price
X_{39} = non-availability of fertilizer at fair price
X_{40} = non-availability of plant protection chemicals at fair price
X_{41} = non-availability of agricultural machinery on hire
X_{42} = lack of drainage facility
X_{43} = complicated process
X_{44} = lack of own bullock

X_{45} = lack of family labour
X_{46} = lack of knowledge about proper recommendation
X_{47} = lack of agro-service centre
X_{48} = lack of good road for transportation
X_{49} = lack of soil testing facility

Linear Programming

In this study it was objected to identify the appropriate rice technologies for the farmers which would be suitable for them. For identifying the appropriate technologies—the alternative available technologies (may be traditional/improved, indigenous or/and imported) need to be tested in the three dimensions of (i) local resource appropriateness; (ii) local need appropriateness; and (iii) social goal appropriateness. A linear programming model had been used in this study for fulfilling the purpose.

Linear programming is a technique that can serve as an important planning tool both at micro and macro levels. This technique can be used to determine (i) the amount of outside financing needed to implement the optimum plan; (ii) the mix of traditional and new agricultural activities that would make the most profitable of land and other resources; (iii) the amount of labour required for a particular plan; and (iv) the sensitivity of the development plan to variations in the values assumed for various economic factors included in the model. In addition, it provides means for testing the effects of alternative policies and guides to investment decisions. Shadow prices generated in the linear programming solutions serve to direct the type of investment which should be made.

The formal structure of the model which was used for identifying the appropriate technologies for the representative farm situations is given below in the mathematical form:

$$\text{Maximize } Z = \sum_{j=1}^{p} C_j X_j \qquad (j = 1, \ldots\ldots\ldots, n) \ldots\ldots\ldots(1)$$

Subject to

$$\sum_{j=1}^{n} a_{ij} X_j \le b_i \qquad (i = 1, 2, \ldots\ldots\ldots, m) \ldots\ldots\ldots(2)$$

$$\sum_{j=1}^{n} a_{ij} X_j = b_i \qquad (i = m+1, \ldots\ldots\ldots, p) \ldots\ldots\ldots(3)$$

$$\sum_{j=1}^{n} a_{ij}X_j \geq b_i \qquad (i = p+1, \text{..........}, r) \text{ .... } (4)$$

Where,

Z = Total profit (Rs.)

C_j = returns over cost A_1 excluding land revenue, cesses, depreciation on implements and farm buildings.

X_j = units of jth technology (activity)

a_{ij} = requirement (a>0) or contribution (a<0) for the jth technology for the ith constraint.

b_i = the ith constraint level, a resource capacity in (2), an accounting balance in (3), and a requirement to be met in (4).

Technologies in the model, X_j, are conceived in terms of group averages of the selected representative farms as are the constraint level, b_i.

We assume that the typical farmer in the study area is trying to maximize returns to fixed resources or returns over variable costs subject to certain lower and upper limits on the level of certain activities. The upper and lower bounds represent the local needs and social goals.

The typical farmer in the study area has several alternatives for the use of his resources. For example, the farmer could choose from a number of different crops, different varieties of crops, different levels of technologies, etc. A list of all technologies that were included in the model is given below.

Technologies included in the linear programming models were:

X_1 = Kharif IR-36 (irrigated)
X_2 = Kharif IR-36 (unirrigated)
X_3 = Kharif IR-50 (irrigated)
X_4 = Kharif IR-50 (unirrigated)
X_5 = Kharif Ratna (irrigated)
X_6 = Kharif Ratna (unirrigated)
X_7 = Kharif Pankaj (irrigated)
X_8 = Kharif Pankaj (unirrigated)
X_9 = Kharif Masuri (irrigated)
X_{10} = Kharif Masuri (unirrigated)
X_{11} = Kharif Sita (irrigated)
X_{12} = Kharif Sita (unirrigated)
X_{13} = Kharif IET-1444 (irrigated)
X_{14} = Kharif IET-1444 (unirrigated)

X_{15} = Kharif IET-5656 (irrigated)
X_{16} = Kharif IET-5656 (unirrigated)
X_{17} = Kharif Panth-IV (irrigated)
X_{18} = Kharif Panth-IV (unirrigated)
X_{19} = Kharif Assam Aush (irrigated)
X_{20} = Kharif Assam Aush (unirrigated)
X_{21} = Kharif Khajurchari (irrigated)
X_{22} = Kharif Khajurchari (unirrigated)
X_{23} = Kharif Gokulshal (irrigated)
X_{24} = Kharif Gokulshal (unirrigated)
X_{25} = Kharif Kadamshal (irrigated)
X_{26} = Kharif Kadamshal (unirrigated)
X_{27} = Kharif Nagrashal (irrigated)
X_{28} = Kharif Nagrashal (unirrigated)
X_{29} = Kharif Laghushal (irrigated)
X_{30} = Kharif Laghushal (unirrigated)
X_{31} = Kharif Radhashal (irrigated)
X_{32} = Kharif Radhashal (unirrigated)
X_{33} = Kharif Hurkashal (irrigated)
X_{34} = Kharif Hurkashal (unirrigated)
X_{35} = Kharif Sundarmukhi (irrigated)
X_{36} = Kharif Sundarmukhi (unirrigated)
X_{37} = Kharif Rajamanik (irrigated)
X_{38} = Kharif Rajamanik (unirrigated)
X_{39} = Kharif Bhasamanik (irrigated)
X_{40} = Kharif Bhasamanik (unirrigated)
X_{41} = Boro IR-36
X_{42} = Boro IR-50
X_{43} = Boro Ratna
X_{44} = Swarna (Recommended)
X_{45} = IET-5656 (Recommended)
X_{46} = IET-4094 (Recommended)
X_{47} = IR-36 (Recommended)
X_{48} = Labour Hired in June
X_{49} = Labour Hired in July
X_{50} = Labour Hired in August
X_{51} = Labour Hired in September
X_{52} = Labour Hired in October

X_{53} = Labour Hired in November
X_{54} = Labour Hired in December
X_{55} = Labour Hired in January
X_{56} = Labour Hired in February
X_{57} = Labour Hired in March
X_{58} = Labour Hired in April
X_{59} = Labour Hired in May

Improved Technologies (Activities): The same list may be used, all the notation were used to indicate the same thing but in different quantities

Resources Restriction: The farmer, like any other decision maker, operates with limited resources. A linear programming problem does not exist unless resources are restricted or limited. For most planning or choice problems, there are restrictions which set limits on the kinds of plans which can be considered. For a farm, restrictions are defined by the fixed quantities of resources; there also can be subjective, technical, institutional or other types of restrictions. For example, the farmer himself may place restrictions on the minimum or maximum size of certain enterprises.

In the present study farmers are constrained from land, labour and capital along with two other non-controlled restrictions such as local need and social goal.

Resources endowments and restriction (b_i) included in the linear programming models are:

Existing Technology: b_1 = kharif paddy land (irrigated)
b_2 = kharif paddy land (unirrigated)
b_3 = rabi land/boro land (irrigated)
b_4 to b_{15} = labour available in the months of June to May
b_{16} = cash available with the farmer
b_{17+p} = predetermined activities *i.e.* local needs (p = 0, 1, 2,...)
b_{18+s} = predetermined activities *i.e.* social goals (s = 0, 1, 2,...)

Sensitivity analysis has also been made to find out the range of changes in the co-efficient with respect to activities and resource constraints so that within that range the response surface remains same.

6

Results and Discussion

The main findings of the present study are presented and discussed in this chapter. The whole chapter has been divided into seven sections. The results of this investigation have been presented and clearly discussed under the following distinct sections:

General characteristics of sample farms.
Extent of yield gap of different rice varieties.
Estimation of relationship between yield gap and technological gap.
Identification of biological factors/cultural practices affecting level of rice production and estimation of their contribution.
Identification and estimation of factors affecting technological gap.
Constraints as perceived by the farmers for the application of improved rice technologies at recommended level.
Identification of appropriate technology for rice production.

General Characteristics of Sample Farms

In this section basic and common characteristics of the sample farmers such as size of holding and tenancy, irrigation status, cropping pattern, information about family labour etc., have been discussed. The discussion was carried out with respect to different farm size groups. Tabular analysis was used to compute and compare the results with respect to different farm categories.

Size of Holding

The sample farmers were classified into four categories on the basis of their respective size of holdings. The unit used to measure the size of land holdings of the farmers was acre. Those farmers, who were having land holdings below one acre were considered in the category-I. The farmers having land holdings between 1 acre and 2.5 acres were considered in category-II. It might be noted that marginal farmers (having land holding upto 1 ha.) were sub-divided into categories-I and II. The farmers of category-III were possessing land between 2.5 acres and 5 acres. In other words, small farmers those having land between 1 ha. and 2 ha. were considered in category-II because 1 ha. is equal to 2.4 acres. The classification was made in such a way to reflect the true picture of the land holdings. The farmers having more than 5 acres were considered in category-IV. The number of farmers under different farm categories presented in Table 6.1.

Table 6.1: Distribution of Sample Farmers into Different Size Groups

Farm Size Groups	*Land Holding (in acre)*	*No. of Farmers*
Category-I	Below 1 acre	14
Category-II	1 to 2.5 acres	26
Category-III	2.5 to 5 acres	40
Category-IV	Above 5 acres	20
Total		100

The number of sample farmers fall in category-I was 14 only. Whereas, 26 farmers were found in category-II. Of the entire sample households surveyed quite a large proportion of the sample farmers were concentrated in category-III farm size accounting 40 households (40 per cent). The proportion of holdings in category-IV was 20. Thus, the distribution of holdings by farm size group showed the predominance of marginal farmers in the study area having 2.5 acres (1 ha.) operational land (categories I and II).

Average Size of Operational Holdings and Tenancy

The average size of operational holdings in different size groups is presented in Table 6.2.

Table 6.2: Average Size of Operational Holdings in Different Size Groups

Size Groups	*Average Operational Holdings (acres)*	*Owned Land (acres)*	*Leased in Land (acres)*
Category-I	0.54 (100.00)	0.45 (83.33)	0.09 (16.66)
Category-II	1.95 (100.00)	1.10 (56.41)	0.85 (43.59)
Category-III	4.20 (100.00)	3.20 (76.19)	1.00 (23.81)
Category-IV	10.45 (100.00)	8.32 (79.62)	2.13 (25.38)
Pooled	4.36 (100.00)	3.30 (75.70)	1.06 (24.30)

Figures in parentheses indicate percentage

The average size of operational holdings as based on the pooled data for the year 1988-89 was 4.36 acres for the sample farmers. Further, when average size of operational holding was calculated according to each farm size group, it came to 0.54 acre for the farmers of category-I, 1.95 acres for the farmers of category-II, and 4.20 acres and 10.45 acres for the farmers of category-III and category-IV respectively.

The details about the land ownership in different size groups of farmers were also presented in Table 6.2. As it was seen from the table, that the overall percentage of owned land and leased in land among the sample farms worked out to be 75.70 and 24.30 respectively. In case of category-I farmers the owned land and leased in land calculated were 83.33 and 16.66 per cent respectively. The calculated percentage of owned land and leased in land for category-II farmers were 56.41 and 43.59 respectively. In case of category-III farmers, the respective figures were 76.19 and 23.81. For the farmers of category-IV the percentage figures of owned land and leased in land were 79.62 and 25.38 respectively. The table showed that in the case of farm category-II, the percentage of leased in land was higher in comparison to other farm categories. It might be noted that in all farm size groups tenant (*Bargadar*) farmers were present. The table also indicated that the system of ownership cultivation was widely prevalent and the extent of tenant cultivation was about 24 per cent of total operated land.

Irrigation Status

The distribution of area under irrigation in different size groups of holdings has been presented in Table 6.3.

Table 6.3: Distribution of Area Under Irrigation Among Different Size Groups of Farms

Size Groups	*Average Size of Operational Holdings (acres)*	*Area under Irrigation (acres)*	*Percentage Area under Irrigation (acres)*
Category-I	0.54	0.25	46.35
Category-II	1.95	0.80	41.00
Category-III	4.20	2.00	47.62
Category-IV	10.45	4.70	44.90
Pooled	4.36	1.98	45.41

In case of category-I farm the percentage of irrigated area of the total operational holding was 46.36 which was the second highest among the four farm categories. The highest percentage of irrigated land was found in case of category-III farm, accounting 47.62 per cent. The percentage area under irrigation of farms in categories II and IV were 41.00 and 44.90 respectively. However, the lowest irrigated area in percentage term was found for farm category-II, though a marked difference in irrigation status was not indicated in the table. The average irrigated area as based on the pooled data was calculated to be 45.41 per cent. The proportion of irrigated area of the sample farms showed a little higher figures in comparison to that in case of district or state figures which might be due to the fact that all the sources of irrigation including pond irrigation were considered for estimation of irrigation status.

Cropping Pattern

The nature of crops grown provides a correct index of the character of the agricultural economy and economic standard of the farmers of an area. It is, therefore, necessary to examine the nature of cropping pattern among various sizes of farms. The cropping pattern followed by the sample farmers of different categories are presented in Table 6.4.

Table 6.4: Cropping Pattern Followed by the Sample Farmers Among Different Size Groups

	Percentage of Net Area Sown				
Crop	*Category-I*	*Category-II*	*Category-III*	*Category-IV*	*Pooled*
HYV paddy	60.00	51.00	32.45	35.50	40.80
Local paddy	40.00	48.00	63.80	61.40	56.90
Sugarcane	-	00.40	02.45	01.50	02.10
Arum	-	00.60	01.30	01.60	01.20
Wheat	02.30	07.35	08.40	07.20	07.80
Potato	01.00	05.20	10.60	08.90	08.60
Mustard	02.80	10.70	15.70	14.90	12.80
Vegetables	02.50	08.80	10.10	10.50	09.00
Pulses	-	-	05.15	04.40	02.10
Onion	-	01.25	05.25	04.40	03.50
Boro paddy	15.60	20.60	20.50	16.50	18.80

The table counting the cropping pattern showed that paddy cultivation in kharif season had an overwhelming importance in the study area. It was also evident from Table 6.4. that a considerable proportion of area had been devoted to cultivation of rice irrespective of the size of farms. This was quite obvious in view of the fact that the farmers had to meet their consumption needs first and hence cultivated about 98 per cent of operated land for growing rice. In kharif season, it had been seen that only 4 crops were grown by the farmers. These were paddy—local and HYV, sugarcane, and arum. In farm category-I only paddy was found to be cultivated in kharif season. The percentage of area under HYV cultivation was 60 per cent which showed the highest figure among the farm categories. More than 50 per cent of the operational holding in farm category-II was under high yielding varieties of rice, and sugarcane and arum account only 1 per cent of the total operational holding. In farm category-III, HYV paddy was cultivated in only about 33 per cent of the total holding which was the lowest among the farm categories. 40 per cent of the total operational holding estimated under HYV paddy cultivation for the farmers of category-IV. The sugarcane and arum of these two farm categories occupied 3.75 and 3.10 per cent respectively. The area under paddy for the pooled sample accounted in about 41 per cent of the total sown area where as only 3.30 per cent of the total area had been occupied by the two non-significant crops-sugarcane and arum in kharif season.

In rabi season, the farmers of category-I were found to cultivate wheat, potato, vegetables, mustard, and boro paddy. The percentage areas under these crops to the net sown area were 2.30, 1.00, 2.50, 2.80, and 15.60 respectively. In category-II all the listed crops except pulses were followed to be grown in rabi season. The percentage area to the total operational holding of these crops was 7.35, 5.20, 1.25, 8.80, 10.70, and 20.60 respectively. The farmers of categories III and IV cultivated all the above listed crops in rabi season. The percentage of area under wheat, potato, onion, vegetables, mustard, pulses, and boro paddy for farm category-III were 8.40, 10.60, 5.25, 10.10, 15.70, 5.15 and 20.50 respectively. The corresponding figures for farm category-IV were 1.20, 8.90, 4.40, 10.50, 14.90, 4.40 and 16.50 respectively. The salient features in the cropping pattern in rabi season was that the area under boro cultivation varied within 20 per cent of the total operational holding and other crops occupied insignificant area in all size groups.

Cropping Intensity

The intensity of cropping as measured by the ratio of grossed sown area to net sown area and expressed in percentage term has been presented in Table 6.5.

Table 6.5: Cropping Intensity Over Different Categories of Farmers

Size Groups	*Net Sown Area (acres)*	*Gross Sown Area (acres)*	*Cropping Intensity*
Category-I	08.64	10.73	124.20
Category-II	50.70	78.53	154.90
Category-III	168.00	295.17	175.70
Category-IV	209.00	334.43	164.80
Pooled	436.34	718.86	166.00

It was revealed from the above table that the highest cropping intensity was found 175.70 per cent for category-III farmers, however, the lowest cropping intensity i.e. only 124.20 per cent was found for category-I farmers. The cropping intensities of categories II and IV were 154.90 and 164.80 respectively. The pooled cropping intensity estimated was 166 per cent. The result indicated a high cropping intensity in comparison to that in case of State or district, which might be due to the fact of higher irrigation index in the study area. Nevertheless, the cropping intensity was found to be higher than the irrigation index which can be explained by the fact that during rabi season many crops were sown in rain-fed condition. The lowest cropping intensities in categories I and II farms can be judged by the fact that the farmers of these two categories were engaged other than farm activities in rabi season, because as rice is staple food, all the farmers cultivated land for rice production in kharif season and rabi cultivation is capital intensive and risk oriented for which the small farmers do not prefer to practice rabi crops as the opportunity cost of rabi crops is higher.

Labour

The average sizes of farm families over different categories of farms were presented in Table 6.6.

Table 6.6: Average Size of Family Among Different Size Groups of Farms

Size Groups	*Average Family Size*	*Adult*	*Children*
Category-I	5.65	2.50	3.15
Category-II	7.86	4.06	3.80
Category-III	7.50	3.72	3.78
Category-IV	6.80	3.95	2.85
Pooled	7.30	3.73	3.57

It had been indicated from Table 6.6. that the number of family members among the different size groups did not differ significantly which implied that farm size might not be considered as the determining factor of family size. The pooled family size of the sample was 7.30 out of which 3.73 were adult and 3.57 were children. The average size of the four farm categories were 5.65, 7.86, 7.50, and 6.80 respectively. However, the farm category-I was the lowest family size and highest family size was found in case of farm category-II.

Occupational Structure

The occupations of the farmers of different farm categories have been presented in the following table.

Table 6.7: Distribution of Sample Farmers According to Occupation Among Different Farm Sizes

Size Groups	*Total No. of Earners (1)*	*No. of Agricultural Earners (2)*	*Percentage of Col. (2) over (1)*
Category-I	2.32	1.96	84.48
Category-II	3.85	3.20	83.12
Category-III	3.50	2.80	80.00
Category-IV	3.30	2.20	66.66
Pooled	3.43	2.70	78.72

Table 6.7. revealed that with regard to the variation in the number of family members engaged in agricultural in different size groups the proportion of earners in agriculture worked out 84.48 per cent for the category-I farmers, 83.12 for category-II, 80.00 per cent for category-III, and 66.66 per cent for category-IV farmers. The average number of family members dependent on agriculture was accounted to be 2.70 (78.72 per cent).

Labour Combination

The proportion of family labour and hired labour for different farm sizes has been presented in Table 6.8.

Table 6.8: Contribution of Labour Days (Family and Hired) Among Different Size Groups

Size Groups	*Percentage of Family Labour*	*Percentage of Hired Labour*	*Total*
Category-I	89.25	10.75	100.00
Category-II	75.60	24.40	100.00
Category-III	48.80	51.20	100.00
Category-IV	33.50	66.50	100.00
Pooled	58.64	41.36	100.00

Table 6.7 shows that in the farm category-I, the percentage of family labour employed was the highest (89.25 per cent) among the different farm categories. The corresponding figures of farm categories II, III, and IV were 75.60, 48.80 and 33.50 respectively. The above analysis made it clear that the farmers of categories I and II employed more family labour in proportion to their farm operation. The proportion of family labour employed had been decreased with the increase of farm size. This negative relationship indicated the fact that the comparatively big farmers were depended on hired labour as they belong to the higher caste community and economically stronger. They did not engage themselves directly in farming activities.

Education

The level of education status of the sample farmers were recorded and analyzed which has been presented in the following table:

Table 6.9: Distribution of Educational Status Among Different Size Groups

Size Group	*Percentage of illiterate*	*Percentage of literate*	*Madhyamik passed*	*H.S. passed*	*Graduate and above*
Category-I	76.20	23.80	—	—	—
Category-II	63.75	36.25	5	2	—
Category-III	54.25	45.75	32	14	5
Category-IV	55.50	44.50	30	18	7
Pooled	59.85	40.15	67	34	12

The above table showed that the highest literacy rate was in case of farm category III. The literacy rate of farm categories I, II, and IV were 23.80, 36.25, and 44.50 per cent respectively. Not a single member of the farm category I was found to have passed Madhyamik (10 Standard) examination. However, 5 members of the farm category II had passed Madhyamik and 2 had passed higher secondary examination. This rate was considerably satisfactory for farm category III, in which 32 mambers had passed Madhyamik, 14 Higher Secondary and 5 Graduate. The figures of Madhyamik and Higher Secondary passed, and Graduates for farm category IV were 30, 18, and 7 respectively. The overall literacy rate calculated as 40.15 per cent which was almost equal to the district average.

Extent of Yield Gap of Rice Varieties

As a matter of fact a substantial difference between potential yield and actual yield of different rice varieties—high yielding varieties as well as local or traditional varieties has been noticed in both the seasons—kharif and boro. There are a large number of rice varieties within the modern improved high yielding varieties as well as in local varieties. In kharif season nine high yielding varieties were adopted by the sample farmers whereas the number of local paddy varieties was eleven. These high yielding varieties were IR-36, IR-50, Ratna, Pankaj, Masuri, IET-1444, IET-5656, Panth-IV, and Sita. The local varieties were Assam Aush, Khajurchari, Gokulshal, Kadamshal, Bashamanik, Nagrashal, Rajamanik, Hurkashal, Laghushal, Sundarmukhi, and Radhashal. In boro season only three high yielding varieties viz. IR-36, IR-50, and Ratna were practiced.

Tabular method was used to measure the magnitude of yield gap. Simple average and aggregation in terms of percentage as well as actual figures were used to estimate the yield gaps of different rice varieties both in kharif and boro seasons. The yield gaps of rice for different farm size groups and varieties as well as overall yield gaps have been presented in Table 6.10. The yield gap is defined as the difference between potential yield expected with full implementation of modern rice technologies recommended in the zone, and actual rice yield of the variety. The information regarding potential yield have been collected from the Adaptive Research Centre and actual yield from the primary data gathered from sample farmers. The yield gap may be written as

$$Y_{ig} = Y_{ip} - Y_{ia}$$

where,

Y_{ig} = yield gap of the rice variety i

Y_{ip} = potential yield of the variety at recommended level of input application

Y_{ia} = actual yield achieved by the sample farmers in respect to i variety

i = 1, 2,..................... , n (different rice varieties)

The estimated figures related to yield gap of different rice varieties have been presented in Table 6.10.

Table 6.10: Estimation of Yield Gaps of Rice Varieties Over Different Categories of Farms

Yield Gap (Quintal/Acre)

Varieties and Season	*Farm Size*				
	Category I	*Category II*	*Category III*	*Category IV*	*Pooled*
Kharif Season (improved Varieties)					
IR-36	6.62(33.16)	5.37(26.90)	5.62 (28.15)	6.10 (30.56)	5.92(29.69)
IR-50	—	1.14(5.71)	5.95(29.80)	7.63(38.22)	4.90(22.02)
Ratna	—	5.25(26.30)	9.92(49.69)	7.67(38.42)	7.61(38.13)
Pankaj	—	5.07(23.42)	5.96(27.54)	4.08(18.85)	5.03(34.27)
Masuri	—	—	8.43(50.53)	7.66(45.92)	8.04(48.22)
IET-1444	—	12.24(67.10)	—	—	12.24(67.10)
IET-5656	—	—	6.96(31.69)	7.71(35.10)	7.73(33.39)
Panth-IV	—	—	8.21(41.08)	3.15(15.78)	5.67(28.45)
Sita	—	11.10(55.61)	6.53(32.71)	5.15(25.80)	7.59(38.04)
Pooled	**6.62(33.16)**	**6.69(34.17)**	**7.20(36.39)**	**6.14(31.08)**	**7.14(36.47)**
Local Varieties					
Assam Aush	—	1.30(12.50)	1.66(15.96)	1.80(17.30)	1.58 (15.25)
Khajurchari	2.18(20.96)	1.47(14.13)	1.47(14.13)	2.12(20.38)	1.81(17.40)
Gokulshal	1.63(15.67)	1.46(14.03)	1.79(17.21)	2.25(21.63)	1.78(17.13)
Kadamshal	—	1.42(13.65)	1.73(16.63)	2.33(22.40)	1.82(17.56)
Bashamanik	—	3.03(29.51)	0.93(8.99)	1.54(14.80)	1.83(17.75)
Nagrashal	—	1.47(14.13)	0.79(7.59)	1.25(12.01)	1.17(11.24)
Rajamanik	—	1.24(11.92)	1.69(16.25)	1.08(10.38)	1.33(12.85)
Hurkashal	0.65(6.25)	1.14(10.96)	1.14(10.96)	1.22(11.73)	1.03(9.97)
Laghashal	—	0.90(8.65)	3.58(34.42)	0.40(3.84)	1.62(15.63)
Sundarmukhi	—	1.24(11.92)	1.40(13.46)	—	1.32(12.69)
Radhashal	2.28(21.92)	—	1.92(18.46)	—	2.10(20.19)
Pooled	**1.67(16.38)**	**1.47(14.14)**	**1.65(15.81)**	**1.55(14.84)**	**1.58(15.24)**
Boro Season					
IR-36	1.79(8.25)	1.77(8.19)	2.15(9.95)	—	1.90(8.79)
IR-50	—	2.26(10.46)	1.54(7.12)	1.99(9.21)	1.93(8.93)
Ratna	—	2.86(13.33)	3.26(15.09)	—	3.06(14.21)
Pooled	**1.79(8.25)**	**2.30(10.66)**	**2.32(10.72)**	**1.99(9.21)**	**2.29(10.69)**

Figures in parentheses indicate the percentage values

Category-wise Analysis of Yield Gaps

Farms of Category-I

The farmers of this category were found to adopt only a single high yielding variety (IR-36) and four local rice varieties viz. Khajurchari, Gokulshal, Hurkashal, and Radhashal in kharif season. The yield gap of IR-36 was estimated 6.62 qtl/ac. (33.16 per cent) and yield gaps calculated with respect to traditional rice varieties were 2.18 qtl/ac. (20.96 per cent), 1.63 qtl/ac. (15.67 per cent), 0.65 qtl/ac. (6.25 per cent), and 2.28 qtl/ac. (21.92 per cent), respectively. The performance record indicated that marginal farmers were most efficient in the adoption of Hurkashal local rice variety since the yield gap of this variety had been found as the lowest one. Radhashal local variety among the local varieties recorded the highest yield gap in this category of farm. In boro season also only IR-36 rice variety was cultivated by the category-I farmers and the estimated yield gap of this variety was only 1.79 qtl/ac. (8.25 per cent). The yield gap of IR-36 in two different seasons differed significantly. The farmers of the same farm category could adopt IR-36 variety successfully in boro season than in kharif season. The reason behind this result may be that in boro season generally the high yielding varieties of rice were grown under controlled irrigation situation with comparatively higher level of inputs application and occurrence of pests and diseases was comparatively very less.

Farms of Category-II

Six types of improved rice varieties were cultivated by the farmers of category-II in kharif season. These varieties were IR-36, IR-50, Ratna, Pankaj, IET-1444, and Sita. The highest yield gap was found in case of IET-1444 estimating 12.24 qtl/ac. (67.10 per cent) and the lowest in case of IR-50 variety, only 1.14 qtl/ac. (5.71 per cent) among all the high yielding varieties grown by the farmers of this category in kharif season. The yield variation ranged from about 2 qtl/ac. to 11 qtl/ac. in other high yielding varieties. The yield gaps of IR-36, Ratna, Pankaj, and Sita rice varieties were 5.37 qtl/ac. (26.90 per cent), 5.25 qtl/ac. (26.30 per cent), 5.07 qtl/ac. (23.42 per cent) and 11.10 qtl/ac. (55.61 per cent), respectively.

The farmers of this category seemed to implement IR-50 variety more efficiently than other modern rice varieties in kharif season. However, they were found less efficient in the production of IET-1444 and Sita varieties. The overall yield gap of improved varieties taken togerher in kharif season of this farm size estimated 6.69 qtl/ac. (34.17 per cent) which was higher than the yield gap of IR-36, IR-50, Ratna, Pankaj but lower than the yield gaps of IET-1444 and Sita varieties.

The farmers of this category grew all the local varieties except Radhashal in kharif season. The highest yield gap among the local varieties was found in case of Bashamanik variety accounting 3.03 qtl/ac. (28.51 per cent) and the lowest yield gap only 0.90 qtl/ac. (8.65 per cent) was recorded in case of Laghushal. The estimated yield gaps were 1.30 qtl/ac. (12.50 per cent) for Assam Aush, 1.47 qtl/ac. (14.13 per cent) for Khajurchari and Nagrashal, 1.45 qtl/ac. (14.03 per cent) for Gokulshal, 1.43 qtl/ac. (13.65 per cent) for Kadamshal, 1.24 qtl/ac. (11.92 per cent) for Rajamanik and Sundarmukhi, 1.14 qtl/ac. (10.96 per cent) for Hurkashal. The yield gap of local varieties as a whole in kharif season calculated only 1.47 qtl/ac. (14.14 per cent). This gap was higher than that in Assam Aush, Gokulshal, Kadamshal, Rajamanik, Hurkashal, Laghushal and Sundarsukhi but lower than that only in Bashamanik and equal with the gap of the two varieties, viz. Khajurchari and Nagrashal. In terms of yield gap these farmers were found expert in the adoption of Laghushal local rice variety but less efficient in case of Bashamanik. However, they were moderately efficient in cultivating other local rice varieties.

In boro season all the three high yielding varieties, viz. IR-36, IR-50 and Ratna were cultivated by these farmers. The estimated yield gaps of these varieties were 1.77 qtl/ac. (8.19 per cent), 2.26 qtl/ac. (10.46 per cent), and 2.86 qtl/ac. (13.33 per cent). It was clear that the farmers of this category could adopt IR-36 variety more efficiently than other varieties in boro season. The yield gaps of IR-36 and Ratna improved rice varieties in boro season were lower in comparison to kharif season. However, the yield gap of IR-50 in kharif season was estimated to be lower than that in boro season. The average gap of boro season's rice varieties was estimated 2.30 qtl/ac. (10.72 per cent) which was substantially lower than the average yield gap of HYV of rice in kharif season, but higher than the average gap of local varieties. This phenomenon proved that the farmers were supposed to be comparatively more efficient in the adoption of local varieties in kharif season.

Farms of Category-III

The farmers of this category practiced all the high yielding varieties except IET-1444 in kharif season. The highest estimated yield gap was 9.92 qtl/ac. (49.69 per cent) in case of Ratna variety in absolute term. Whereas in percentage figure Masuri variety recorded the highest yield gap 8.43 qtl/ac. (50.33 per cent) in kharif season. The lowest gap accounting 5.62 qtl/ac. (28.15 per cent) in absolute figure in case of IR-36 but percentage calculation Pankaj variety was found to have the lowest yield gap 27.54 per cent (5.96 qtl/ac.) among the high yielding varieties cultivated by this category farmers in kharif season. The yield gap of IR-50 was recorded 5.95 qtl/ac. (29.80 per cent), this gap is 6.96 qtl/ac. (31.69 per cent) in case of IET-5656 variety, 8.20 qtl/ac. (32.71 per cent) in case of Sita variety. The average yield gap of all the high yielding varieties of this farm size in kharif season was estimated to be 7.20 qtl/ac. (36.39 per cent).

In kharif season all the eleven local rice varieties commonly grown in the area were cultivated by the farmers of category III. The highest gap among the local varieties was estimated in case of Laghushal traditional rice variety figuring 3.58 qtl/ac. (34.42 per cent) and the lowest gap was recorded in case of Nagrashal i.e. 0.79 qtl/ac. (7.59 per cent) only. The yield gaps of other local varieties calculated to be 1.66 qtl/ac. (15.96 per cent) for Assam Aush, 1.47 qtl/ac. (14.13 per cent) for Khajurchari, 1.79 qtl/ac. (17.21 per cent) for Gokulshal, 1.73 qtl/ac. (16.63 per cent) for Kadamshal, 0.93 qtl/ac. (8.99 per cent) for Bashamanik, 1.69 qtl/ac. (16.25 per cent) for Rajamanik, 1.14 qtl/ac. (10.96 per cent) for Hurkashal, 1.40 qtl/ac. (13.46 per cent) for Sundarmukhi, and 1.92 qtl/ac. (18.46 per cent) for Radhashal. The average yield gap of the local varieties was 1.65 qtl/ac. (15.81 per cent). A small value of yield gap for local rice varieties implied that the medium farmers could adopt local rice varieties more successfully than the high yielding varieties.

Like farmers of category II, the farmers of category-III also adopted all the three improved varieties of rice in boro season. The highest yield gap in boro season for this farm size was 3.26 qtl/ac.

(15.09 per cent) in case of Ratna variety, and the lowest yield gap was 1.54 qtl/ac. (7.12 per cent) in case of IR-50 variety. The estimated gap of IR-36 variety in boro season was 2.15 qtl/ac. (9.95 per cent). The average yield gap in this season was only 2.32 qtl/ac. (10.72 per cent) which was substantially lower than the average yield gap of improved varieties in kharif season though higher in absolute figure than kharif season but lower in percentage figure.

Farms of Category-IV

In kharif season all the improved modern rice varieties recorded in sample farmers except IET-1444 were found to be adopted by the farmers of large farm category. The highest gap in terms of absolute figure was 7.71 qtl/ac. (35.10 per cent) for the IET-5656 variety. In terms of percentage, Masuri variety had the highest yield gap 7.66 qtl/ac. (45.92 per cent). The lowest yield gap was recorded in Panth-IV which was 3.15 qtl/ac. (15.78 per cent). The yield gaps of IR-36, IR-50, Pankaj, Ratna, and Sita varieties were 6.10 qtl/ac. (30.56 per cent), 7.63 qtl/ac. (38.22 per cent), 4.08 qtl/ac. (18.85 per cent), 7.67 qtl/ac. (38.42 per cent), and 5.15 qtl/ac. (25.80 per cent) respectively. The average yield gap of all the improved varieties was 6.14 qtl/ac. (31.08 per cent) which was higher than Sita, Panth-IV, Pankaj, and IR-36 but lower than IR-50, Ratna, Masuri, and IET-5656.

Large farmers were found to practice nine out of eleven local varieties in kharif season. These varieties and their respective yield gaps recorded were Assam Aush 1.80 qtl/ac. (17.30 per cent), Khajurchari 2.12 qtl/ac. (20.38 per cent), Gokulshal 2.25 qtl/ac. (21.63 per cent), Kadamshal 2.33 qtl/ac. (22.40 per cent), Bashamanik 1.54 qtl/ac. (14.80 per cent), Nagrashal 1.25 qtl/ac. (12.01 per cent), Rajamanik 1.08 qtl/ac. (10.38 per cent), Hurkashal 1.22 qtl/ac. (11.73 per cent) , and Laghushal 0.40 qtl/ac. (3.84 per cent). They were more efficient in the production of Laghushal and least efficient in the production of Kadamshal local rice variety as the lowest gap was found in former variety and the highest gap in the latter variety. The overall yield gap of local rice varieties taken together was only 1.55 qtl/ac. (14.84 per cent),

In boro season large farmers had grown only a single improved rice variety IR-50 and the yield gap of this variety was only

1.99 qtl/ac. (9.21 per cent). This result indicated that in boro season the category-IV farmers could produce IR-50 rice variety more efficiently than in kharif season. Because the yield gap of this variety was lower in boro season than in kharif. Though the yield gap of boro season was higher in absolute figure than in kharif season's local varieties, but the gap in former season was lower than that in latter season when considered in percentage term.

Variety-wise Analysis of Yield Gap

Kharif IR-36: All the four farm size categories practiced this variety in kharif season. The estimated gaps of these farm categories were 6.62 qtl/ac. (33.16 per cent) in case of category-I farmers, 5.37 qtl/ac. (26.90 per cent) in case of category-II farmers, for category-III and IV farmers the figures were 5.62 qtl/ac. (28.15 per cent) and 6.10 qtl/ac. (30.56 per cent) respectively. The highest gap was found in case of category-I farm size and the lowest gap in category-II farm size. The pooled yield gap of this high yielding variety was recorded 5.92 qtl/ac. (26.69 per cent) irrespective of farm size which was higher than the gap recorded in category-II and III farms but lower than the gaps in the category-I and IV farms.

Kharif IR-50: Except the farmers of category-I other three farm size groups adopted this variety in kharif season. The highest yield gap among the farm sizes was 7.63 qtl/ac. (38.22 per cent) in case of category-IV farmers and the lowest gap was found in case of category-II farmers accounting only 1.14 qtl/ac. (5.71 per cent). The magnitude of the yield gap for the category-III farm size group was estimated 5.95 qtl/ac. (29.80 per cent). The overall gap of this variety in kharif season was 4.90 qtl/ac. (22.02 per cent) which was higher than the lowest yield gap found in category-II farm, but higher than the gap in category-III and IV farm groups.

Kharif Ratna: Like IR-50 variety, the farmers of category-II, III, and IV cultivated this variety in kharif season. The yield gap of Ratna variety ranged from 5.25 qtl/ac. to 9.92 qtl/ac. The highest yield gap 9.92 qtl/ac. (49.69 per cent) recorded in case of category-III farmers and the lowest gap was calculated to be 5.25 qtl/ac. (26.30 per cent) in category-II farms. The estimated yield gap of this variety for category-IV farm size group was 7.67 qtl/ac. (38.42 per cent) which was slightly higher than the overall gap 7.61 qtl/ac. (38.13 per cent).

Kharif Pankaj: This variety was practiced by all the farm size groups except category-I farmers in kharif season. The yield gaps in respect to farm size area were 5.07 qtl/ac. (23.42 per cent), 5.98 qtl/ac. (27.54 per cent), and 4.08 qtl/ac. (18.08 per cent) respectively. This result indicated that category-IV farmers were most efficient in the adoption of Pankaj high yielding variety in kharif season than the farmers of other two categories. The overall yield gap of this variety estimated to be only 5.03 qtl/ac. (23.27 per cent), which was higher than the gap in category-IV farm size but lower than the gaps in categories II and III farmers.

Kharif Masuri: Only the farmers of the two size groups, viz. category-III and IV cultivated Masuri rice variety. The estimated yield gaps were 8.43 qtl/ac. (50.53 per cent) and 7.66 qtl/ac. (45.92 per cent) respectively. The overall yield gap of this variety calculated to be 8.04 qtl/ac. (48.22 per cent) which was higher than the gap in category-IV farm size, but lower than the gap in category-III farm size.

Kharif IET-1444: This high yielding rice variety was practiced only by the farmers of category-II and the calculated gap was 12.24 qtl/ac. (67.10 per cent) which was the highest gap found among the high yielding varieties in kharif season. This result also explains the cause of non-adoption of this variety by the farmers of all size groups.

Kharif IET-5656: The farmers of categories-III and IV cultivated this variety in kharif season. The respective yield gaps were 6.96 qtl/ac. (31.69 per cent) and 7.71 qtl/ac. (35.10 per cent). The overall yield gap accounted to be 7.33 qtl/ac. (33.39 per cent).

Kharif Panth-IV: Panth-IV high yielding rice variety was cultivated by the farmers of categories-III and IV. The yield gap 8.20 qtl/ac. (41.08 per cent) of category-III farm size was significantly higher than the gap 3.15 qtl/ac. (15.78 per cent) of the farmers of category-IV. The estimated overall yield gap was only 5.67 qtl/ac. (28.43 per cent).

Kharif Sita: Except the farmers of category-I, the farmers of all other three farm sizes grew this variety in kharif season. The highest gap was 11.10 qtl/ac. (55.61 per cent) recorded in category-II farms and the lowest gap was 5.15 qtl/ac. (25.80 per cent) in category-IV. The estimated yield gap of category-III was 6.33 qtl/ac. (32.71 per cent). The overall gap of this variety accounting 7.59 qtl/ac. (38.04 per cent), which was higher than that in case of categories-III and IV, and lower than that in category-II.

In kharif season IR-36 rice variety was widely accepted by the farmers of all size groups. IR-50, Ratna, Pankaj, Sita high yielding rice varieties were adopted by the farmers of categories-II, III and IV. Only categories-III and IV farmers adopted Masuri, IET-5656 and Panth-IV varieties, IET-1444 was adopted only by the farmers of category-II. The performance record in terms of yield gap of the farmers of all the categories established the fact that large farmers were more efficient in the adoption of high yielding rice varieties in kharif season as they were economically strong. The yield gap of the high yielding varieties in kharif season irrespective of farm size calculated and it was found that IR-50 variety had the lowest yield gap accounting only 4.90 qtl/ac. (22.02 per cent). The yield gap of Pankaj variety i.e. 5.03 qtl/ac. (23.27 per cent) was also substantially low in comparison to the gaps of other varieties. The highest gap was found in case of IET-1444 variety accounting 12.24 qtl/ac. (67.10 per cent). The overall yield gap of these high yielding varieties irrespective of farm size was 7.14 qtl/ac. (36.47 per cent) which was higher than the yield gap of IR-50 but significantly lower than the yield gap of IET-1444.

Assam Aush (Kharif): This local rice variety was grown by the farmers of categories-I, III, and IV. The highest yield gap recorded as to be only 1.80 qtl/ac. (17.30 per cent) in case of large farm size group. The lowest yield gap accounting only 1.30 qtl/ac. (12.50 per cent) in case of category-II farmers. The overall yield gap was calculated to be 1.58 qtl/ac. (15.25 per cent) which was higher than the gap in category-II farm but lower than the categories-III and IV farms. The estimated yield gap of category-III farmers was 1.66 qtl/ac. (15.96 per cent).

Khajurchari (Kharif): The farmers of all the four size groups cultivated this local rice variety in kharif season. The calculated yield gaps according to farm size group were 2.18 qtl/ac. (20.96 per cent), 1.47 qtl/ac. (14.13 per cent), 1.47 qtl/ac. (14.13 per cent) and 2.12 qtl/ac. (20.38 per cent) respectively. The highest yield gap was recorded in case of category-I farmers and the lowest yield gap was found in case of the farmers of both the categories-II and III. The estimated overall yield gap of this variety was only 1.81 qtl/ac. (17.40 per cent).

Gokulshal (Kharif): Except category-I, the farmers of all other categories grew this local rice variety in kharif season. The highest yield gap of Gokulshal was 2.25 qtl/ac. (21.63 per cent) and it was found in case of large farmers. The lowest yield gap accounting only 1.46 qtl/ac. (14.03 per cent) in case of farmers of category-II. The yield gap of this variety in case of the farmers of category-III was estimated to be 1.79 qtl/ac. (17.21 per cent). The overall yield gap was only 1.78 qtl/ac. (17.13 per cent) which was higher than the yield gaps of categories-I and II farms but a little lower than the gap in category-III farms.

Kadamshal (Kharif): Kadamshal traditional rice variety was cultivated by the farmers of the farm size groups namely categories-II, III, and IV. The estimated yield gaps of this rice variety were 1.42 qtl/ac. (13.63 per cent), 1.73 qtl/ac. (16.63 per cent) and 2.33 qtl/ac. (22.40 per cent) respectively. The lowest yield gap was found in category-II farms and the highest yield gap was found in category-IV farms. This result implied that the production efficiency of Kadamshal variety was comparatively higher in case of category-II farms than other farm groups. The estimated yield gap of this variety irrespective of farm size was only 1.82 qtl/ac. (17.56 per cent) which was lower than the gap of large farm size, but higher than the gaps of both the categories-II and III farms.

Bashamanik (Kharif): Except marginal farmers, the other three farm categories cultivated this local rice variety in kharif season. The yield gap of this variety in small farm size was significantly high estimating 3.03 qtl/ac. (29.51 per cent) and the lowest gap was found in case of medium farm size accounting only 0.93 qtl/ac. (8.99 per cent). The gap of the large farmers was 1.54 qtl/ac. (14.80 per cent). The overall yield gap of this variety was 1.83 qtl/ac. (17.75 per cent).

Nagrashal (Kharif): Nagrashal local rice variety was cultivated by categories-II, III, and IV farms. The highest gap of this variety accounting to be 1.47 qtl/ac. (14.13 per cent) was found in case of category-II farms. The yield gap in case of category-III was only 0.79 qtl/ac. (7.59 per cent) which was the lowest one among all the farm sizes. The yield gap of category-IV farms was calculated to be 1.25 qtl/ac. (12.01 per cent). The pooled yield gap irrespective of farm size of this variety was 1.17 qtl/ac. (11.24 per cent) which was found to be higher than the gap in category-III farms but lower than in category-II and category-IV farm size groups.

Rajamanik (Kharif): The farmers of categories-II, III and IV cultivated this local rice variety. The estimated yield gap was found to be more than 1 qtl/ac. in all the farm size groups. The yield gaps of Rajamanik with respect to different farm sizes were 1.24 qtl/ac. (11.92 per cent), 1.69 qtl/ac. (16.25 per cent), and 1.08 qtl/ac. (10.38 per cent) respectively. The farmers of category-III farm size were found inefficient and category-IV farmers were found to be relatively efficient in comparison to other farm sizes with respect to the production of this local rice variety in kharif season. The overall yield gap of this variety was calculated to be 1.33 qtl/ac. (12.85 per cent).

Hurkashal (Kharif): The farmers of all the four farm size groups grew this local rice variety in kharif season. The lowest yield gap was found in case of farmers of category-I accounting to be 0.65 qtl/ac. (6.25 per cent) and the highest yield gap was recorded as 1.22 qtl/ac. (11.73 per cent) in case of category-IV farms. The yield gap was calculated to be 1.14 qtl/ac. (10.96 per cent) in both the cases of farmers belonging to categories-II and III. The overall yield gap of this variety was only 1.03 qtl/ac. (9.97 per cent).

Laghushal (Kharif): This local rice variety was cultivated by the farmers of all the farm size groups except the farmers in category-I. The yield gaps recorded were 0.90 qtl/ac. (8.65 per cent), 3.58 qtl/ac. (34.42 per cent, and 0.40 qtl/ac. (3.84 per cent) respectively. The overall yield gap of this variety was calculated to be 1.62 qtl/ac. This result indicated that the category-III farms were most efficient in the adoption of this variety but farmers of categories-II and IV were more efficient in the production of this variety though the farmers of category-IV were comparatively more efficient than the farmers of category-II.

Sundarmukhi (Kharif): The farmers of categories-II and III cultivated Sundarmukhi local rice variety in kharif season. The yield gap of the farmers in category-II was 1.24 qtl/ac. (11.92 per cent) and 1.40 qtl/ac. (13.46 per cent) was recorded as the magnitude of yield gap for the farmers of category-III size. The pooled yield gap of this variety was accounted as only 1.32 qtl/ac. (12.69 per cent).

Radhashal (Kharif): The farmers of categories-I and III were found to adopt this local rice variety in kharif season. The yield gaps were 2.28 qtl/ac. (21.92 per cent) and 1.92 qtl/ac. (18.46 per cent) respectively. The overall yield gap (all the farm sizes taken together) was 2.10 qtl/ac. (20.19 per cent).

In kharif season among the local varieties; Khajuchari, Gokulshal, Hurkashal, varieties were widely adopted by the farmers of all the four farm size groups. The farmers except category-I adopted Assam Aush, Kadamshal, Bashamanik, Nagrashal, Rajamanik, and Laghushal varieties. Sundarmukhi variety was practiced by the farmers of categories-II and III whereas categories-I and III farmers cultivated Radhashal rice variety. The yield gap of local rice with respect to farm size were 1.67 qtl/ac. (16.38 per cent), 1.47 qtl/ac. (14.14 per cent), 1.65 qtl/ac. (15.81 per cent), and 1.55 qtl/ac. (14.84 per cent) respectively. It was found that the farmers of category-II were relatively more efficient in traditional rice production, whereas farmers of category-III were seemed to be more inefficient in the production of high yielding rice in kharif season.

The yield gap among the local varieties in kharif season ranged between 1.03 qtl/ac. (9.97 per cent) in case of Hurkashal to 2.10 qtl/ac. (20.19 per cent) in case of Radhashal variety. This result indicated that Hurkashal local rice variety was adopted successfully whereas production inefficiency was found in Radhashal variety.

It was interesting to note that the yield gap of local varieties in comparison to high yielding variety in kharif season was lower in all farm size groups. The yield gap of improved rice was 7.14 qtl/ac. (36.47 per cent) whereas only 1.58 qtl/ac. (15.24 per cent) was recorded as yield gap of local rice irrespective of variety and farm size.

Boro IR- 36: IR-36 as Boro high yielding variety was selected for adoption by the farmers of categories-I, II, and III farm size accounting to be 2.15 qtl/ac. (9.95 per cent). The lowest yield gap was only 1.77 qtl/ac. (8.19 per cent) and it was found in category-II farms. The estimated yield gap of category-I farmers was 1.79 qtl/ac. (8.25 per cent). The overall yield gap irrespective of farm size was calculated only 1.90 qtl/ac. (8.79 per cent) which was higher than the gaps of farmers of categories-I and II but lower than the category-III farms' yield gap of Boro IR-36 variety.

Boro IR-50: Not a single farmer in category-I reported to cultivate this high yielding variety but the farmers of other farm categories adopted this variety in Boro season. The calculated gaps of this variety were 2.26 qtl/ac. (10.46 per cent), 1.54 qtl/ac. (7.12 per cent) and 1.99 qtl/ac. (9.21 per cent) respectively. The overall gap of this variety in Boro season was only 1.93 qtl/ac. (8.93 per cent) which was higher than the gap in category-III but lower than the gaps in both categories of I and IV farm sizes.

Boro Ratna: Only the farmers of categories-II and III cultivated Ratna rice variety in boro season. The calculated yield gap of farmers in category-II was 2.86 qtl/ac. (13.33 per cent) and for the category-III farms the gap was recorded as 3.20 qtl/ac. (15.09 per cent). The overall yield gap of this variety was 3.06 qtl/ac. (14.21 per cent), which was higher than the category-II farms' gap but lower than the gap of the category-III farm size.

In Boro season the highest gap (irrespective of variety) of high yielding varieties was recorded in category-III farms size and the lowest gap was found in case of category-I farms. Ratna variety was found as maximum gap recording variety in Boro season. However, the lowest gap was recorded for IR-36 variety. This result established the fact that the large number of farmers chose the variety which recorded the lowest yield gap and *vice versa.* It was to be noted that in Boro season the yield gaps of all the high yielding varieties were substantially lower than the yield gaps of respective varieties in kharif season. This phenomenon explained the fact that in Boro season all the production inputs could be applied successfully and high yielding varieties were suitable in physical environment in summer.

Yield Gap and Technological Gap

In the preceding section a marked difference between potential yield of a rice variety and its actual yield in farmers' field has been noticed. The yield gap of rice variety is a common feature in Indian agriculture for all varieties—high yielding as well as traditional and in all seasons—kharif and boro. However, there is a substantial variation in the yield gap over farm size, variety and season. It is a well established fact that the low level of yield of rice varieties is mainly due to the sub-optimal or non-application of many of the essential input factors such as seed rate, ploughing, manuring, application of fertilizer and pesticides, weeding, etc. by the farmers in their rice fields. In other words, technological gap might be considered as the main cause of yield gap. The difference between recommended level and actual level of inputs application is termed as technological gap. A traditional belief is that the yield of a particular rice variety depends upon the inputs of production. That is, the level of inputs determines the level of output. In this section the relationship between yield gap and technological gap over farm size groups and varieties has been explained.

To estimate the casual relationship between yield gap and technological gap zero order correlation matrix was constructed. The results are summarized in Tables 6.11 and 6.12. Table 6.11 represents the correlation coefficients of yield gap and technological gap over farm size. Variety-wise correlation coefficients are presented in Table 6.12.

Yield gap of a farmer is calculated taking average of the yield gaps of all the rice varieties cultivated by the farmer in a particular year. Similarly, technological gap of the farm is the average gap in the application of production inputs in the adoption of all the rice varieties.

The functional relationship may be written as

$$Y = f(X)$$

where,

Y = yield gap and

X = technological gap

The yield gap has been considered as dependent variable and technological gap as independent variable.

Farm Size-wise Yield Gap and Technological Gap

The estimated correlation coefficient of yield gap and technological gap was 0.72350 for category-I farm size which explained the fact that the level of yield of marginal farmers depended upon the level of inputs application by 72 per cent on an average.

In case of category-II farmers the correlation coefficient of yield gap and technological gap was calculated as only 0.59218. This was the lowest value of correlation coefficient among the farm size groups. Only 59 per cent of the yield gap was explained by the low level of input application.

The correlation coefficient of yield gap and technological gap for category-III farms was calculated as 0.61742 which was slightly higher than that of category-II farms but lower than both of categories-I and IV farmers' correlation coefficient. The correlation coefficient of category-II farmers indicated that 61 per cent yield gap depended upon the technological gap.

For the large farmers the calculated correlation coefficient between yield gap and technological gap was 0.80472 which was the highest coefficient among the farm size classes. It implied that 80 per cent yield gap of rice was explained by the low level of inputs application by the farmers.

The pooled correlation coefficient was estimated to be 0.66014 which was smaller than that in category-I and category-IV farms but bigger than the coefficients in categories-II and III farms.

Table 6.11: Correlation Coefficient Between Yield Gap and Technological Gap (Farm Size-wise)

Sl. No.	*Farm Size Category*	*Correlation Coefficient*
1.	Category-I	0.72350
2.	Category-II	0.59218
3.	Category-III	0.61742
4.	Category-IV	0.80472
5.	Pooled	0.66014

In all the four farm size classes positive correlation coefficient were estimated which implied that there was a direct relationship between yield gap and technological gap though the degree of association was not equally strengthened in all farm sizes. However, the yield gap of rice could be narrowed down by decreasing the technological gap. In other words, yield gap increased with the increase in technological gap and *vice versa.*

A high correlation coefficient indicated a close association between yield gap and technological gap. The relationship between yield gap and technological gap was strong in case of category-I and large farmers than it was in case of small and medium farmers. This result also explained that the level of rice production did not totally depend upon the biological factors only. There were many other factors which influenced the level of rice production. Farm management, supervision, etc. were such non-biological factors which affected the level of output.

Variety-wise Relationship Between Yield Gap and Technological Gap

In kharif season the correlaton coefficient between yield gap and technological gap of high yielding rice varieties showed marked differences. The highest correlation coefficient among the high yielding varieties was estimated as 0.83750 in case of Pankaj variety. This result implied that for Pankaj variety 83 per cent yield gap was due to technological gap. The lowest correlation coefficient was 0.59068 in case of Panth-IV variety. The second highest correlation coefficient was calculated in case of IR-50 variety where 76 per cent yield gap was explained by the technological gap. The correlation coefficients between yield gap and technological gap for IR-36, Ratna, Masuri, IET-1444, IET-5656, and Sita varieties were 0.70294, 0.63940, 0.64039, 0.60721, 0.71532 and 0.66350 respectively. The correlation coefficient between yield gap and technological gap for combined high yielding varieties in kahrif season was calculated 0.69304 which implied that the yield gap can be reduced by 0.79 by decreasing the technological gap by one. In other words this correlation coefficient showed a high degree of association between technological gap and yield gap.

Though correlation coefficient between yield gap and technological gap with respect to local rice varieties is not very meaningful from economic and statistical point of view but the exercise was done to have some idea about the responsiveness of local rice varieties to the modern technologies which were not used by the farmers few years back. So far the traditional rice varieties cultivated by the sample farmers are concerned, the correlation coefficients between yield gap and technological gap were 0.40425 for Assam Aush, 0.49306 for Khajurchari, 0.42595 for Nagrashal, 0.53062 for Gokulshal, 0.54781 for Laghushal, 0.50247 for Sundarmukhi, 0.59313 for Radhashal, 0.43040 for Bashamanik, 0.47932 for Rajamanik, and 0.49176 for Hurkashal rice variety during Kharif season. In case of Radhashal 59 per cent yield gap was caused due to low level of inputs application. This was the highest correlation coefficient among the local varieties. The lowest correlation coefficient was estimated in case of Assam Aush. In the production of Assam Aush local rice variety non-biological factors affected significantly. The overall correlation coefficient for combined local varieties was only 0.48907. This explained that less than 50 per cent yield gap of local varieties was associated with technological gap. It should be noted that the correlation coefficient of local rice varieties were in general lower than that of high yielding varieties. This phenomenon established the fact that the biological factors had more influence on yield gaps of high yielding varieties than that in case of local varieties.

Table 6.12: Correlation Coefficient Between Yield Gap and Technological Gap (Variety-wise)

Sl. No.	*Farm Size Category*	*Correlation Coefficient*
	Kharif Season (HYV)	
1.	IR-36	0.70294
2.	IR-50	0.76368
3.	Ratna	0.63940
4.	Pankaj	0.83750
5.	Masuri	0.64039
6.	IET-1444	0.60721
7.	IET-5656	0.71532
8.	Panth-IV	0.59068
9.	Sita	0.66350
	Pooled	0.69304
	Kharif Season (L. Varieties)	
1.	Assam Aush	0.40425
2.	Khajurchari	0.49306
3.	Nagrashal	0.42595
4.	Gokulshal	0.53062
5.	Lagushal	0.54781
6.	Sundarmukhi	0.50247
7.	Radhashal	0.59313
8.	Bashamanik	0.43040
9.	Rajamanik	0.47932
10	Hurkashal	0.49176
	Pooled	0.48907
	Boro Season (HYV)	
1.	IR-36	0.83934
2.	IR-50	0.76010
3.	Ratna	0.70462
	Pooled	0.75841

In boro season the correlation coefficient between yield gap and technological gap for IR-36 variety was 0.83934 which was the highest among the correlation coefficients of high yielding varieties in boro season and also higher than that of kharif season for the same variety. The technological gap was responsible by 83 per cent for yield gap for this variety. The correlation coefficient for IR-50 in boro season was estimated 0.76010 which was smaller than that of kharif season. In case of Ratna variety the correlation coefficient was calculated 0.70462 which was the lowest in boro season but higher than that of kharif season. The correlation coefficient for combined high yielding varieties in boro season was estimated 0.75841 which explained that on an average 75 per cent yield gap as caused due to technological gap. This combined correlation coefficient of high yielding varieties in boro season was higher in comparison to kharif season. The result supported the fact that the same high yielding variety in boro season was more input/culture practices responsive than in kahrif season.

The results of this section supported the hypothesis of 2 of this study that there was a positive and significant relationship between yield gap and technological gap.

Identification and Evaluation of Different Production Factors Responsible for Yield Gap

The relationship between yield gap of different rice varieties and technological gap has been discussed in the previous section where we found a very strong association between the two gaps. The present analysis was carried out to identify and evaluate the various production factors affecting the yield of different rice varieties in kharif season as well as in boro season. Multiple regression models were used to identify and measure the respective contribution to the yield gap.

Simple correlation coefficient matrix was worked out for the explanatory variables to examine the multicollinearity problem. However, the result did not exhibit the existence of multicollinearity in any of the case and therefore, the data in original form were put through regression analysis in the computer.

Based on the literature and prior knowledge from the survey of the area it was hypothesized that the level of output of a particular variety of rice depends upon the level of input application and other essential treatments. In other words, the yield gap of rice is directly and positively related with the input gaps and gaps in other cultural treatments. In the present case variety-wise yield gap was used as depended variable. The explanatory variables included in the analysis were those gaps in the seed rate, seed treatment, method of sowing, ploughing, application of organic manure, application of Nitrogenous,

Phosphoric and Potassic fertilizers, weeding, and application of plant protection chemicals. The functional relationship of the model in order of the variables in the equation developed for various rice varieties separately was

$$Y_i = f(X_{i1}, X_{i2}, \ldots\ldots\ldots, X_{i10})$$

where,

Y_i = yield gap of the rice variety i

X_{i1} = gap in the seed rate of the variety

X_{i2} = gap in the seed treatment of the variety

X_{i3} = gap in the method of sowing of the variety

X_{i4} = gap in the ploughing for the variety

X_{i5} = gap in the application of organic manure in the cultivation of the variety

X_{i6} = gap in the application of N-fertilizer for the variety

X_{i7} = gap in the application of P-fertilizer for the variety

X_{i8} = gap in the application of K-fertilizer for the variety

X_{i9} = gap in weeding for the variety, and

X_{i10} = gap in the application of plant protection chemicals for the variety.

All the variables, both dependent and independent variables, were measured in percentage terms.

The above mentioned 10 factors/cultural practices were considered to have an effect on rice production. The original data envisaged that there was no gap at all in seed rate and method of sowing. However, 100 per cent gap was recorded in case of seed treatment. Not a single sample farmer in either season was found to apply seed treatment practice. Therefore, the expected effect of these three factors on yield were not found as it could not be considered in the model. Hence, the multiple regression equations were fitted without considering these factors having no variations over observations.

Regression coefficient of the explanatory variables estimated through multiple regression analysis along with t-values and coefficient of multiple determinations (R^2) are presented in tables 6.13, 6.14, and 6.15.

Variety-wise Analysis

Kharif Season (High Yielding Varieties): In the study area nine high yielding varieties were found to be adopted by the sample farmers in the reference year. But due to inadequacy of number of observations (and consequently the lack of degrees of freedom) three varieties namely IET-1444, IET-5656, and Panth-IV had to be dropped from this regression analysis. The results of the multiple regression analysis for the rest of the varieties, viz. IR-36, IR-50, Ratna, Pakaj, Masuri, and Sita are presented in table 6.4.1.

IR-36: The result of multiple regression for this variety showed that the regression coefficients of the gaps in ploughing, manuring, NPK fertilizers, weeding, and plant protection chemical application were 0.56923, 0.20675, 0.10264, 0.23796,0.13992, 0.49815, and 0.08310 respectively. The coefficients expressed in the model were found positively related with the yield gap, but all were not significant at certain level of probability. Weeding was found significant at 1 per cent level of probability, ploughing was significant at 10 per cent level of probability. The non-significant factors/treatment were N-fertilizer, K-fertilizer, and plant protection chemicals. The highest coefficient among all factors/treatments was found in the treatment of ploughing. Hence, it is concluded that if the gap in the ploughing decreases by 1 per cent the yield gap of IR-36 will also decreased by 0.56923 per cent. The value of multiple regressions (R^2) expressed that 57 per cent of the variation in yield gap was caused due to gaps in independent variables.

IR- 50: The gap in the application of plant protection chemical was excluded with the first three factors since the original data envisaged no variation in the application of plant protection chemicals in the adoption of IR-50 improved rice variety in kharif season. The result of multiple regressions revealed that the gap in ploughing, phosphates fertilizer, and potassic fertilizer did not have any significant impact on yield gap in case of IR-50. The coefficients of these three non-significant factors were 0.02166, 0.04562, and 0.08212 respectively. The highest coefficient was found in case of gap in N-fertilizer application among all the factors and treatments. If the gap in the application of N-fertilizer was increased by 1 per cent the yield gap of the variety would have also increased by 0.407 per cent and vice-versa. This was significant at 5 per cent level of probability. The coefficient of the gap in organic manure application (X_5) was also found significant at 5 per cent level of probability. The other significant coefficient was (X_9) showing significant at 10 per cent level of probability. All these explanatory variables explained 67 yield gap variations for this variety in kharif season. The significant coefficients of X_5, X_6, and X_9 supported the hypothesis 3 which stated that there was a significant relationship between yield gap and gaps in manuring, nitrogenous fertilizer, and weeding. All the variables included in the model were positively related with yield gap. The coefficients of X_5, X_6, and X_9 were 0.31389, 0.40759, and 0.23189 respectively.

Ratna: In case of Ratna rice variety all the variables included in the model were found significant. Variable (X_8) was excluded from the model due to invariability of magnitude over the sample observations. The coefficient of X_5, X_7, X_9, and X_{10} were significant at 1 per cent level of probability. The coefficients of X_6 and X_4 were significant at 5 per cent and 10 per cent level of probability respectively. The values of the coefficients of these explanatory variables X_5, X_6, X_7, X_8, X_9, and X_{10} were 0.25324, 0.48709, 0.38766, 0.34172, 0.32673, and 0.37345. The result supported the hypothesis of the study. It was evident that the impact of manuring on yield of Ratna variety was its highest level among all factors/treatments. If there was an increase by one per cent in the gap of organic manure, yield gap would have increased by 0.48 per cent and vice versa. The value of the coefficient of determination (R^2) showed that in case of Ratna variety 87 per cent variation in yield gap was explained by the explanatory variables included in the equation.

Pankaj: The value of the coefficient of multiple determinations (R^2) for Pankaj variety was 0.82978 which indicated that about 83 per cent yield gap variation of this variety was determined by the explanatory factors/treatments included in the model. The coefficients of X_5, X_7 were significant at 1 per cent level of probability. The other significant coefficient was X_{10} at 20 per cent level of probability. The coefficients of these variables were 0.63259, 0.37528, and 0.37654 respectively. Variables X_4, X_6, X_8, and X_9 were non-significant and the coefficients were 0.12904, 0.26060, 0.04336, and 0.05641 respectively. All the explanatory variables included in the model were positively related with yield gap which explained a direct relationship between dependent and independent variables. The hypothesis 3 of the study was supported by this result. The coefficient of X_5 was the highest among all the explanatory variables which revealed that 0.63 per cent of yield gap variation was due to 1 per cent variation in manuring in case of Pankaj high yielding variety in kharif season.

Masuri: In case of Masuri the regression coefficients of X_5, X_6, X_7, X_8, X_{10} were 0.38734, 0.02475, 0.37666, 1.000, and 0.25886 respectively. All the explanatory variables were positively related with the yield gap of Masuri rice variety though not significant at a specified level of probability. However, X_4 and X_9 were excluded from the model for this variety due to constant gaps over the observations in case of these two factors. The coefficients of X_5 and X_{10} were found to be higher and significant at 5 per cent level of probability. The coefficient of X_7 was significant at 10 per cent level of probability. Factors like X_6 and X_8 did not have any significant impact on yield gap. The coefficient of multiple determinations (R^2) for this variety was 0.92398 which was the highest among all high yielding varieties in kharif season. The value of R^2 explained that about 92 per cent variation in yield gap was caused due to the joint effect of the explanatory variables included in the model.

Sita: Variable X_{10} was excluded from the model with the first three explanatory factors in case of Sita variety. The significant variables were X_5, X_6, X_7, X_8. The coefficients of X_5, X_7, and X_8 were significant at 5 per cent level of probability. The coefficient of X_6 was significant at 10 per cent level of probability. The regression coefficients of these significant factors were 0.77499, 0.44703, 0.66317, and 1.38876 respectively. The coefficients of non-significant factors were 0.83102 for X_4 and 0.19714 for X_9. The value of the coefficient of multiple determinations (R^2) for Sita variety was 0.78876 which revealed that the explanatory variables explained jointly about 79 per cent yield gap variation of the variety.

The Summary: In kharif season for high yielding varieties the gap in the organic manure application (X_5) in rice field was found to be the most important factor in determining the yield gaps for all the varieties in the analysis. However, the level of significance for different varieties was different. The coefficient of X_5 was significant at 1 per cent level of probability in case of Ratna and Pankaj varieties, it was significant at 5 per cent level of probability for IR-50, Masuri and Sita varieties, and in case of IR-36, it was significant at 10 per cent level of probability.

The second most important factor having the effect on yield gap of high yielding varieties was the gap in the application of P-fertilizer (X_7). The coefficient of X_7 was significant at 1 per cent level of probability for Ratna and Pankaj varieties, for Sita variety it was significant at 5 per cent level of probability. In case of Masuri and IR-36, the coefficient of X_7 was significant at 10 per cent probability level.

The coefficient of the gap in ploughing (X_4) was significant at 5 per cent level and 10 per cent level of probability for IR-36 and Ratna varieties respectively. The coefficient of X_6 was found to be significant at 5 per cent level of probability for IR-50 and Ratna varieties. It was significant at 10 per cent level of probability in case of Sita variety. The coefficient of X_8 was significant at 5 per cent level of probability for Sita variety only. Weeding was found to be one of the important factors affecting yield gap. The coefficient of X_9 was significant at 1 per cent level of probability. The coefficient of plant protection chemical was also found significant for three rice varieties. It was significant at 1 per cent level of probability for Ratna variety. It was also significant at 5 per cent and 10 per cent level of probability for Masuri and Pankaj varieties respectively.

The regression results of this section showed that the production inputs/cultural treatments were significantly related at different levels of probability with the yield gaps of high yielding rice varieties. It can be concluded that all the factors which were included in this model were responsible for yield gap of high yielding rice varieties which supported the hypothesis 3 of this study that there was a significant relationship between yield gap of a rice variety and production inputs/treatments for rice cultivation.

Local Varieties: Eleven local varieties were reported to be adopted by the sample farmers during the reference year in kharif season. Three varieties, viz. Laghushal, Sundarmukhi, and Hurkashal were dropped from the regression analysis due to insufficient degree of freedom as the number of observations was small. However, the other local varieties namely Assam Aush, Khajurchari, Gokulshal, Nagrashal, Kadamshal, Bhasamanik, Rajamanik, and Hurkashal were considered for multiple regression analysis and the results were presented in Table 6.13.

Assam Aush: The result of multiple regression analysis of this variety showed that the coefficients of X_4, X_5, X_6, X_7, X_8, X_9, and X_{10} were 0.05584, 0.15691, 0.12942, 0.09643, 0.79078, 0.14781, and 0.10105 respectively. All the varieties were found to have positive relationship with the yield gap of Assam Aush. X_8 was the most important determinant of the yield gap of the variety. The coefficient of X_5 and X_9 were significant at 1 per cent level of probability indicating high influence on yield gap. The coefficients of X_6 and X_8 were significant at 5 per cent and 10 per cent level of probability respectively. The coefficients of X_4, X_7, and X_{10} were not significant. The coefficient of X_8 showed the highest value among the explanatory variables which indicated that the yield gap would decrease or increase by 0.79078 per cent if the gap of the K-fertilizer application decreased or increased by 1 per cent. The coefficient of multiple determinations (R^2) showed that about 52 per cent variation in yield gap of Assam Aush was explained by the explanatory variables included in the model.

Khajurchari: The coefficients of X_4, X_5, X_6, X_9, and X_{10} were found significant and indicated that the gap in ploughing, organic manure application, weeding, and plant protection chemicals had significant impact on yield gap of Khajurchari rice variety. The coefficient of X_9 was significant at 1 per cent level of probability. The coefficient of X_4, X_5, X_6, and X_{10} were significant at 5 per cent level of probability. The coefficients of X_7 and X_8 were not significant. The regression coefficients of X_4, X_5, X_6, X_7, X_8, X_9, and X_{10} were 0.17631, 0.12790, 0.16315, 0.14720, 0.03926, 0.16856, and 0.12729 respectively. The yield gap of this variety was influenced highly by ploughing gap as the regression coefficient of X_4 was the highest among all the explanatory variables. The yield gap of Khajurchari local variety was affected by 0.17631 per cent due to 1 per cent change in this explanatory variable. The value of the coefficient of multiple determinations (R^2) was 0.64686 for this variety which indicated that about 64 per cent yield gap variation was explained by the explanatory variables of the model.

Nagrashal: The factor X_{10} (gap in the application of plant protection chemicals) were excluded from the regression model as no variation was found over observations in Nagrashal cultivation. The value of the multiple determinations (R^2) was estimated 0.94216 which explained that about 94 per cent yield gap variation of this variety was determined by the independent variables of the regression equation. All the explanatory variables were positively related with yield gap of this variety but not significant. The gaps in the application of organic manure (X_5) and N-fertilizer (X_6) were found to have significant impact on yield gap of Nagrashal variety. The coefficients of these two variables were significant at 20 per cent level of probability. The value of the coefficients of X_5 and X_6 were 0.98419 and 0.65469 respectively. The non-significant factors were ploughing, P-fertilizer, K-fertilizer, and weeding and their coefficients were 0.64590, 0.65469, 0.35405, and 0.71527 respectively.

Kadamshal: In case of Kadamshal local rice variety all the explanatory variables included in the equation was significant and positively related with its yield gap. The regression coefficients of X_4, X_5, X_6, X_7, X_8, X_9, and X_{10} were 0.19586, 0.30564, 0.18436, 0.38850, 1.21426, 0.04648, and 0.07021 respectively. The coefficients with respect to the gaps in manuring (X_5). P-fertilizer (X_7), and K-fertilizer (X_8) were significant at 1 per cent level of probability. The coefficients of gaps in ploughing (X_4) and plant protection chemical (X_{10}) were significant at 5 per cent probability level. The coefficient of gap in the application of N-fertilizer and coefficient of the gap in weeding (X_9) was significant at 20 per cent level of probability. This result showed that all the explanatory variables had have influence on the yield gap of the variety. The value of the coefficient of multiple determinations (R^2) was estimated 0.88168 which explained the fact that 88 per cent variation in yield gap was caused due to gaps in the different factors/treatments included in the model.

Bashamanik: Independent factor X_7 (P-fertilizer) was excluded from the equation of regression for this variety in the same logic of the exclusion of the first three factors/treatments. All the explanatory variables were positively related but not significant. Only the gap in weeding (X_9) and the gap in plant protection chemicals application (X_{10}) were estimated significant variables for this variety. The coefficient of X_9 and X_{10} were significant at 5 per cent level of probability. The regression coefficients of these significant variables were 0.20505 and 0.14465 respectively. However, there was no impact of other factors (X_4, X_5, X_6, X_8) on the yield gap of Bashamanik variety. The respective regression coefficients of these non-significant variables were 0.08295, 0.30416, 0.04065, and 0.23826. The coefficient of K-fertilizer (X_8) was found having the highest value which indicated the biggest impact on yield gap. The value of the coefficient of multiple determinations (R^2) was 0.57647 showing that the variation in yield gap of Bashamanik local rice variety was influenced about 57 per cent by joint effect of the explanatory variables included in the equation.

Table 6.13: Estimated Relationship Between Yield Gap and Gaps in the Production Inputs/Cultural Practices

Variety Kharif (HYV)	*Intercept*	*Regression Coefficients*							
		X_4	X_5	X_6	X_7	X_8	X_9	X_{10}	R^2
IR-36	-42.13961	0.56923**	0.20675@	0.10264	0.23796@	0.13992	0.49815*	0.08310	0.57147
		(2.295)	(1.422)	(0.515)	(1.769)	(0.637)	(2.749)	(0.930)	
IR-50	-43.94398	0.02166	0.31389**	0.40759**	0.04562	0.08212	0.23189@	—	0.67589
		(0.073)	(2.174)	(2.505)	(0.298)	(0.442)			
Ratna	-107.4142	0.25324@	0.48709	0.38766**	0.34172*	—	0.32673*	0.37345	0.87808
		(1.402)	(5.249)	(2.928)	(3.451)		(4.886)	(4.269)	
Pankaj	-97.56478	0.12904	0.63259*	0.26069	0.37528*	0.04356	0.05641	0.37654@@	0.82978
		(0.685)	(2.979)	(0.775)	(1.711)	(0.211)	(0.216)	(1.257)	
Masuri	-40.44441	—	0.38734**	0.02475	0.37666@	1.00000	—	0.25886**	0.82978
			(5.240)	(0.025)	(2.965)	(0.000)		(3.825)	
Sita	-409.2454	0.83102	0.77499**	0.44703@	0.66317**	1.38876**	0.19714	—	0.78896
		(1.392)	(4.906)	(3.176)	(3.817)	(4.776)	(0.722)		
LOCAL VARIETIES									
Assam Aush	-113.1427	0.05584	0.15691*	0.12942**	0.09643	0.79078@	0.14781*	0.10105	0.52387
		(0.557)	(3.282)	(1.985)	(1.046)	(1.689)	(2.823)	(0.932)	
Khajurchari	-51.97350	0.17631**	0.12790**	0.16315**	0.14720	0.03926	0.16856*	0.12729**	0.64686
		(1.714)	(2.374)	(2.276)	(1.183)	(0.168)	(3.561)	(1.760)	
Gokulshal	-164.7780	0.19244	0.16930	0.04879	1.08540**	0.45507@	0.79951*	0.39335*	0.90579
		(0.674)	(0.819)	(0.689)	(2.138)	(1.551)	(6.382)	(3.332)	
Nagrashal	-38.03582	0.64590	0.71652@@	0.98419@@	0.65469	0.35405	0.71517	—	0.94216
		(1.992)	(3.094)	(3.446)	(1.992)	(0.597)	(2.850)		

(contd.)

(Contd. table 6.13)

Variety *Kharif (HYV)*	*Intercept*	*Regression Coefficients*							
		X_4	X_5	X_6	X_7	X_8	X_9	X_{10}	R^2
Kadamshal	-42.33665	0.19586** (2.100)	0.30564* (5.120)	0.18436@ (1.824)	0.38850* (3.108)	1.21426* (4.526)	0.04648@@ (1.481)	0.07021** (2.123)	0.88168
Bashamanik	-5.39900	0.08295 (0.346)	0.30416 (1.045)	0.04065 (0.128)	—	0.23826 (1.009)	0.20505** (2.498)	0.14465** (2.386)	0.57647
Rajamanik	-20.57819	0.70106** (3.552)	0.08703 (0.546)	0.34403@ (2.421)	0.44200 (1.208)	0.29904@ (2.348)	0.06654 (1.085)	0.14788@@ (1.601)	0.91597
Hurkashal	-9.34432	0.11631 (0.947)	0.04646 (0.916)	0.09817 (1.256)	0.37466 (1.367)	0.37335@ (1.555)	0.03736 (1.074)	0.03934 (0.979)	0.82892
BORO SEASON									
IR-36	-0.51345	0.00159 (0.043)	0.16516* (3.880)	0.07963@@ (1.665)	0.07121** (2.703)	0.04875** (2.445)	0.03558** (2.762)	0.00660 (0.563)	0.96964
IR-50	-1.32427	0.01556 (0.395)	0.04301@@ (1.665)	0.08603** (2.651)	0.00312 (0.068)	0.01722 (0.761)	0.03491* (2.925)	0.01573 (1.227)	0.92892

Figures in parentheses indicate the t-values
* Significant at 1 per cent level of probability
** Significant at 5 per cent level of probability
@ Significant at 10 per cent level of probability
@@ Significant at 20 per cent level of probability

Rajamanik: All the explanatory variables included in the model had positive effect on yield gap of Rajamanik local rice variety. The coefficients with respect to X_4, X_5, X_6, X_7, X_8, X_9, and X_{10} were 0.70106, 0.08703, 0.34403, 0.44200, 0.29904, 0.06654, and 0.14788 respectively. The gap in the level of ploughing was found to have a significant impact on the yield gap of this variety. This was significant at 5 per cent level of probability. The coefficients of X_6 and X_8 were significant at 10 per cent level of probability. The coefficient with respect to gap in the plant protection chemical (X_9) was significant at 20 per cent level of probability. There was found no significant impact of the gap in manuring, the gap in P-fertilizer application and the gap in weeding on the yield gap of this local rice variety. The highest regression coefficient was estimated in the case of the gap in the level of ploughing (X_4) which showed that the level of yield gap was decreased or increased by 0.70 per cent depending upon the decrease or increase in the gap of the level of ploughing. The value of the coefficient of multiple determinations (R^2) was 0.91597 which explained the fact that 91 per cent yield gap variation was determined by the explanatory variables included in the model.

Hurkashal: The value of the coefficient of multiple determinations (R^2) for Hurkashal local rice variety was estimated 0.82892. The value showed that the explanatory variables jointly explained the variation in the yield gap of this variety by about 82 per cent. In the case of this variety only K-fertilizer had significant impact on the yield gap at 20 per cent level of probability. The regression coefficient of this significant factor was 0.37335. The other explanatory variables were positively related with the yield gap but not found significant at a specified level of probability. The regression coefficients of these independent variables were 0.11631, 0.04646, 0.09817, 0.37466, 0.03736, and 0.03934 respectively. The highest coefficient was estimated with respect to the gap in the P-fertilizer. This explained that if the gap in application of P-fertilizer decreases by 1 per cent the yield gap will also decrease by 0.37466 per cent, For the Hurkashal local rice variety the estimated value of the coefficient of multiple determinations (R^2) was 0.82892. The value indicated that about 83 per cent variation in the yield gap was explained by the explanatory variables included in the model.

The Summary: The gap in the level of ploughing for local rice varieties in kharif season was found to be statistically significant determinant of the yield gap. The yield gap of local rice was affected by the gap in the level of ploughing. However, this was not highly influential for all local rice varieties equally. It was significant at 5 per cent level of probability in case of Khajurchari and Kadamshal varieties. But the impact of this treatment or culture was not found to be significant for other local rice varieties.

The coefficient with respect to organic manure application in local rice field was also significant for Assam Aush, Khajurchari, Nagrashal, and Kadamshal varieties. It was significant at 1 per cent level of probability in case of Assam Aush and Kadamshal varieties; in case of Khajurchari it was significant at 5 per cent level of probability. This explanatory variable was also significant at 20 per cent level of probability for Nagrashal variety. But manuring had no significant impact in the production of Gokulshal, Bhasamanik, Rajamanik, and Hurkashal varieties.

The gap in the application of N-fertilizer was most influential factor and had a significant relation with the yield gap of local rice varieties. The coefficient of X_6 was significant at 5 per cent level of probability in case of Assam Aush and Khajurchari rice varieties. It was also significant at 10 per cent level of probability in case of Kadamshal and Rajamanik varieties. It was found significant at 20 per cent level of probability in the case of Nagrashal rice variety.

The regression coefficient with respect to the gap in the application of P-fertilizer (X_7) was significant at 1 per cent level and 5 per cent level of probability in case of Kadamshal and Gokulshal respectively. In other cases P-fertilizer had no impact on the level of yield of local rice varieties.

The coefficient with respect to the gap in the application of K-fertilizer (X_8) was significant at 1 per cent level of probability for Kadamshal variety. This regression coefficient was also significant at 10 per cent level of probability in case of Assam Aush, Gokulshal and Rajamanik varieties. It was also significant at 20 per cent level of probability in the case of Hurkashal. For other local varieties it had no significant impact on the yield gap.

The gap in the level of weeding had a great impact on the yield gap. The coefficient with respect to the gap in weeding (X_9) was found significant at 1 per cent level for Assam Aush, Khajurchari and Gokulshal rice varieties. This was also significant at 5 per cent and 20 per cent level of probability for Bhasamanik and Kadamshal varieties respectively. This factor, however, had no significant impact on yield gap of Nagrashal, Rajamanik and Hurkashal rice varieties.

The coefficient with respect to the gap in the plant protection chemical application was significant at 1 per cent probability level in case of Gokulshal rice variety. It was significant at 5 per cent level of probability for Khajurchari, Kadamshal and Bhasamanik varieties. The coefficient was also significant at 20 per cent level of probability in case of Rajamanik local rice variety in kharif season.

The regression result of the local varieties showed that all the production factors/cultural practices had significant influence on yield gap at different levels of probability which supported the hypothesis 3 of the present investigation.

Boro Season: In this season only three high yielding varieties were found to be adopted by the sample farmers. No local variety was grown in this season. These high yielding varieties were IR-36, IR-50, and Ratna. The number of observations of Ratna variety was not sufficient and hence, this variety was dropped from the analysis.

IR-36: The regression coefficients with respect to the gap in ploughing, the gap in manuring, the gaps in N, P and K fertilizers application, the gap in weeding, and the gap in the application of plant protection chemicals were 0.00159, 0.16516, 0.07963, 0.07121, 0.047121, 0.04875, and 0.03558 respectively. The gap in the application of organic manure, the gaps in the application of N-fertilizer, P-fertilizer, K-fertilizer, the gap in weeding for this rice variety were positive and significant which indicated that these factors contributed significantly in the yield gap of IR-36 variety. The coefficient with respect to the gap in manuring (X_5) was found to be significant at 1 per cent level of probability. The regression coefficients of the gap in the application of P and K-fertilizers and the gap in weeding were significant at 5 per cent level of probability. The regression coefficient with respect to the gap in N-fertilizer (X_6) for IR-36 variety was significant at 20 per cent probability level. The non-significant factors/treatments were the gap in the ploughing (X_4), and the gap in the application of plant protection chemicals (X_{10}). All the explanatory variables were positively related with the yield gap of this variety in boro season. The value of the coefficient of multiple determinations (R^2) was 0.96964 which indicated that 96 per cent variation in yield gap of the variety was explained by the explanatory variables. The highest value of the coefficient of explanatory variable was estimated in case of the gap in manuring (X_5) which indicated that the yield gap decreased or increased by 0.16 per cent if the gap in manuring decreased or increased by 1 per cent.

IR-50: In case of IR-50 three factors were found to be statistically significant. These factors were the gap in the application of N-fertilizer (X_6), the gap in the organic manure application (X_5), and the gap in weeding (X_9). The regression coefficients of these three variables were 0.0860, 0.0430, and 0.0349 respectively. The coefficient with respect to the gap in manuring was significant at 20 per cent level of probability. The coefficients with respect to the gap in N-fertilizer application (X_6) and the gap in weeding (X_9) were also significant at 5 per cent and 1 per cent level of probability respectively. The gap in the level of ploughing, the gaps in the application of P and K fertilizers and the gap in the application of plant protection chemical were found insignificant in the yield gap of IR-50 variety. The regression coefficients of these factors were 0.0155, 0.0031, 0.0172, and 0.0157 respectively. The positive and significant coefficients revealed that these factors had influence on the yield gap. The value of the coefficient of multiple determinations (R^2) was 0.9289 which showed that about 92 per cent variation in yield gap was explained by the explanatory variables included in the regression model.

The Summary: In boro season, the gap in the manuring, the gap in the application of N-fertilizer, the application of P-fertilizer, the gap in the application of K-fertilizer and the gap in weeding were found positively and significantly related with the yield gap of high yielding varieties. However, the gap in the level of ploughing and the gap in the application of plant protection chemicals were found to be non-significant in this season, which might be due to the fact that for favourable weather condition in summer season this factor was not influential which was true in kharif season. However, all the explanatory variables were positively related with yield gap but not significant in this season.

The regression result of yield gap and the factors/cultural practices related with it showed that all the factors were positively and significantly related irrespective of variety and season. However, all the variables were not significant equally and for all varieties.

Therefore, the hypothesis 2 of this study was supported by this result which stated that there was a positive and significant relationship between the yield gap and the factors/treatments considered in the analysis.

Factors Determining the Technological Gap in Rice Production

In this section an attempt has been made to identify and examine different factors determining the technological gap in rice production. Multiple linear regression equations were fitted to the set of data for identifying and examining the factors having influence on the technological gap in rice cultivation in the study area.

Prior to the fitting of regression equation zero order correlation coefficients were estimated with a view to examine the existence or otherwise, of multicollinearity among the independent variables. It was found that there was no problem of multicollinearity in this set of data and hence, the data of original form were put through the computer for regression analysis.

Based on the literature and prior knowledge from the survey of the area it was hypothesized that the technological gap (i.e. transfer of technological gap) in rice cultivation dependent upon several independent factors, viz. age of the farmer, caste of the farmer, family size, farm size, educational level, the economic status of the family, social participation of the farmer, percentage irrigated area to total cropped area, index of outstanding credit, status of land ownership, utilization of mass media, utilization of cosmopolite sources of information and participation in training programme. This may be mathematically expressed as given below:

$$Y = f(X_i), i = 1, 2, 3, \ldots\ldots\ldots\ldots 13$$

where,

X_1 = age of the farmer
X_2 = caste of the farmer
X_3 = family size
X_4 = farm size
X_5 = education
X_6 = economic status
X_7 = social participation
X_8 = percentage of irrigated area to total cropped area

X_9 = index of outstanding credit
X_{10} = status of land ownership
X_{11} = utilization of mass media
X_{12} = utilization of cosmopolite sources of information
X_{13} = participation in training programme

Separate regression equations were fitted to different sets of data concerning from different farm categories respectively and also for the overall farm situation. The regression coefficients of the fitted equations with their respective t-values in parenthesis, and the value of the coefficient of multiple determinations (R^2) over different farm categories have been presented in Table 6.14.

Farm Category-I

In this farm category the regression coefficients with respect to the age of the farmer (X_1), utilization of mass media (X_{11}), utilization of cosmopolite sources of information (X_{12}), and participation in training programme (X_{13}) were found significantly related to the technological gap. The coefficient with respect to age of the farmer (X_1) was positively related and significant at 1 per cent level of probability. The coefficient of utilization of mass media (X_{11}) was also significant at 1 per cent level of probability but negatively related with the technological gap. The positive relation of age of the farmer with technological gap indicated that higher the age higher would be the technological gap. In other words, young farmers were found to adopt all the practices in higher degree for rice cultivation than the older farmers. This might be due to the fact that the old farmers were motivated by the traditional attitude and beliefs whereas the young farmers were more flexible in the adoption of all practices in the best possible level. The utilization of mass media (X_{11}) was negatively related with the technological gap and significant at 1 per cent level of probability. It indicated that higher the utilization of mass media lower the technological gap was and vice versa. The other significant regression coefficients were utilization of cosmopolite sources of information (X_{12}) and participation in training programme (X_{13}). Both the regression coefficients were found to be positive and significant at 20 per cent probability level. The result concluded that higher the utilization of cosmopolite sources of information and participation in training programme higher would be the technological gap, which was found contrary to our expectation. It was found that the regression coefficients with respect to the caste of the farmer (X_2), family size (X_3), farm size (X_4), education (X_5), family economic status (X_6), social participation (X_7), percentage of irrigated area to total cropped area (X_8), index of outstanding credit (X_9), and Status of land ownership (X_{10}) did not appear to have exercised any significant baring on technological gap. However, the coefficients of caste, family size, farm size, education were positive but not significant. The non-significant negative relation of technological gap was found with economic status, social participation, percentage of irrigated area to total cropped area, index of outstanding credit, and status of land ownership. The value of the coefficient of multiple determinations (R^2) was estimated as 0.76132 which indicated that the 76 per cent variation in technological gap was explained by the explanatory variables included in the analysis.

Farm Category-II

The coefficient of multiple determinations (R^2) in case of category-II farms was estimated to be 0.93239 indicating 93 per cent of the total variation in the technological gap which was explained by the factors included in the model. The coefficient with respect to the percentage of irrigated area to total cropped area (X_8), status of land ownership (X_{10}), and utilization of mass media (X_{11}) were found significant at 1 per cent level of probability. The values of these coefficients were -4.17034, -0.05393, and -2.71227 respectively. All these three significant factors were negatively correlated with the technological gap as it was expected. The negative relation of percentage of irrigated area to total cropped area with the technological gap indicated that the gap would be decreased if the irrigated area increased. Similarly, the technological gap was supposed to be affected in opposite direction with the status of land ownership and utilization of mass media. The technological gap would be lower/higher depending upon whether the land was owned, leased in or leased out by the respondent. The coefficient of outstanding credit (X_9) was found significant at 5 per cent level of probability. The

Table 6.14: Factors Determining Technological Gap Over Different Categories of Farms

Farm Category	Intercepts	Regression Coefficients of													
		X_1	X_2	X_3	X_4	X_5	X_6	X_7	X_8	X_9	X_{10}	X_{11}	X_{12}	X_{13}	R_2
Category-I	54.10063	0.29726*	0.02036	0.06000	0.33492	0.05332	-0.09822	-0.24132	-0.10184	-0.14167	-0.5390	-2.30510*	0.81932@@	0.47393@@	0.76132
		(2.916)	(0.124)	(0.345)	(0.201)	(0.253)	(-0.556)	(-0.505)	(-0.530)	(-0.897)	(-0.396)	(-3.059)	(1.433)	(1.372)	
Category-II	78.43051	-6.741E-03	0.05578@@	0.07607@@	0.07245	0.06512	0.08882@@	-0.03940	-4.17034*	-3.42960**	-0.05393*	-2.71227*	0.03292	-0.15683	0.93239
		(-0.085)	(1.266)	(1.349)	(1.175)	(1.127)	(1.521)	(-0.383)	(-4.322)	(-2.405)	(-3.794)	(-15.571)	(0.226)	(-1.037)	
Category-III	58.53192	-0.12207@@	-0.02931	9.1663E-03	0.01281	0.02715	-.09908	-0.07546	-0.09846	-0.16397@	-0.02765*	-1.25080*	-0.27679@@	-0.10550	0.66235
		(-1.232)	(-0.250)	(0.092)	(1.127)	(1.176)	(-0.888)	(-0.489)	(-0.934)	(-1.691)	(-2.811)	(-6.333)	(-1.245)	(-0.994)	
Category-IV	61.93144	0.15536*	0.13808@	0.06247	-0.07198	-0.06178	-0.02869	0.07195	-0.09267	-0.03101	0.13351@@	-0.28261@@	-2.19809*	0.02803	0.88653
		(3.524)	(1.779)	(-0.710)	(-0.639)	(-0.642)	(-0.260)	(0.474)	(-0.976)	(-0.350)	(1.523)	(-1.254)	(-4.140)	(0.118)	
Pooled	67.09926	0.06619**	0.02099	0.01858	0.28532*	-2.333E-05	0.0794	-0.08765	-3.06908	-0.07125@@	-0.10488@	-1.05604*	0.01958	-0.07930	0.70343
		(2.357)	(0.361)	(0.301)	(2.408)	(-0.000)	(0.956)	(-0.982)	(-3.824)	(-1.242)	(-1.763)	(-4.856)	(0.109)	(-0.931)	

Figures in parentheses indicate the t-values
* Significant at 1 per cent level of probability
** Significant at 5 per cent level of probability
@ Significant at 10 per cent level of probability
@@ Significant at 20 per cent level of probability

estimated value of the coefficient was -3.42960. Caste of the farmer (X_2), family size (X_3), and economic status (X_6) of the family were found to have positive relation with the technological gap. The regression coefficients of these variables were significant at 20 per cent probability level. The estimated values of the regression coefficients for these three explanatory variables were 0.07578, 0.07607 and 0.08882 respectively. The positive relation of technological gap with caste, family size, and economic status indicated that the gap was high with higher caste, big family size, and high economic status and *vice versa.* However, the insignificant coefficients with their values were age of the farmer (-6.741E-03), farm size (0.07245), education (0.6512), social participation (-0.03940), utilization of cosmopolite sources of information (0.03292), and participation in training programme (0.15683). However, none of these coefficients was found to be statistically significant but age, social participation and participation in training programme were negatively related with technological gap. The positive relationship with technological gap and farm size indicated that the higher the farm size higher would be the technological gap. The small farmers were found to be technically efficient than the large farmers. Similarly it was revealed that formal education was remained ineffective in narrowing down the technological gap.

Farm Category-III

In category-III farms, the coefficients of the status of land ownership (X_{10}) and utilization of mass media (X_{11}) were found to be negatively related with the technological gap and significant at 1 per cent level of probability. The values of these two regression coefficients were -0.02765 and -1.25080 respectively. The negative coefficients indicated that the technological gap was higher in case of leased in/leased out land and lower of utilization of mass media and *vice versa.* The coefficient with respect to the index of outstanding credit (X_9) was also significant at 10 per cent level of probability and negatively related with technological gap. The value of the regression coefficient (X_9) was estimated to be -0.16397. The other statistically significant regression coefficients were related with age of the farmer (X_1) and utilization of cosmopolite sources of information (X_{12}). Both the coefficients were found to be negative. The numerical values of these two coefficients were -0.12207 and -0.27679 respectively. The statistically non-significant factors in case of farm category-III were caste of the farmer (X_2), family size (X_3), farm size (X_4), education (X_5) family's economic status (X_6), social participation (X_7), index of irrigation (X_8), and participation in training programme (X_{13}). It could be concluded that these factors had no impact in the application of inputs/treatments for rice production. The regression coefficients of these factors were -0.02931, 0.1663E-03, 0.01281, 0.02713, -0.9908, -0.07545, -0.09846, and -0.10550 respectively. The coefficient of multiple determinations (R^2) was estimated as 0.66235 which expressed that about 66 per cent of the total variation in the technological gap was affected by those factors included in this model.

Farm Category-IV

Age of the farmer (X_1), caste of the farmer (X_2), status of land ownership (X_{10}), utilization of mass media (X_{11}) and utilization of cosmopolite sources of information (X_{12}) were found to be statistically significant determinants of technological gap in case of farm category-IV. The coefficient with respect to the age (X_1) and utilization of cosmopolite sources of information (X_{12}) were significant at 1 per cent level of probability and their numerical values were 0.15536 and -2.19809 respectively. The positive coefficient of age signified that the relationship between the technological gap and the age of the farmer was direct. The technological gap would be increased with the increase of age of the farmer which revealed that a greater technological gap would be found for the older farmers. This conclusion was similar to the farmers of category-I but contradictory to that in farm category-III. On the other hand, the negative relationship between technological gap and utilization of cosmopolite sources of information (X_{12}) indicated that the gap was lower in case of higher utilization of cosmopolite sources of information.

The caste of the farmer (X_2) in this farm category was found to be positively related and statistically significant at 10 per cent level of probability. This result showed that the technological gap was higher in case of higher caste farmers and *vice versa.* The same conclusion was drawn in farm category-II where it was found significant. The value of the regression coefficient was 0.13808. The coefficients of status of land ownership (X_{10}) and utilization of mass media (X_{11}) were also statistically significant at 20 per cent level of probability. Status of land ownership was positively related to the technological gap which indicated that the gap would be increased with the increase in the status of ownership of land. However, this result was contradictory to the earlier results regarding ownership of land in categories-II and III. The negative coefficient of utilization of mass media indicated that the technological gap would be found to decrease with increase in utilization of mass media and *vice versa* as it was expected. The value of the regression coefficients of these two factors were 0.13351 and -0.28261 respectively. Family size (X_3), farm size (X_4), education (X_5), economic status (X_6), irrigation index (X_8), index of outstanding credit (X_9) were negatively related with the technological gap but found statistically insignificant. The values of these regression coefficients were -0.06247, -0.06247, -0.07198, -0.0678, -0.02869, -0.09267, -0.03101 respectively. Positively related insignificant factors were social participation and participation in training. Their respective coefficient values were estimated as 0.07195 and 0.02803.

The coefficient of multiple determinations (R^2) was estimated as 0.88653 which expressed that 88 per cent of the total variation in technological gap was explained by the factors included in the regression equation.

Pooled: In pooled data the coefficients with respect to age of the farmer (X_1), farm size (X_4), irrigation index (X_8), index of outstanding credit (X_9), status of land ownership (X_{10}), utilization of mass media (X_{11}) were statistically significant. The coefficients of farm size, irrigation index and utilization of mass media were found to be significant at 1 per cent level of probability. Farm size was positively related with technological gap, and irrigation index and utilization of mass media were negatively related. Age of the farmer was found to be positively related and its regression coefficient was significant at 5 per cent level of probability. The coefficient of the status of land ownership was statistically significant at 10 per cent level of probability and it was negatively related with the technological gap. Index of outstanding credit was also found to have negative relationship with technological gap and its regression coefficient was statistically significant at 20 per cent level of probability. The castes of the farmers (X_2), family size (X_3), economic status (X_6) and utilization of mass media (X_{11}) were positively related with technological gap but their coefficients were insignificant. Education level (X_5), social participation (X_7), and participation in training programme (X_{13}) were negatively related but their regression coefficients were not found to be statistically significant.

The value of the overall coefficient of multiple determinations (R^2) was 0.70343. It indicated that 70 per cent of the total variation in technological gap was explained by the independent variables included in the equation.

Brief Summary: The regression coefficient of the age of the farmer (X_1) was found to be statistically significant at 1 per cent level in case of farm categories-I and IV and in case of farm category-III it was significant at 20 per cent level of probability. The first two coefficients were positive which indicated the direct relationship with the technological gap. However, it is negatively related with technological gap in case of farm category-III. But the coefficient was not found significant in case of farm category-II. The overall coefficient of the age of the farmer was statistically significant at 5 per cent level of probability. The positive value of the coefficient (0.06619) indicated that the technological gap was directly related with the age of the farmer. In other words, the technological gap was supposed to be increased with the increase of the age of the farmer. The conclusion might be that the older farmers were found to be less efficient in the application of production inputs and application of other cultural treatments at optimal level for rice production. The result supported the hypothesis 4 of the study which stated that there was a positive relationship between technological gap of the farmers and their age. This result may be judged by the fact that the younger farmers are more dynamic and interested in the adoption of modern agricultural technology package for rice cultivation, whereas older farmers were motivated by traditional belief and practices.

The coefficient with respect to the caste of the farmer (X_2) was found statistically significant at 10 per cent and 20 per cent level of probability in farm category-IV and II respectively and positively related with the technological gap but it was found statistically insignificant when the farm categories were pooled.

The coefficient of family size (X_3) was found to be statistically significant at 20 per cent level of probability in case of farm category-II only. The positive value of the coefficient showed direct relationship between technological gap and family size. There was higher technological gap with bigger family size and *vice versa.* However, this coefficient was not found statistically significant in case of pooled data.

The coefficient with respect to farm size (X_4) was found statistically significant in none of the farm categories but in pooled result it showed statistically significant at 1 per cent level of probability. The positive regression coefficient indicated that the relationship between technological gap and farm size was direct. The technological gap was supposed to be varied in the same direction with the farm size. A higher technological gap in case of bigger farm size might be due to the fact that the larger farmers did not have direct relationship with the agricultural practices. This result supported the fact of inverse relationship between farm size and productivity.

The regression coefficient of education of the farmer (X_5) was not found significant at all in the application of inputs and practices for rice cultivation. It could be concluded that formal education had no bearing in the adoption of improved rice practices at recommended level.

The economic status of the family (X_6) was found positively related with the technological gap in farm category-II. It implied that higher technological gap would be found for the well-to-do farmers. The coefficient of economic status was significant at 20 per cent level of probability. In other farm categories it was negatively related with technological gap but none of the coefficients was significant. The overall coefficient of economic status was found to be positively related but insignificant.

It might be noted that a negative relationship between technological gap and economic status of the farmer was expected. But the result contradicted the expectation. This might be explained by the fact that economic condition of the farmer could play an important role in the transfer of technology from the traditional to modern along with other factors such as land situation, irrigation facilities and availability of inputs. That is, in the selection of capital intensive practices economic condition might play a crucial role. In other words, the choice of technology was guided by the economic condition of the farmer. But economic status might not have significant influence on the practices/treatments of the production process. Less variation in different practices over different observations was noticed. Thus in general more or less a common practice was followed in the application of inputs and treatments in rice cultivation irrespective of farm size groups and economic condition. It seemed that a general culture among the rice farmers for a particular variety with respect to different practices were in existence, which was obviously sub-optimal. This type of behaviour of rice producers generalizing the improved practices in a state of divergence from the recommended one might be viewed as if transforming improved practices to traditional practices. The whole process was a reverse of Prof. Sultz's observation that "transforming traditional agriculture into a modern one".

The coefficient with respect to social participation (X_7) was not found statistically significant in any case. The coefficients were negative in all categories except category IV where it was positive.

The regression coefficient with respect to percentage of irrigated area to total cropped area (X_8) was found to be statistically significant at 1 per cent level of probability in farm category-II. The negative value of the coefficient indicated a reverse relationship between technological gap and irrigation index. In other farm categories also negative regression coefficients were recorded but they were not statistically significant. The overall coefficient of irrigation index was also statistically significant at 1 per cent level of probability. The inverse relationship between technological gap and irrigation index might explain that irrigation facilities played an important role in adoption of rice technologies at recommended level. In case of assured irrigation risk in the production process was lower and application of inputs was higher. Consequently technological gap became lower and *vice versa.*

The regression coefficient of the index of outstanding credit (X_9) was significant at 5 per cent and 10 per cent level of probability in farm categories-II and III respectively. In both cases the value of the coefficients were negative. It was found to be negatively correlated and significant at 20 per cent level of probability for pooled data. This result indicated that the technological gap would be decreased with the increase in outstanding credit.

The coefficient with respect to the status of land ownership (X_{10}) was significant at 1 per cent level of probability in case of farm categories-II and III. In both the cases the magnitude of the coefficient was negative. In case of farm category-IV the regression coefficient was positively related and significant at 20 per cent level of probability. However, the overall regression coefficient of land ownership status was statistically significant at 10 per cent level of probability. The negative value of the regression coefficient indicated that the technological gap in case of owned land was lower than in case of leased in/leased out land.

The coefficient of the mass media (X_{11}) was found to be statistically significant in all farm categories and pooled data. It was significant at 1 per cent level of probability for farms I, II and III categories but in the case of farm category-IV it was significant at 20 per cent level of probability in pooled data. In all cases the value of the regression coefficient was found negative which indicated the inverse relationship between technological gap and utilization of mass media.

The coefficient of the utilization of cosmopolite sources of information (X_{12}) was found to be statistically significant at 20 per cent level of probability in farm categories-I and III. It was also significant at 1 per cent level of probability in category-II farms but it was not statistically significant for irrespective of farm categories. It was negatively related with technological gap in farm categories-III and IV but positively related in farm category-I.

In case of farm category-I, the coefficient of the participation in training programme (X_{13}) was statistically significant at 20 per cent level of probability but positively related with technological gap. The other categories it was negatively related but insignificant. The overall result showed a negative coefficient but not statistically significant. It indicated that participation in training programme had no impact in the application of improved rice technologies.

The result of the regression analysis for determining the factors responsible for technological gap revealed that age of the farmer (X_1), farm size (X_4), irrigation index (X_8), index of outstanding credit (X_9), status of land ownership (X_{10}), and utilization of mass media (X_{11}) were related with technological gap which established the hypothesis 4 of the present exercise where the result was expected. But the hypothesis that technological gap was related with caste (X_2), family size (X_3), education (X_5), economic status (X_6), social participation (X_7), personal cosmopolite sources of information (X_{12}), and participation in training programme (X_{13}) was not supported by the findings of the regression as these factors were not found statistically significant. However, all the factors except education and social participation were found to be statistically significant at least in one farm category. Hence, with respect to farm size groups the hypothesis 4 was supported excluding statistically insignificant factors, viz. education and social participation from the model.

Constraints in the Adoption of Recommended Rice Technologies as Perceived by the Farmers

In the previous section various factors affecting the technological gap has been discussed. In this section an attempt has been made to identify the constraints perceived by the farmers in the adoption of improved rice technologies in their fields. For this purpose factor analysis technique was applied. The various factors considered in the study have been listed in Chapter 5 discussing the methodological aspects.

The factors which are considered as the causes of non-adoption of the improved rice technologies in the field perceived by the farmers were scored in four-point scale. The factor responsible vary much for non-adoption was scored - 3, much scored -2, not so much -1, and not at all -0.49 variables were considered for factor analysis and the data were processed through computer. The technological gap was considered as dependent variable. The results of the factor analysis have been presented in Table 6.15.

From the table it is found that out of 49 factors considered for the analysis 12 variables are most influential with Eigen value greater than one. These 12 variables according to importance were lack of ownership (X_1), lack of irrigation facilities (X_4), non-availability of irrigation at time (X_6), lack of capital (X_{10}), lack of adequate credit (X_{12}), lack of marketing facilities (X_{15}), low market price of rice (X_{18}), high labour wages (X_{23}), not profitable (X_{24}), lack of technological knowledge for field application (X_{25}), lack of advice and guidance (X_{29}), and lack of knowledge about proper recommendation (X_{46}).

Lack of ownership of land (X_1) has been found the most important factor perceived by the farmers for non-adoption of improved rice technologies at recommended level. The highest Eigen value related with this factor accounts to 4.19749 and the percentage of variance is 10.8. The result indicated that if the owner of the land was the cultivator, the percentage of technological gap would have been minimal. As a matter of fact, the farmers generally take proper care for the permanent improvement of land reflecting for higher productivity on own plot and consequently the percentage adoption of improved rice technologies is increased. However, farmers can take independent decisions in the adoption of improved rice technologies at recommended level in case of own land only.

Table 6.15: Constraints in the Adoption of Recommended Rice Technologies as Perceived by the Farmers

Constraints	*Communality*	*Eigen value*	*Percentage of variance*	*Cumulative Percentage*
Lack of land ownership (X_1)	0.49105	4.19749	10.8	10.8
Lack of irrigation facilities (X_{14})	0.49694	4.02686	10.3	21.1
Non-availability of irrigation in time (X_6)	0.43451	3.66439	9.4	30.5
Lack of capital (X_{10})	0.40737	3.04092	7.8	38.3
Lack of adequate credit (X_{12})	0.59482	1.66157	4.3	42.5
Lack of marketing facilities (X_{15})	0.30471	1.59030	4.1	46.6
Low market price of rice (X_{18})	0.52711	1.41601	3.6	50.3
High labour wages (X_{23})	0.58466	1.38052	3.5	53.8
Not profitable (X_{24})	0.55664	1.36702	3.5	57.3
Lack of technological knowledge for field application (X_{25})	0.88863	1.19561	3.1	60.4
Lack of advice and guidance (X_{29})	0.57737	1.07798	2.8	63.1
Lack of knowledge about proper recommendation (X_{46})	0.32387	1.01711	2.6	65.7

The second most influential factor is lack of irrigation (X_4). Eigen value of this variable is 4.02686 and the percentage of variance is 10.3. The first two factors namely lack of land ownership and lack of irrigation facilities are having Eigen value greater than 4. The first two factors only explained 21.1 per cent of total variation. Irrigation is considered as the key factor of modern package of rice technology. Due to lack of assured irrigation facilities, farmers could not take decision in the adoption of improved rice technologies which require all the necessary inputs for higher productivity. Irrigation itself may prevent, though all other factors are available, from the adoption of rice technologies at recommended level.

Non-availability of irrigation at time (X_6) and lack of capital (X_{10}) are having Eigen value greater than 3 in each case. They together explain 17.2 per cent of total variation. The first four factors explain 38.3 per cent of total variation. Lack of capital has been rightly found as one of the most influential factors in the adoption of improved rice technologies. Because improved rice technologies are capital intensive and are to purchase from the market. More capital is required for the implementation of rice technologies at recommended level. Non-availability of irrigation at time has also rightly been found as a hindrance of adoption of the improved rice technologies, because timely irrigation is related with application of other production inputs and practices such as fertilizer and weeding.

Eigen value of each of the remaining eight variables are greater than 1. But percentage variation of these factors varies. Percentage variation of the variables, viz. lack of credit (X_{12}) and lack of marketing facilities (X_{15}) have been found greater than 4. It is greater than 3 for the variables like low market price of rice (X_{18}), high labour wages (X_{23}), non-profitability (X_{24}), and lack of technological knowledge about proper recommendation (X_{46}) has been found greater than 2 in each case. The selected 12 factors together explained 65.7 per cent of total variation. It explained that the technological gap can be narrowed down by 65.7 per cent by controlling these 12 constraints.

Lack of adequate credit, as perceived by the farmers, is a constraint in the adoption of recommended rice technologies as it is capital intensive. Hence, credit availability helps farmers to adopt more of recommended rice technology. Lack of marketing facilities is also another constraint as perceived by the farmers. Production inputs as well as final product require strong and adequate marketing facilities. Hence, the lack of proper marketing facilities might hinder the adoption of recommended rice technologies.

Low market price of rice, not profitable and high wages of labour are the constraints as perceived by the farmers. They feel that in comparison to other commodities the price of rice is lower. On the other hand due to sharp rise in wage rate of labour, profit margin in the rice production becomes tapering.

Lack of technical knowledge for field application (X_{25}), lack of advice and guidance (X_{29}), and lack of knowledge about recommendation (X_{46}) have been found influential factors as perceived by the farmers for the adoption of recommended rice technologies. These constraints played crucial role in the adoption of modern production inputs and practices in the production process. The farming situation may permit the implementation of modern rice technologies, but if farmers are not aware about these improved production inputs and the method of application, the whole efforts in this direction is nullified. In the village society farmers do not get the proper and sufficient information about the improved rice technologies. They are interested to implement the improved rice technologies but the lack of information and guidance prevent the farmers from adoption of recommended rice technologies.

Identification of Appropriate Technologies in Rice Production for Different Synthetic Farm Situations

The yield gap which was resultant of technological gap has been discussed earlier. The technologies which are available, perhaps, are not suitable *in toto* for the farmers and hence, they can not exploit the full potential of these technologies. Therefore, it is imperative to identify the best suited alternative technologies and the appropriate one from among the available farm technologies. For this purpose to identify the appropriate technologies, technologies available from different levels (may be traditional or improved and indigenous or imported) need to be tested in the three dimensions of: (i) resource appropriateness—the technologies should be exactly consistent with the present resource endowment of the farmers, (ii) needs appropriateness—the technologies should envisage the farmers' preference and choice, and (iii) goals appropriateness—the technologies should satisfy the needs and objectives of the society.

It has been assumed that the typical farmer in the study area intends to maximize return to fixed resources or return over variable costs subject to certain lower and upper limits on the level of certain activities. For identifying appropriate technologies envisaging farmers' preferences and social goals for the representative synthetic farm situation, linear programming method has been used.

The typical farmer in the study area has several alternatives for the use of the resources which are most efficient way in converting resources into product from various levels of technologies.

For this purpose, considering two types of technologies, viz. Existing Technologies (obtained from synthetic farm situation) and Recommended Technology (obtained from Block and Zonal Adaptive Research Station of the study area), an optimum set of technologies which is appropriate has been identified separately for different categories of farms.

Identification of Appropriate Technologies for Category-I Farmers

A list of activities (Xi) drawn from the existing and recommended technologies for incorporation in the linear programming models for this category is given below:

Activities (Technologies)

Existing Technology
Kharif Season
HYV Paddy

Irrigated	*Unirrigated*
IR-36	IR-36

Local Paddy

Irrigated	Unirrigated
Khajurchari	Khajurchari
Gokulshal	Gokulshal
Hurkashal	Radhashal
Radhashal	

Boro Season
IR–36

Recommended Technology
IR–36
Swarna
IET–1444
IET–5656

Resources Restriction: The average size of holding of this category of farmers has been recorded as 0.54 acre. The area exposed for kharif irrigated situation is 0.26 and 0.28 acre has been allocated to kharif paddy with normal rainfall condition. The boro paddy occupied 0.26 acre of land. The average labour supply for every month has been accounted as 54.11 man-days. This has been treated as labour restriction every month of a crop year. The cash in hand has been estimated as Rs. 7498.68 and used as cash restriction in the model.

The area allocated to different crops with their percentage over total cropped area under identified set of appropriate technologies for different categories of farms have been depicted in Table 6.16.

It has been found from the table that in kahrif season only three varieties have been occupied in the entire kharif land. Three varieties are IR-36, Hurkashal, and IET-5656. Kharif IR-36 with normal rainfall only occupied 35 per cent (0.28 acre) of total cropped area. The second important variety is IET-5656 which occupies 28.75 per cent (0.23 acre) of total cropped area in kharif season. The local variety Hurkashal has occupied only 3.75 per cent (0.03 acre) of total cropped area in kharif season. The result indicates that category-I farmers should cultivate high yielding varieties in maximum area with little local variety in kharif season to fulfil the local need. In boro season IR-36 variety occupied the entire irrigated land which is 32.50 per cent (0.26 acre) of total cropped area.

Return Over Variable Costs: Table 6.17 showed that in the appropriate set of rice technologies the ROVC increased to Rs. 2445.78, only 29.50 per cent increase over ROVC of existing set of rice technologies which should not be considered as a significant increase.

Human Labour Requirement: Monthly human labour (family and hired) used by the farmers of different categories has been presented in Table 6.18. For category-I farmers, it has been found that only a little percentage of total family labour has been used, there was no need to hire labour for cultivation of rice. It is justified because category-I farmers are having little land and they are used to hire out their surplus labour power.

The total land has been used and the cash in hand was sufficient to meet the expenditure incurred for cultivation of the appropriate set of rice technologies.

Identification of Appropriate Technologies for Category-II Farmers

For the farmers of category-II, a list of activities (Xi) drawn from existing and recommended technologies for incorporation the linear programming models has been given below:

Activities (Technologies)

Existing Technologies
Kharif Season
HYV Paddy

Irrigated	*Unirrigated*
IR-36	IR-36
IR-50	IR-50
Ratna	Ratna
Pankaj	Pankaj
IET-1444	
Sita	

Table 6.16: Area Allotted to the Appropriate Set of Rice Varieties in Different Farm Categories

Category	*Activity (Technology)*	*Area Sown (in acre)*	*Percentage of total area*
I	Kharif IR-36 (unirrigated, X_2)	0.28	35.00
	Kharif Hurkashal (irrigated, X_{33})	0.03	03.75
	Boro IR-36 (X_{41})	0.26	32.50
	Recommended IET-5656 (X_{45})	0.23	28.75
II	Kharif Pankaj (unirrigated, X_8)	0.17	06.25
	Assam Aush (unirrigated, X_{20})	0.97	35.66
	Kharif Laghushal (irrigated, X_{29})	0.05	01.84
	Hurkashal (irrigated, X_{33})	0.06	02.20
	Boro Ratna (X_{43})	0.79	29.05
	Recommended IET-5656 (X_{45})	0.68	25.00
III	Kharif Sita (irrigated, X_{11})	1.51	24.83
	Kharif Sita (unirrigated, X_{12})	0.87	14.31
	Laghushal (irrigated, X_{29})	0.06	00.98
	Hurkashal (irrigated, X_{33})	0.08	01.31
	Hurkashal (unirrigated, X_{34})	1.42	23.35
	Boro IR-36 (X_{41})	1.90	31.25
	IET-5656 (Recommended, $_{45}$)	0.24	03.94
IV	Kharif Panth-IV (unirrigated, X_{18})	5.80	38.66
	Laghushal (irrigated, X_{29})	0.15	01.00
	Hurkashal (irrigated, X_{33})	0.25	01.67
	Boro IR-50 (X_{42})	4.60	30.66
	IET-5656 (Recommended, X_{45})	4.20	28.00

Local Paddy

Irrigated	*Unirrigated*
Assam Aush	Assam Aush
Khajurchari	Khajurchari
Gokulshal	Gokulshal
Kadamshal	Kadamshal
Bhasamanik	Bhasamanik
Rajamanik	Rajamanik
Hurkashal	Hurkashal
Sundarmukhi	Nagrashal
Laghushal	Laghushal

Boro Season

IR-36
IR-50
Ratna

Recommended Technology

IR-36
Swarna
IET-5656
IET-4094

Resources Restriction: The accounted average size of holding of the farmers of category-II is 1.94 acres. The irrigated area in kharif season has been accounted as 0.79 acre only and 1.15 acres has been allotted to kharif paddy with normal rainfall situation. The boro paddy may be cultivated in the area irrigated which is 0.79 acre. The average labour supply for every month has been estimated as 33.89 man-days. This has been treated as labour restriction every month of the given year. The cash in hand has been estimated as Rs. 20378.00 and used as cash restriction in the model.

It can be seen from the appropriate set of rice technologies that only one high yielding variety, that is, Pankaj should be cultivated in kharif season with other three local rice varieties to maximize the net return. These local varieties are Assam Aush, Laghushal and Hurkashal. However, Hurkashal and Laghushal were cultivated by the farmers to fulfil the local needs. In boro season only a single rice variety was found to be appropriate to cultivate which was Ratna variety. The farmers of this category should cultivate only one variety, namely IET-5656 out of four recommended varieties.

Table 6.16 of appropriate set of rice technologies of different farm categories showed that Pankaj, Assam Aush, Laghushal, Hurkashal, and IET-5656 have occupied the entire kharif rice land. Kharif Pankaj with normal rainfall has occupied (0.17 acre) 6.25 per cent of total cropped area. Assam Aush has occupied the maximum land in Kharif season with normal rainfall accounting (0.97 acre) 35.66 per cent of total cropped area. In kharif season IET-5656 has occupied the maximum amout of irrigated land accounting (0.68 acre) 25 per cent of total cropped area. The local need fulfilling varieties together have occupied only (0.11 acre) 4.04 per cent of total cropped area. In boro season Ratna variety has occupied the entire irrigated land and accounting (0.79 acre) 29.05 per cent of total cropped area. However, in Kharif season the high yielding varieties have been cultivated only in (0.85 acre) 30.25 per cent of total cropped area.

Return Over Variable Costs: In this farm category the estimated ROVC in the appropriate set of rice technologies increased to Rs. 8842.70. The ROVC in the existing set of rice technologies was Rs. 4388.75 (Table 6.17). It indicates that ROVC increases by 101.46 per cent over the existing set of rice technologies, which is a significant increase. It means that the farmers of category-II could double their ROVC by adopting the appropriate set of rice technologies.

Table 6.17: Return Over Variable Costs of Different Farm Categories (in Rs.)

Category	*ROVC in Existing Technology*	*ROVC in Appropriate Technology*	*ROVC of Appropriate Technology as Percentage of Existing Technology*
I	1824.25	2445.78	29.50
II	4388.75	8842.70	101.46
III	5689.86	15628.23	174.67
IV	11849.55	42906.87	262.00

Human Labour Requirement: It has been found from Table 6.18 of human labour used in different farm categories that the farmers of this category did not hire human labour to cultivate rice. It has been also found that only a little percentage of total family labour used by them. In the month of August, November and December, the

Table 6.18: Monthly Human Labour Used in Different Farm Categories (Man Days)

Month	*Category-I*			*Category -II*			*Category-III*			*Category-IV*		
	F. Lbr.	*H.Lbr*	*Total*	*F.Lbr*	*H.Lbr*	*Total*	*F.Lbr*	*H.Lbr*	*Total*	*F.Lbr*	*H.Lbr*	*Total*
January	2.73	00.00	2.73	3.16	00.00	3.16	13.31	00.00	13.31	18.40	00.00	18.40
February	7.02	00.00	7.02	1.58	00.00	1.58	22.80	00.00	22.80	28.46	81.94	110.40
March	1.31	00.00	1.31	2.37	00.00	2.37	19.00	00.00	19.00	28.46	40.54	69.00
April	4.16	00.00	4.16	11.85	00.00	11.85	3.80	00.00	3.80	28.46	59.34	87.80
May	3.69	00.00	3.69	33.36	00.00	33.36	31.11	3.08	34.19	19.80	00.00	19.80
June	5.01	00.00	5.01	8.08	00.00	8.08	15.24	00.00	15.24	28.46	12.74	41.20
July	7.69	00.00	7.69	6.08	00.00	6.08	31.11	34.03	65.14	28.46	152.54	181.00
August	8.81	00.00	8.81	33.89	00.00	33.89	31.11	00.00	31.11	28.46	9.89	38.35
September	1.00	00.00	1.00	27.24	00.00	27.24	12.68	00.00	12.68	14.87	00.00	14.87
October	3.50	00.00	3.50	5.53	00.00	5.53	31.11	1.29	32.40	28.46	26.14	54.80
November	3.59	00.00	3.59	33.89	00.00	33.89	31.11	00.00	31.11	28.46	34.74	63.20
December	0.23	00.00	0.23	33.89	00.00	33.89	6.19	00.00	6.19	2.70	00.00	2.70

F.Lbr = Family Labour
H.Lbr = Hired Labour
Human Labour Availability:
Category-I: 54.11 man days
Category-II: 33.89 man days
Category-III: 31.11 man days
Category-IV: 28.46 man days

total family labours have been used. In these busy months family labours were sufficient to manage the requirement of labour for different rice activities. The reason behind this might be that the average size of holding is small which is insufficient to absorb the total family labour. Generally they hire out their surplus labour power for livelihood.

It has been found that total land in kharif season has been used for cultivation of appropriate set of rice technologies. The cash in hand was sufficient to meet the expenditure incurred for cultivation of appropriate set of rice technologies in this farm category.

Identification of Appropriate Technologies for Category-III Farmers

A list of rice activities (Xi) drawn from existing and recommended technologies for incorporation the linear programming model for the farmers of category-III, has been given below:

Activities (Technologies)

Existing Technology
Kharif Season
HYV Paddy

Irrigated	*Unirrigated*
IR-36	IR-36
IR-50	IR-50
Ratna	Ratna
Pankaj	Pankaj
IET-5656	Sita
Sita	Masuri
Panth-IV	
Masuri	

Local Paddy

Assam Aush	Assam Aush
Khajurchari	Khajurchari
Gokulshal	Gokulshal
Kadamshal	Kadamshal
Bhasamanik	Bhasamanik
Nagrashal	Nagrashal

Irrigated	*Unirrigated*
Rajamanik	Hurkashal
Hurkashal	Laghushal
Laghushal	Sundarmukhi
Sundarmukhi	Radhashal
Radhashal	

From the table it has been seen that the total irrigated area in kharif season has been occupied by Sita, IET-5656 and two local varieties meeting the local needs, whereas, Sita and Hurkashal varieties have occupied the total unirrigated area in case of the category-III farms. The maximum irrigated land has been occupied by Sita variety accounting (1.51 acres) 24.83 per cent of total cropped area. IET-5656 has occupied only (0.24 acre) 3.94 per cent of total cropped area. Laghushal and Hurkashal both irrigated together fulfilling the local needs have occupied (0.14 acre) 2.29 per cent of the total cropped area. Unirrigated Sita variety has occupied (0.87 acre) 14.31 per cent, whereas unirrigated Hurkashal has occupied (1.42 acres) 23.35 per cent of total cropped area. In boro season the total irrigated area has been occupied by IR-36 variety accounting (1.90 acres) 31.25 per cent of total cropped area. In kharif season the percentage area of total cropped area occupied by high yielding varieties accounting 43.08 per cent, whereas the local varieties together accounting only 25.64 per cent. This result indicated that the farmers of category-III should cultivate the high yielding varieties in greater percentage in combination to local varieties which is permitted by other restriction.

Return Over Variable Costs (ROVC): The estimated ROVC for the farmers of category-III in the appropriate set of rice varieties increased to Rs. 15628.23 (175 per cent increase of existing ROVC). The ROVC in the exsiting set of rice varieties cultivated by the farmers was Rs. 5689.86.

Human Labour Requirement: It is evident from the table of monthly human labour used in different farm categories that the farmers of category-III have hired the human labour in the months of May, July, and October. These three months, perhaps, were busy in rice cultivation. In the months of August and November the entire family labours have been used to cultivate rice. The family labour was found surplus in rest of the months.

The whole land of the farmers of category-III has been used for the cultivation of the optimum set of rice technologies in kharif season. The cash in hand in this category of farms was found to be sufficient to meet the cultivation expenditure.

Identification of Appropriate Technologies for the Category-IV Farmers

A list of rice activities (Xi) has drawn from the existing and recommended technologies for incorporation of the linear programming model for the farmers of category-IV is mentioned below:

Activities (Technologies)

Existing Technologies
Kharif Season
HYV Paddy

Irrigated	*Unirrigated*
IR-36	IR-36
IR-50	IR-50
Ratna	Pankaj
Pankaj	Masuri
Masuri	Panth-IV
Sita	
Panth-IV	

Local Paddy

Assam Aush	Assam Aush
Khajurchari	Khajurchari
Kadamshal	Kadamshal
Gokulshal	Gokulshal
Bhasamanik	Bhasamanik
Nagrashal	Nagrashal
Hurkashal	
Laghushal	

Boro Season
IR-50
Recommended Technology
IR-36
Swarna
IET-5656
IET-4094

Resources Restriction: The average size of holding of category-IV farmers has been calculated as 10.40 acres. In kharif season 4.60 acres gpt irrigation and remaining 5.80 acres allotted for rice cultivation with normal rainfall condition. In boro season the entire irrigated land has been allotted for growing high yielding rice varieties. The average labour supply in every month of the farmers of this category has been accounted as 28.46 man-days. This has been treated as labour restriction. The cash in hand of category-IV farms has been estimated as Rs. 51399.39 and used as cash restriction in the model.

Appropriate Set of Rice Technologies: It has been observed from the table of appropriate set of rice technologies that only one high yielding variety should be practiced in kharif season by the farmers of category-IV. This variety is Panth-IV. In kahrif season the local rice varieties which were found to be appropriate were Laghushal and Hurkashal. However, both these varieties would meet the local needs of the farmers. In boro season, IR-50 was found to be appropriate rice variety to practice for maximizing the net return. Out of four recommended varieties only one variety, namely IET-5656 is found to be appropriate variety to cultivate by the farmers of category-IV farmers.

The area allotted to different crop varieties under the appropriate set of rice technologies in different farm categories has been presented in Table 6.16. From the table it has been found that the total irrigated land in kharif season has been occupied by IET-5656, Laghushal, and Hurkashal varieties. Whereas, Panth-IV high yielding variety alone has occupied the total unirrigated land of the category-IV farms accounting (5.80 acres) 38.66 per cent of the total cropped area. 28.00 per cent (4.20 acres) of total cropped area has been occupied by IET-5656 in kharif season. The two local varieties meeting the local needs in kharif season together occupied (0.40 aces) 2.67 per cent of total cropped area. In boro season the total irrigated area has been occupied by IR-50 high yielding variety accounting (4.60 acres) 30.66 per cent of total cropped area. In kharif season the percentage of total cropped area occupied by high yielding varieties accounting (10.00 acres) 66.66 per cent. Whereas, in the same season the local varieties occupied only (0.40 acres) 2.67 per cent of total cropped area to meet the local need of the farmers of category-IV. This result established the fact that the large farmers should cultivate high yielding varieties in high percentage of total cropped area, since their resources would permit to cultivate those varieties.

Return Over Variable Costs (ROVC): The estimated ROVC for the farmers of category-IV in the appropriate set of rice technologies increased to Rs. 42906.87. The ROVC in the existing set of rice technologies was calculated as Rs. 11849.55. An increase of ROVC by 262.00 per cent over existing ROVC has been recorded. This result indicates that the farmers of category-IV could increase the ROVC by 262.00 per cent by adopting the appropriate set of rice technologies in their fields.

Human Labour Requirement: It has been found from the table of human labour used under different farm categories that the farmers of category-IV have hired human labour round the year except in the months of January, May, September, and December. Family labour in these four months were sufficient to meet the labour requirement for rice cultivation in category-IV farms.

The total land was found to be used for the production of appropriate set of rice varieties. The cash in hand with the farmers of this class was found to be sufficient to meet the expenditure incurred to adopt the appropriate set of rice technologies.

In this context it should be noted that farmers responded that lack of capital was an important constraint in the adoption of recommended rice technologies, but in this case calculated cash in hand was found to be sufficient to meet the expenditure. The reason of non-borrowing for the adoption of rice technologies by the farmers of even a single farm category may be that the seed is supplied from the home; human labours as well as bullock labour are supplied from family. These two inputs—seed and labour involve maximum costs of production and hence, the capital required for the adoption of rice technologies is met by the cash in hand with the farmers.

Though one of the three dimensions for testing appropriate technologies is social goal, but in this analysis no specific social goal has been considered. However, covering the total rice area with high yielding varieties for optimum production and maximum profit has been considered as the social goal in this work.

7

Summary and Conclusions

In Indian economy agriculture plays an important role. It contributes a substantial share to the GNP of the country. Rice is the most important crop of Indian agriculture. Continuous increase in the size of the country's population and change of economic condition create additional demand for rice. It would be impossible to meet this additional demand for rice if the present rate of productivity is not increased substantially. As a matter of fact, an attempt has been made to replace traditional agriculture by modern one since mid-sixties through the introduction of high yielding varieties with assured irrigation and other necessary production inputs such as fertilizer, pesticides, etc. Since then a large number of improved rice production technologies have been innovated in our country. Currently, there are sufficient modern technologies in the market for rice production which are meant for high yield. The Green Revolution was concerned with the application of high yielding varieties and other inputs package for higher yield. But it has been noticed that farmers do cultivate high yielding varieties to some extent but other inputs are not used in the same tune as they are recommended. It is also true for the cultivation of local rice varieties. Though there is no dearth of improved rice technologies, only a part of the available technologies for rice production has been accepted by the farmers. As a result, rice yield in the farmers' field still remains below the potential level and consequently there exists a significant yield gap of rice. The low yield and the consequent yield gap can be explained by the low rate of adoption of improved technologies for rice production by the farmers. In one hand, the responsible factors which prevent farmers from the exploitation of full potential of the improved technologies may be of socio-economic, infrastructural, agro-biological, managerial, and technological in nature; on the other hand, the available technologies might not be appropriate for the farmers with respect to their resource endowments, local needs and social goals. Hence, the yield gap can be narrowed down either by removing the constraints responsible for application of improved rice technologies at recommended level or/by identifying the appropriate technologies for rice production which are suitable for local resource endowments and consistent with local needs and social goals. The appropriate technologies may be improved or traditional, imported or indigenous.

In the present study, attempt has been made to measure the yield gap of different rice varieties and to determine the important factors with their relative contribution on yield gap. It has also been emphasized to identify the constraints related to the adoption of improved rice technologies of its recommended level and to identify appropriate technologies for rice production. The specific objectives of the investigation are as follows:

(1) To estimate the gap between potential yield and actual yield of rice.
(2) To identify the factors responsible for yield gap in rice production and their relative contribution therein.
(3) To identify the field level constraints in the adoption of recommended rice production technologies.
(4) To identify the appropriate technologies for rice production over different farm categories.
(5) To implicate some policy measures based on the study.

Summary

A summary of the results along with major conclusions reached in the foregoing chapters is recapitulated as follows:

General Characteristics of the Sample Farmers

A comparison of various farm characteristics among different farm categories regarding size of holding, tenancy, irrigation index, cropping pattern, cropping intensity, occupational classification, educational status, information about family labour, etc. was made.

It was observed that there was predominance of marginal and

small farmers in the study area. In terms of land holding, out of 100 sample farmers the number of small and marginal farmers was 80. In true sence there was absence of big farmers which reflected the land reforms record of West Bengal State.

The average operational holdings of different farm categories varied from 0.54 acre to 10.45 acres. The average size of operational holdings for overall farm category was only 4.36 acres. It was also noticed that the system of ownership cultivation was widely prevalent accounting more than 75 per cent and the extent of tenant cultivation was negligible among the farmers. However, the share croppers recorded as bargadars and there were also patta holders.

About 46 per cent of the total sown area was found to get irrigation facilities from different sources. However, the highest irrigation index was found in category-III farms and that of the lowest in category-II. It may be noted that there was no significant difference in irrigation index over different farm categories. It may be concluded that the lack of proper irrigation facilities was one of the main causes of non-adoption of improved rice technologies in farmers' field at recommended level.

In kharif season, paddy occupied the largest area that was about 98 per cent of the total sown area. The other recorded crops were sugarcane and arum and the area covered by these two crops were negligible. In rabi season quite a large number of crops is recorded to be cultivated by the sample farmers. These crops were wheat, potato, mustard, vegetables, onion, pulses, and boro paddy. In this season also paddy was found to be the largest area occupying crop. The area occupied by boro paddy was 18.80 per cent of the total sown area. The cropping intensity of the sample farmers irrespective of farm categories was 166 per cent which indicated a good trend of double cropping in the study area and supported by higher irrigation index.

Occupational distribution of the sample farmers showed that agriculture was the main source of income and about 78 per cent of the earning members were engaged in agriculture and allied activities. However, it is interesting to note that there was a negative relationship between operational holdings and percentage of agricultural earners to total earners. Farmers with small land holding were depended very much on agriculture and allied activities and *vice versa.*

Extent of Yield Gap of Rice Varieties

The yield gap of different rice varieties was estimated through tabular method. Simple average and aggregation in terms of percentage as well as actual figures were used to estimate the yield gaps of all the rice varieties both in kharif and boro seasons. The yield gap is defined as the difference between potential yield expected from full implementation of modern rice technologies recommended and actual rice yield in farmers' field of the variety. The information regarding potential yield have been collected from the Adaptive Research Station and actual yield recorded from the fields of the sample farmers.

A substantial difference between potential yield and actual yield of different rice varieties, high yielding varieties as well as local varieties has been noticed in both the crop seasons—kharif and boro. In kharif season nine high yielding varieties were found to be adopted by the farmers whereas the number of local varieties cultivated was eleven. These high yielding varieties were IR-36, IR-50, Ratna, Pankaj, Masuri, IET-1444, IET-5656, Panth-IV, and Sita. The local varieties were Assam Aush, Khajurchari, Gokulshal, Kadamshal, Bashamanik, Nagrashal, Rajamanik, Hurkashal, Laghushal, Sundarmukhi, and Radhashal. In boro season only three high yielding varieties, viz. IR-36, IR-50, and Ratna were practiced.

In kharif season IR-36 rice variety was widely accepted by the farmers of all size groups. IR-50, Ratna, Pankaj, Sita high yielding varieties of rice were adopted by the farmers of categories-II, III, and IV. Only categories-III and IV farmers adopted Masuri, IET-5656 and Panth-IV varieties, IET-1444 was adopted only by the farmers of category-II. The performance record in terms of yield gap of the farmers of all the categories established the fact that large farmers were more efficient in adoption of high yielding rice varieties in kharif season. The reason may be that big farmers are economically stronger which helped in adoption of capital intensive rice varieties.

The highest yield gap in kharif season of high yielding varieties was found to be 7.20 qtl/ac. (36.30 per cent) in category-III. The average yield gap of category-IV farmers was recorded as 6.14 qtl/ac. (31.08 per cent), which was the lowest. The average yield gaps of HYV in kharif season in category-I and II farms were 6.62 qtl/ac.

(33.16 per cent) and 6.69 qtl/ac. (37.17 per cent) respectively. The overall yield gap of HYV in kharif season irrespective of farm size groups was recorded as 7.14 qtl/ac. (36.47 per cent). The yield gap of the high yielding varieties in kharif season irrespective of farm size was calculated and it was found that IR-50 variety had the lowest yield gap accounting only 4.90 qtl/qc. (22.02 per cent). The yield gap of Pankaj variety, i.e. 5.03 qtl/ac. (23.27 per cent) was also found substantially low in comparison to the gaps of other varieties. The highest yield gap was found in case of IET-1444 variety accounting 12.24 qtl/ac. (67.16 per cent). The yield gaps of other high yielding varieties such as IR-36, Ratna, Masuri, IET-5656, Panth-IV and Sita were calculated to be 5.92 qtl/ac. (29.69 per cent), 7.61 qtl/ac. (38.13 per cent), 8.04 qtl/ac. (48.22 per cent), 5.67 qtl/ac. (28.45 per cent) and 7.59 qtl/ac. (38.04 per cent) respectively.

Among the local rice varieties Khajurchari, Gokulshal, Hurkashal varieties were widely adopted by the farmers of all the four size groups. The farmers except category-I adopted Assam Aush, Kadamshal, Bashamanik, Nagrashal, Rajamanik, and Laghushal varieties. Sundarmukhi variety was practiced by the farmers of category-II and category-III. Categories-I and III farmers cultivated Radhashal rice variety. The yield gaps of local rice varieties with respect to farm size were 1.67 qtl/ac. (16.38 per cent), 1.47 qtl/ac. (14.14 per cent), 1.65 qtl/ac. (15.81 per cent), and 1.55 qtl/ac, (14.84 per cent) respectively. It was found that the farmers of category-II were relatively more efficient in local rice production, whereas farmers of category-III were seemed to be more inefficient in the production of traditional varieties of rice in kharif season. The yield gap of local varieties ranged between 1.03 qtl/ac. (9.97 per cent) in case of Hurkashal and 2.10 qtl/ac. (20.19 per cent) in case of Radhashal variety. This result indicated that Hurkashal local rice variety was adopted successfully whereas production inefficiency was found in Radhashal variety. The second lowest yield gap was recorded for Nagrashal rice variety accounting 1.17 qtl/ac. (11.24 per cent). The yield gap of other local varieties were calculated as 1.58 qtl/ac. (15.25 per cent) for Assam Aush, 1.81 qtl/ac. (17.40 per cent) for Khajurchari, 1.78 qtl/ac. (17.13 per cent) for Gokulshal, 1.82 qtl/ac. (17.75 per cent) for Bashamanik, 1.33 qtl/ac. (12.85 per cent) for Rajamanik, 1.62 qtl/ac. (15.63 per cent) for Laghushal, and 1.32 qtl/ac. (12,69 per cent) for Sundarmukhi variety.

In boro season the highest gap (irrespective of variety) was recorded in category-III accounting 2.32 qtl/ac. (10.72 per cent) and the lowest gap was found in category-I accounting 1.79 qtl/ac. (8.25 per cent). Ratna variety was found as maximum gap recording variety in boro season accounting 3.06 qtl/ac (14.21 per cent). The lowest gap was found in IR-36 variety accounting 1.90 qtl/ac. (8.79 per cent). The calculated yield gap of IR-50 was 1.93 qtl/ac. (8.93 per cent). This result established the fact that the large number of farmers adopted the varieties having lower yield gap in boro season.

The above result indicated that the yield gaps of the local rice varieties in kharif season were lower than that of high yielding varieties. The overall yield gap of HYVs in kharif season was 7.14 qtl/ac. (36.47 per cent) whereas; it was only 1.58 qtl/ac. (15.24 per cent). Hence the yield gap of high yielding varieties in boro season was substantially lower than that of kharif season. The overall yield gap of HYVs in boro season was recorded only 2.29 qtl/ac. (10.69 per cent). This might be due to the fact that in boro season all the production inputs were used intensively under better environmental situation and controlled irrigation. It was possible because only a part of the total cultivable land was taken for boro paddy. The local paddy needs the lower input dozes which may be the cause of lower yield gap of these varieties.

Yield Gap and Technological Gap

The yield gap of rice is a common feature in Indian agriculture for all varieties high yielding as well as local and in all seasons—kharif and boro. However, there is a substantial variation in the yield gap over farm size, variety and season. It is a well established fact that the low level of yield of rice varieties is mainly due to sub-optimal or non-application of many of the necessary input factors such as seed rate, ploughing, manuring, application of fertilizers and pesticides, weeding, etc., by the farmers in their rice fields. In other words, technological gap might be considered as the main cause of yield gap. The difference between recommended level and actual level of inputs application is termed as technological gap. A traditional belief is that the yield of a particular rice variety totally depends upon the inputs of production. That is, the level of inputs determines the level of outputs. To estimate the casual relationship between yield gap and technological gap zero order correlation matrixes was constructed. The yield gap of a farmers calculated taking average of the yield gaps of all the rice varieties cultivated by the farmer in a particular year. Similarly, technological gap of the farmer is the average gap in the application of production inputs in the adoption of all the rice varieties.

The estimated correlation coefficient of yield gap of rice and technological gap was 0.72350 for category-I farms. The correlation coefficients of categories-II, III, and IV farms were calculated as 0.59218, 0.617426, and 0.80472 respectively. The figure of the correlation coefficient of pooled data was 0.6614 which explained the fact that the level of yield gap of rice depended upon the level of inputs application by 66 per cent on an average.

In all the four categories of farms, positive correlation coefficient were established which implied that there was a direct relationship between yield gap and technological gap though the degree of association was not equally strong in all farm sizes. A high correlation coefficient indicated a close association between yield gap and technological gap. The relationship between yield gap and technological gap was stronger in categories-I and IV farmers than in categories-II and III. The result also explained that the level of rice production did not totally depend upon the biological factors only. There were many other factors which influenced the level of rice production. Farm management, supervision, etc. were such non-biological inputs which also affected the level of output.

In kharif season the correlation coefficient showed a marked difference. The highest correlation coefficient among the high yielding varieties was estimated as 0.83750 in case of Pankaj variety and the lowest correlation coefficient was 0.59068 in case of Panth-IV variety. In case of local varieties the corresponding figures were 0.5913 and 0.40425 for Radhashal and Assam Aush respectively. The overall correlation coefficient of high yielding varieties in kharif season was estimated as 0.69304, the corresponding figure for local variety was 0.48907. In boro season the highest correlation coefficient was calculated as 0.83734 for IR-36 and it was the lowest in case of Ratna variety accounting 0.70462. The overall value of the correlation coefficient in boro season was 0.75841 which was higher than both of the figures in kharif season for high yielding and local varieties. This result indicated that the high yielding varieties are more inputs/

cultural practices responsive particularly in boro season than the local rice varieties.

Identification and Evaluation of Various Production Factors Responsible for Yield Gap

As a matter of fact the level of output of rice variety depends upon the level of input application and other essential cultural practices. That is, the yield gap of rice is directly and positively related with the input gaps and gaps in other cultural treatments. In the present study yield gap was considered as dependent variable and gaps in different inputs and cultural practices such as seed rate, seed treatment, method of sowing, ploughing, application of organic manure, application of Nitrogenous and Potassic fertilizers, weeding, and application of plant protection chemicals were considered as independent variables. Multiple regression models were used to identify and measure the respective contribution to the yield gap. There was no gap at all in the seed rate and method of sowing but 100 per cent gap was recorded in case of seed treatment. Hence, these three factors were dropped from the final analysis.

In kharif season for high yielding varieties the gap in the organic manure application in rice field was found to be the most important factor in determining the yield gap for all the rice varieties in the analysis. However, the level of significance for different varieties was different. The regression coefficient of organic manure was significant at 1 per cent level of probability in case of Ratna and Pankaj varieties, it was significant at 5 per cent level of probability for IR-36, Masuri, and Sita varieties, and in case of IR-36, it was significant at 10 per cent level of probability.

The second most important factor having the effect on yield gap of high yielding varieties was the gap in the application of P-fertilizer. The coefficient of the variable was significant at 1 per cent level of probability for Ratna and Pankaj varieties, for Sita variety it was significant at 5 per cent level of probability. In case of Masuri and IR-36 varieties, the coefficient was significant at 10 per cent level of probability.

The coefficient of the gap in ploughing was significant at 5 per cent level and 10 per cent level of probability for IR-36 and Ratna variety respectively. The coefficient of N-fertilizer was found to be significant at 5 per cent level of probability for IR-50 and Ratna varieties. It was also significant at 10 per cent level of probability in case of Sita variety. The coefficient of K-fertilizer was significant at 5 per cent level of probability for Sita variety only. Weeding was found to be one of the important factors affecting yield gap and it was significant at 1 per cent level of probability for Ratna variety. The coefficient of plant protection also found significant for three varieties. It was significant at 1 per cent level of probability for Ratna variety, 5 per cent level of probability for Masuri variety and 10 per cent level of probability for Pankaj variety.

The gap in the level of ploughing for local rice varieties in kharif season was found to be statistically significant determinant of the yield gap. It was found significant at 5 per cent level of probability in case of Khajurchari and Kadamshal varieties, but the impact of this treatment was not found to be significant for other local rice varieties. The coefficient with respect to the gap in organic manure application in local rice field was also significant for Assam Aush and Kadamshal varieties at 1 per cent level of probability, in case of Khajurchari it was significant at 5 per cent level of probability and for Nagrashal variety it was significant at 20 per cent level of probability. The coefficient with respect to N-fertilizer was significant at 5 per cent level of probability in case of Assam Aush and Khajurchari rice varieties. It was also significant at 10 per cent level of probability in the case of Kadamshal and Rajamanik varieties. In case of Nagrashal variety it was found significant at 20 per cent level of probability. The regression coefficient with respect to P-fertilizer was significant at 1 per cent and 5 per cent level of probability in case of Kadamshal and Gokulshal varieties respectively. The coefficient with respect to the gap in the application of K-fertilizer was significant at 1 per cent level of probability for Kadamshal variety, and 10 per cent level of probability for Assam Aush, Gokulshal and Rajamanik varieties. It was also significant at 20 per cent level of probability in case of Hurkashal variety. The coefficient of weeding was found significant at 1 per cent level of probability for Assam Aush, Khajurchari and Gokulshal rice varieties. This was also significant at 5 per cent level of probability for Bashamanik and Kadamshal varieties respectively. The coefficient with respect to the gap in the plant protection chemical application was significant at 1 per cent probability level in case of

Gokulshal rice variety. It was significant at 5 per cent level of probability for Khajurchari, Kadamshal and Bashamanik varieties. The coefficient was also significant at 20 per cent level of probability in case of Rajamanik local rice variety.

In boro season the coefficients of the gap in manuring, the gap in the application of N-fertilizer, the gap in the application of P-fertilizer, the gap in the application of K-fertilizer, and the gap in weeding were found positively and significantly related with the yield gap of high yielding varieties. But the coefficients with respect to the gap in the level of ploughing and the gap in the application of plant protection chemicals were found insignificant. The coefficient of organic manure was significant at 1 per cent and 20 per cent level of probability for IR-36 and IR-50 varieties respectively. For IR-50 variety, the coefficient of N-fertilizer was significant at 5 per cent level of probability and it was significant at 20 per cent level of probability for IR-36. The coefficient with respect to P-fertilizer was significant at 5 per cent level of probability in case of IR-36 variety only. The coefficients of K-fertilizer and weeding both were significant at 5 per cent level of probability for IR-36 variety. In case of IR-50 variety the coefficient of weeding was significant at 1 per cent level of probability.

Factors Determining the Technological Gap in Rice Production

The productivity of rice depends upon the degree of adoption of different inputs at recommended level. But all the inputs/cultural treatments are not used as per the recommendation by the farmers There are many factors such as age of the farmers, caste of the farmer, family size, farm size, education, the economic status of the family, social participation of the farmer, percentage of irrigated area to total cropped area, index of outstanding credit, status of land ownership, utilization of mass media, utilization of cosmopolite sources of information, and participation in training programme are related with the adoption of improved rice production technologies in its recommended level. Multiple linear regression equations were fitted to the set of data for identifying and examining the factors having influence on the technological gap in rice cultivation in the study area.

The regression coefficient of the age of the farmer was found to be statistically significant at 1 per cent level in case of farm categories-I and IV and in case of category-III it was significant at 20 per cent level of probability. The overall coefficient of age of the farmer was positive and significant at 5 per cent level of probability which indicated that technological gap was supposed to be increased for old farmers.

The coefficient with respect to the caste of the farmers was found statistically significant at 10 per cent level and 20 per cent level of probability in farm categories-IV and II respectively and positively related with the technological gap but it was not found significant when the farmers were pooled.

The coefficient of family size was found to be statistically significant at 20 per cent level of probability in case of farm category-II only. The positive value of the coefficient showed higher the technological gap with bigger family size and *vice versa.* However, this coefficient was not found statistically significant in pooled data.

The coefficient with respect to farm size also statistically significant in none of the farm categories but in pooled result it showed statistically significant at 1 per cent level of probability. The positive value of this coefficient indicated that a higher technological gap in case of bigger farm size might be due to the fact that the larger farmers did not have direct relationship with the agricultural practices.

The regression coefficient of education was not found significant at all in the application of inputs and practices for rice cultivation. The economic status of the family was found positively related with the technological gap in farm category-II at 20 per cent level of probability. The overall coefficient of economic status was also found to be positively related and significant.

The coefficient with respect to social participation was not found statistically significant in any case. The coefficient was negative in all categories except category-IV farm.

The coefficient with respect to percentage of irrigated area to total cropped area was found to be statistically significant at 1 per cent level of probability in farm category-II. The negative value of the coefficient indicated an inverse relationship between technological gap and irrigation index. In other farm categories also negative regression value of the coefficient was recorded but it was not significant. The overall coefficient of irrigation index was also statistically significant at 1 per cent level of probability. The inverse relationship between technological gap and irrigation index might explain that irrigation facilities played an important role in adoption of rice technologies at recommended level. In case of assured irrigation risk in the production process was lower and application of inputs was higher. Consequently technological gap becomes lower and *vice versa.*

The regression coefficient of the index of outstanding credit was significant at 5 per cent level of probability in farm categories-II and III respectively. In both cases the value of the coefficient was negative. It was found to be negatively correlated and significant at 20 per cent level of probability for pooled data. This result indicated that the tehnological gap would decrease with the increase of outstanding credit.

The coefficient with respect to the result of land ownership was significant at 1 per cent level of probability in case of farm categories-II and III. In case of farm category-IV the regression coefficient was significant at 20 per cent level of probability. However, the overall regression coefficient of land ownership status was negative and statistically significant at 10 per cent level of probability. The negative value of the regression coefficient implied that the technological gap in case of the owned land was lower than in case of leased in/leased out land.

The coefficient of the mass media was found to be statistically significant in all farm categories and as well as pooled data. It implied that mass media can play a crucial role by informing the farmers to implement the improved rice technologies at recommended level. It was significant at 1 per cent level of probability for the farmers of categories-I, II, and III, and at 20 per cent for category-IV farmers. It was also statistically significant at 1 per cent level of probability in pooled data. The negative value of the regression coefficient indicated that higher the utilization of mass media lower would be the technological gap.

The coefficient of the utilization of cosmopolite sources of information was found to be statistically significant at 20 per cent level of probability in farm categories-I and III. It was also significant at 1 per cent level of probability in case of category-IV farmers.

In case of category-I farm the coefficient of the participation in training programme was statistically significant at 20 per cent level of probability but positively related with technological gap. In other categories it was negatively related but insignificant. The overall result showed a negative coefficient but statistically not significant. It indicated that participation in training programme had no impact in the application of modern technologies for rice production. The reason may be the other factors of non-adoption are too strong.

Constraints in the Adoption of Recommended Rice Technologies as Perceived by the Farmers

In the market there are sufficient improved as well as local technologies for rice production. But it has been estimated that the farmers accept in some cases only a part of the improved rice technologies packages, and in other cases, they do not implement at all the technologies required for higher production. There are different constraints which prevent the farmers from the exploitation of full potential of improved rice technologies. 49 such constraints were scored on the basis of 4-point scale. The factors responsible very much as perceived by the farmers was scored-3, much-2, not so much-1, and not at all-0. Factor analysis technique has been used to identify the most influencial factors which were the cause of non-adoption of improved rice technologies at prescribed rate. In the present study 12 such variables were selected on the basis of Eigen value. The Eigen value of each of these 12 variables was greater than 1. The technological gap was considered as dependent variable of this set of analysis.

It has been seen that 12 variables which were alleged by the farmers as more important to prevent them from implementation of improved rice technologies. These factors were lack of land ownership (X_1), lack of irrigation facilities (X_4), non-availablity of irrigation in time (X_6), lack of capital (X_{10}), lack of adequate credit (X_{12}), lack of marketing facilities (X_{15}), low market price of rice (X_{18}), high labour wages (X_{23}), not profitable (X_{24}), lack of technical knowledge for field application (X_{25}), lack of advice and guidance (X_{29}) and lack of knowledge about proper recommendation (X_{29}).

Lack of land ownership (X_1) has been found to be the most important factor with Eigen value accounts to 4.19749 and its percentage of variation is 10.8. It has been rightly found because the farmers take much care and independent decision in the implementation of improved rice technologies at recommended level.

The second most important factor is the lack of irrigation facilities (X_4). The Eigen value of this factor is 4.02686 and its percentage of variation accounts to 10.3. This factor has also been rightly selected because without assured irrigation facilities improved rice technologies cannot be implemented as prescribed.

Non-availability of irrigation at time (X_6) and lack of capital (X_{10}) both are having Eigen value more than 3. The Eigen value of X_6 was 3.66439 and its percentage of variation was 9.4. The corresponding figures of X_{10} are 3.04092 and 7.8.

The Eigen values of lack of adequate credit (X_{12}), lack of marketing facilities (X_{15}), low market price of rice (X_{18}) were 1.66157, 1.59030 and 1.41601 respectively. The corresponding figures of percentage of variation were calculated as 4.3, 4.1, and 3.6. The factors have been influenced as perceived by the farmers in the adoption of recommended rice technologies.

The Eigen values of high wages of labour (X_{23}) and non-profitability are estimated as 1.38052 and 1.36702 respectively. The corresponding figures of the percentage of variation are 3.5 in each case.

The last three factors namely lack of technical knowledge for field application(X_{25}), lack of advice and guidance (X_{29}) and lack of knowledge about proper recommendation (X_{46}) were also important. The Eigen values of these factors were 1.19561, 1.07798, and 1.01711 respectively. The corresponding figures of the percentage of variation have been estimated as 3.1, 2.8, and 2.6. The selected 12 factors together explained 65.7 per cent variation. This figure explained the fact that these twelve factors are responsible for technological gap by 65.7 per cent. That means, the technological gap can be reduced by 65.7 per cent if these 12 constraints are removed.

Identification of Appropriate Technologies in Rice Production for Different Synthetic Farm Situation

The available rice technologies, perhaps, are not suitable *in toto* for the farmers and hence, they can not implement the recommended rice technologies in their fields. Therefore, it is imperative to identify the best suited alternative technologies and the appropriate one from among the available farm technologies. To identify the appropriate technologies for rice production linear programming technique has been used. The appropriate technologies may be traditional or improved and indigenous or imported, need to be tested in the three dimensions of (i) resource appropriateness, (ii) needs appropriateness, and (iii) goals appropriateness.

For this purpose, considering two types of technologies, viz. Existing Technology (obtained from synthetic farm situation) and Recommended Technology (obtained from Block and Zonal Adaptive Research Station of the study area), an optimum set of technologies which is appropriate for the particular setting of synthetic farm has been identified separately for different categories of farms.

Category-I: The average size of holding of this category of farmers has been recorded as 0.54 acre only. Nearly 50 per cent land was recorded as irrigated. Boro paddy was practiced by the farmers of this category. The average labour supply from the family for every month has been accounted as 54.11 man days. Cash in hand has been estimated as Rs. 7498.68 and treated as cash restriction.

In kharif season for the farmers of category-I IR-36 (unirrigated), Hurkashal (irrigated) and IET-5656 (recommended) are found to be the appropriate set of rice technologies which maximizes the net return over variable costs. The area occupied by unirrigated IR-36 was (0.28 acre) 28.75 per cent of total cropped area and Hurkashal occupied only (0.03 acre) 3.75 per cent of total cropped area. This result indicated that category-I farmers should allot the entire land for high yielding varieties after meeting the local need. In boro season IR-36 has occupied the entire irrigated land which is (2.6 acres) 32.50 per cent of total cropped area.

The Return Over Variable Cost (ROVC) of category-I farm of the appropriate set of rice technologies has been calculated as Rs. 2445.78. It was Rs. 1624.25 in existing set of rice technologies. The ROVC increases by 29.50 per cent. The family labours of this category farmer are sufficient to meet the labour demand to implement the appropriate set of rice technologies. The surplus labour, generally hired out by the farmers of this category. The cash in hand is also found to be sufficient for rice production in appropriate set of technologies.

Category-II: The average size of holding of the farmers of this category has been recorded as 1.94 acres. In kharif season the irrigated area has been accounted as 0.79 acre and 1.15 acres has been allocated to kharif paddy with normal rainfall situations. The average monthly family labour supply has been estimated as 33.89 man-days. The cash in hand of this farm category has been recorded as Rs. 20378.00.

In kharif season the appropriate set of rice technologies for the farmers of category-II would be Pankaj (unirrigated), Assam Aush, Laghushal, Hurkashal, Boro Ratna, and recommended IET-5656. Laghushal and Hurkashal satisfied the local need of the farmers. Kharif Pankaj with normal rainfall has occupied (0.17 acre) 6.25 per cent of total cropped area. Assam Aush has occupied the maximum kharif land with normal rainfall accounting (0.37 acre) 35.66 per cent of the total cropped area. In this season recommended IET-5656 has occupied the maximum irrigated land accounted as (0.68 acre) 25 per cent of the total cropped area. The local need meeting varieties together have occupied only (0.11 acre) 4.04 per cent of the total cropped area. In boro season the entire irrigated land (0.79 acre) 29.05 per cent has been occupied by Ratna high yielding variety.

For this farm category the estimated ROVC is Rs. 8842.70 with appropriate set of technologies. The ROVC with existing set of technologies is Rs. 4388.75, that is, an increase by 101.46 per cent. The human labour required to cultivate the appropriate set of technologies has been supplied from the family. There was no need to hire labour. The cash in hand was also found to be sufficient for the cultivation of appropriate set of rice technologies.

Category-III: The average size of holding of the farmers of category-III has been accounted as 4.20 acres. The area covered under irrigation is 1.90 acres and 2.30 acres has been allotted to kharif paddy with normal rainfall situation. The average monthly labour supply of the farmers of category-III has been estimated as 31.11 man-days. The cash in hand has been estimated as Rs. 20806.75

The appropriate set of rice tehnologies for the category-III farm in kharif season would be Sita (irrigated), Sita (unirrigated), Laghushal (irrigated), Hurkashal (irrigated), Hurkashal (unirrigated), and recommended IET-5656. However, Laghushal and Hurkashal (irrigated) satisfy the local needs of the farmers. In boro season only IR-36 is the appropriate paddy variety.

The highest irrigated land has been occupied by Sita variety accounting to (1.51 acres) 3.04 per cent of the total cropped area. Laghushal and Hurkashal both irrigated together fulfilling the local needs have occupied (0.14 acre) 2.29 per cent of the total cropped area. Unirrigated Sita variety has occupied (0.87 acre) 14.31 per cent, whereas unirrigated Hurkashal has occupied (1.42 acres) 23.35 per cent of total cropped area. IR-36 only occupied the entire boro land accounts to (1.90 acres) 31.25 per cent. The high yielding varieties (kharif and boro) have occupied about 75 per cent of total cropped area.

The estimated ROVC for the farmers of category-III in the appropriate set of rice technologies increased to Rs. 15628.23 (175 per cent increase over existing ROVC). In the months of May, July and October, the farmers of category-III have hired human labour for the production of rice in appropriate set. In all other months, family labours are sufficient to meet the labour demand of the farm.

The total land of the farmers of category-III has been used in kharif season for the cultivation of the optimum set of rice technologies. The cash in hand was also sufficient to meet the expenditure incurred for the adoption of appropriate set of rice technologies.

Category-IV: The average size of holding of category-IV farmers has been calculated as 10.40 acres. The size of irrigated land is 4.60 acres and the balance 5.80 acres are unirrigated. The average family labour supplied in every month of this category has been recorded as 28.46 man-days. The cash in hand of the farmers of category-IV has been estimated as Rs. 51399.39.

In kharif season the appropriate set of rice technologies in category-IV farms would be Panth-IV (unirrigated), Laghushal and Hurkashal both irrigated and recommended IET-5656. The total kharif irrigated land has been occupied by recommended IET-5656 with two local rice varieties, namely Hurkashal and Laghushal fulfilling local needs of the farmers. The area occupied by IET-5656 is recorded as (4. 20 acres) 28 per cent of total cropped area. The local varieties occupied the area (0.40 acre) 2.67 per cent of total cropped area. 5.80 acres (38.66 per cent) of the total cropped area has been occupied by unirrigated Panth-IV in kharif season. In boro season the total irrigated area has been occupied by IR-50 variety accounting

(4.60 acres) 30.66 per cent. Meeting the local needs the farmers of category-IV should practice high yielding varieties in kharif season to maximize profit.

The estimated ROVC for the farmers of category-IV in the appropriate set of rice technologies has increased to Rs. 42906.87, an increase of Rs. 262.00 per cent over the ROVC of the existing set of rice technologies. The existing ROVC has been recorded as Rs. 11849.55. In the category-IV farm human labour is to be hired round the year except the months of January, May, September, and December to implement the appropriate set of rice technologies in fields.

The total land has been used and the cash in hand would be sufficient to meet the expenditure incurred for the adoption of appropriate set of rice technologies.

In this context it should be noted that cash in hand is found to be sufficient for the adoption of appropriate set of rice technologies for all categories of farms though according to farmers lack of capital was an important constraints in the adoption of improved rice technologies as perceived by the farmers. The reason of non-borrowing for cultivation of rice may be that farmers do use the seed from home, bullock labour, and human labour both are supplied from family. Hence, a little capital is necessary to purchase the other production inputs and practices; since, seed and labour include maximum production costs.

Conclusions

The following conclusions have been drawn on the basis of the results of the present study.

(i) A substantial difference between potential yield and actual farm yield of different rice varieties—high yielding as well as traditional varieties, has been noticed in both the crop seasons—kharif and boro. However, the yield gap of different high yielding varieties is not uniform. Some high yielding varieties are having bigger gap in comparison to other. The yield gap of local varieties in comparison to high yielding varieties in kharif season was lower in all categories of farms.

It can be concluded that high yielding varieties required more inputs package at recommended level which are not met by the farmers, whereas local varieties can be grown with less capital investment and these varieties are less susceptible to pest and diseases. Moreover, the farmers are having vast experience in the cultivation of local varieties by traditional method but the modern rice varieties require the knowledge about the appropriate method of inputs application. Consequently, the yield gap of the local varieties is lower than the high yielding varieties.

(ii) The yield gap of all the high yielding rice varieties in boro season are substantially lower than those of respective varieties in kharif season. This may indicate that in boro season farmers can apply production inputs and other cultural practices more intensively because in that time only a part of the total farm size is cultivated for boro paddy. Moreover, in this season rice is practiced only under assured irrigation. In boro period farmers can look after the boro rice field more carefully and all the inputs can be applied in time.

(iii) There is a direct relationship between yield gap and technological gap with varied degrees of association. It may be concluded that the gap can be narrowed down by decreasing the technological gap. The correlation coefficient of high yielding varieties in kharif season is higher than that of local rice varieties. But it is lower than that of high yielding varieties in boro season. This may imply that boro rice are more input responsive than high yielding varieties in kharif season.

(iv) No farmer in the study area adopted the seed treatment practice which might be an important cause of the yield gap of rice varieties.

(v) Gaps in the use and application of inputs and methods considered in this analysis have significant impact on the variation of yield gaps of different rice varieties in kharif season though the level of significance of various factors is not uniform.

(vi) In boro season all the inputs/practices except gaps in ploughing and application of plant protection chemicals have the significant bearing on rice yield at different levels of significant.

(vii) Except education and social participation all the factors considered do have significant bearing on the transfer of new rice production technologies. It may be concluded that formal education and social participation need not be given emphasis in the adoption of improved rice technologies.

(viii) It can be concluded that the lack of ownership of land prevents the farmers from the adoption of recommended rice technologies. Lack of irrigation facilities also discourages the farmers to implement the improved rice technologies. Non-availability of irrigation in time is another factor which prevents farmers from the adoption of improved technologies for rice production. It can be concluded that the economic factors such as lack of capital, lack of adequate credit, lack of marketing facilities, low market price of rice, high wages of labour and non profitability are also responsible for non-adoption of improved rice technologies as perceived by the farmers. But economic condition was not related with the technological gap. It seems that the infrastructural constraints are more prominent than the socio-economic and biological constraints. Lack of knowledge about proper recommendation, lack of advice and guidance, and lack of technical knowledge for field application also prevent farmers in the application of modern inputs and practices for rice production in a prescribed manner.

(ix) In all the four categories of farms, the appropriate set of rice technologies include high yielding varieties in higher percentage with local varieties in a small area to fulfil the local needs of the farmers. In category-II, Assam Aush and in category-III, Hurkashal (unirrigated) were found appropriate in local rice varieties. This appropriate set includes both local and high yielding varieties which maximizes the profit of the farmers.

(x) Only one recommended rice variety that is IET-5656 is found to be appropriate in all the four categories of farms.

(xi) The family labours are recorded as surplus in the categories-I and II farms. In categories-III farm only a few labours have been hired. Only in category-IV farms the size of hired labour is bigger.

(xii) The cash in hand in all four categories of farms are sufficient to meet the expenditure incurred for implementation of appropriate set of rice technologies. There is no need of borrowing for this purpose.

(xiii) The total land in kharif season in all categories has been exhausted in the implementation of appropriate set of rice technologies. There is no surplus land in any of the farm categories.

(xiv) It can be concluded that the Return Over Variable Costs (ROVC) can be increased by a significant extent by implementing the appropriate set of rice technologies in all the four categories of farms.

Policy Implications

The results of the study have several implications which are discussed below:

(i) The yield gap of the high yielding varieties as well as local varieties can be decreased by increasing the adoption of all the inputs required for rice production at its recommended level.

(ii) Farmers in the study area may undertake IR-50 and Pankaj varieties as these two high yielding varieties were found lower in comparison to other high yielding varieties in kharif season.

(iii) As the yield gaps of local rice varieties are lower in comparison to high yielding varieties, farmers should increase the land under local rice particularly Hurkashal and Nagrashal whenever possible after satisfying the objective function of the producers.

(iv) The land under boro cultivation may be increased to get more profits as the productivity of high yielding varieties in boro season is higher than the corresponding varieties in kharif season. Policies should be framed to encourage the boro rice cultivation by supplying the necessary inputs along with irrigation facilities.

(v) Farmers may increase the application of manure in rice fields to increase the productivity of rice, since it has higher degree of correlation with productivity of different rice varieties.

(vi) Seed treatment practice is a necessary input of better yield. So farmers should be encouraged to follow this treatment.

(vii) Irrigation facilities, status of land ownership, index of outstanding credit and utilization of mass media facilities may be increased which were found significantly related with adoption behaviour of the farmers.

(viii) As the lack of ownership of land is one of the causes of non-adoption of improved technologies for rice production. Government can frame the policy to transfer the ownership to the cultivators—maybe tenancy farmers or registered *bargadars,* so that they will take care for permanent improvement of land for higher productivity with the implementation of appropriate set of rice technologies.

(ix) Irrigation facilities should be extended. Less than 50 per cent cultivable land has been covered under irrigation. Efforts should be made to increase the percentage of irrigated area so that improved rice technologies are adopted. This will also help to increase the area under boro cultivation which is more profitable. All the sources of irrigation should be given importance to extend the irrigation facilities.

(x) Government can also frame policy related with price of the rice, wages, marketing facilities and provision of easily available credit so that farmers can earn profit by producing more rice with improved rice technologies.

(xi) As lack of information about improved technologies, lack of advice and guidance and lack of technical knowledge for field application were found to be the causes of non-adoption of improved rice technologies, government should take decision to employ the Krishi Projukti Sahayak (KPS) in the Panchayat level so that he can provide the current information about modern rice technologies to the farmers with proper advice and guidance. He also can help the farmers for the application of these technologies in the rice field. If not Government should abolish the department of agriculture except its research branch and its resources can be merged with irrigation department with sufficient importance.

(xii) The efficacy of any technology should not be straightaway discarded which is apparently not befitting with the constraint matrices. They should irrespective of their genesis (indigenous or imported, local or improved) and nature, be properly tested for their appropriateness.

(xiii) The appropriateness of the rice technologies can be tested with respect to resources endowment only.

Bibliography

Abalu, G. and Yayock, J. (1980), Adoption of Improved Farm Technology in Northern Nigeria, *Quarterly Journal of International Agriculture,* Vol. 19., No.3.

Adgaonkar, D.A. (1978), *The Problems of New Land Holders in Adoption of Agricultural Technology,* Unpublished M.Sc. (Ag.) Thesis; N.A.U., Parbhani.

Adhikari, S.R. and Patel, A.A. (1987), Socio Psychological Correlation of Technology Utilization by Nepalese Farmers, Gujarat Agril. *University Research Journal,* 11(2): 52-54 (c.f.) World Agril. Economic Rural Sociology Abstract, 29(B): 592).

Agarwal, U. (1967), *Social Consequences of Technology Change,* Nie Heights; Delhi.

Ahmed, I (1977), *Appropriate Rice Production Technology for Bangladesh, Agricultural Mechanization in Asia* (197); 8(4), 38-44.

Ali, M.I. and Barthakur, G.C. (1973), *An Assessment of Small and Marginal Farmers Development Programme in Assam: A Case Study of Kharif Programme of Kamrup District, Assam.;* Assam Agricultural University; Agro-Economic Research Centre for North-East India, Jorhat.

Allport, G.W. (1935), *Attitudes and A Hand Book of Social Psychology (Ed.)* C. Murchison, Clark University Press, Worchester.

Arya, S.R.S. and Shah, S.L. (1984), *New Technology for Rainfed Agriculture and Identification of Constraints on its Adoption in Mid-Hills of U.P., Agricultural Situation in India;* 39(7): 487-496.

Asian Development Bank (1977), *Asian Agricultural Survey,* 1976, Manila; Philippines; 490.

Athavale, M.C. (1973), *Small Farmers Development Agency in M.P.,* Agro-Economic Research Centre, Jabalpur.

Balasubramanian, U.A. (1980), *A Study on Innovativeness in relation to Adoption of High Yielding Rice Technology and Sequential Socio-Economic Changes in Farming Community of Tamil Nadu,* Unpublished Ph.D. Thesis; Division of Agricultural Extension, I.A.R.I., New Delhi.

Balasubramanian, U.A. (1981), *An Analysis of Socio-Technological Gap in Lab to Land Programme,* Research Report, Centre for Agricultural and Rural Development Studies, Tamil Nadu Agricultural University, Coimbatore.

Ballav Sri and Prasad Guru (1985), Lack of Technical Knowledge Attributed to Gap in Technology, *Journal of Extension System:* 78-80.

Barker, R. (1978), *Yield and Fertilizer Input in I.R.R.I., Interpretive Analysis of Selected Papers from Changes in Farming in Selected Areas of Asia,* Los Banos; Philippines.

Basrur, R.S. (1949), Notes on Economics of Mechanized Agriculture, *Indian Journal of Agricultural Economics,* Vol. IV(i); 78-84.

Bhardwaj, K. (1974), *Production Conditions in Indian Agriculture, A Study Based on Farm Management Surveys,* Syndicate of the Cambridge University Press, London.

Bhaskaran, K. and Praveena, C. (1982), Adoption of Improved Dryland Agricultural Technology in an Integrated Dryland Agricultural Development Project in Andhra Pradesh, *Indian Journal of Extension Education,* 18 (3&4); 37.

Bhilegaonkar, M.G. (1976), *A Study of Fertilizer Utilization Behaviour of Farmers and Communication Patterns Under Constraints,* Unpublished Ph.D. Thesis; Division of Agricultural Extension; I.R.R.I., New Delhi.

Biggs, S.D. (1976), *Appropriate Agricultural Technology in Bangladesh Two Papers: Discussion Paper,* Institute of Development Studies, Sussex University (1976); No. 90, pp. 37, Ford Foundation, Dacca, Bangladesh.

Bordolai, N. (1978), *Extent of Adoption of Selected Improved Paddy Cultivation Practice by Small Farmers in the Nowgaon District of Assam,* Unpublished M.Sc. (Ag.) Thesis, P.A.U., Ludhiana.

Bose, A.N. (1982), *Appropriate Technology and Appropriate Socio-Economic Structures,* Paper Presented at the National Workshop on Appropriate Rural Technology at NIRO, Hyderabad, August 19-22.

Bose, S.P., Dasgupta, S., and Das, S.P. (1963), *Beyond the Economic Frontier Bulletin,* Cultural Research Institute, I: 20-30.

Bose, S. (1967), *Orissa's Agricultural Condition: A Case Study with Reference to the Rice Crop,* AICC Economic Review; 18(18); pp. 23-31.

Bowonder, B. (1981), The Myth and Reality of High Yielding Varieties in Indian Agriculture, *Development and Change,* 12(2), pp. 293-313.

Bruce, F. Johnston and Soren T. Nielsen (1966), Agricultural Structural Transformation in Developing Economy, *Economic and Cultural Change,* 14(3); pp.279-301.

Byerlee, D., Collinson, M. (*et al.*), (1980), *Planning Technologies Appropriate to Farmers—Concepts and Procedures,* Mexico, D.F.; Mexico Economic Programme, CIMMYT.

Cattell, R.B. (1966), *'The Screen Test for the Number of Factors Multivariate Behavioural Research,* 1; 245-276.

Cernuda, J.C. (1980), Appropriate Technology and Community Development in Haiti, In *Desarrallo Rural En Las Americas* (1980), 12(2), 125-139.

Chaddha, G.K. (1978), *The HYV Technology and the Changing Farm Size-Productivity Relationship, A Study of Punjab,* India, (14); 1-13.

Chand, D.B. (1984), *A Study of the Constraints Interacting the Transfer of Rice Technology in Nepal,* Unpublished Ph.D. Thesis, Gujarat Agricultural University, Navasari Campus; Gujarat.

Chand, D.B. (1986), *A Study of the Constraints Interacting the Transfer of Rice Technology in Nepal, Thesis Abstract, Directorate of Publications,* HAU, Hissar, 12(1); 20.

Chapman, J.A. (1984), *Design and Analysis of Appropriate Technology for Small Farmers,* Cropping System Research in the Philippines, In Dissertation Abstracts International; 44(7), p. 2205.

Chavan, B.M. (1979), *Social and Economic Implication of HYV Programmes in Aurangabad Division,* M.Sc. (Ag.) Thesis, Division of Agricultural Extension; N.A.U., Parbhani.

Chidambaram, M.A. (1977), Agricultural Technology for Small and Marginal Farmers, *ARDC News* (1977), 6(1), pp. 3-8.

Choudhury, B.K. and Ghosh, M.G. (1968), HYV's in Birbhum, West Bengal—Its Achievement and Prospect, *I.J.A.E.* 23(4); pp. 141-142.

Choudhury, B.N. (1973), *A Study of Factors Related to the Effectiveness of Communication in Fertilizer Promotion,* Unpublished Ph.D Thesis, Division of Agricultural Extension; I.A.R.I., New Delhi.

Choudhury, K.P. (1967). *Farmers' Response to Farm Planning Programme in an IADF Block, Proceedings of Research Foundation Bulletin,* Birsa Agricultural University, Sabour; (8 & 9); pp. 109-112.

Choudhury, S. (1988), *Impact of National Transfer Technology Programme of Visva-Bharati,* Unpblished Ph.D. Thesis; P.S.B., Institute of Agriculture, Visva-Bharati.

Choudhury, S. and Dasgupta, D. (1986), *Farm Level Constraints in a Transfer of Improved Varieties of Major Crops Due to a Transfer of Technology Programme,* Paper Presented at the 74th Session of Indian Science Congress at Bangalore.

Central Rice Research Institute (1980), *Annual Report,* CRRI, Cuttack.

Central Rice Research Institute (1981), *Annual Report,* CRRI, Cuttack.

Dakshinamurthi, C. (1973), Recent Trend in Water Management, *Agricultural Mechanization in Asia,* 4(2), pp. 27-28.

Dasgupta, Biplab (1980), Panchayat, Bhumi-Sanskar Gramonnyan, Calcutta, W.B., Comprehensive Area Development Corporation, pp. 77-80.

Dasgupta, Biplab (1980), *The New Agrarian Technology and India,* The Macmillan Company of India Limited, Madras.

Dasgupta, D. and Sarkar, A. (1983), *Towards a Better Agriculture in the Sub-humid Tracts of W.B.—An Overview of the Infrastructural and Socio-Economic Constraints.* Paper Presented at the National Seminar on Constraints in the Crop Prodcution of Sub-humid Zones, at College of Agriculture, Visva-Bharati, Nov. 26-28.

Davidson, B.R. and Martin, B.R. (1965), The Relationship Between Yields on Farms and in Experiments, *Australian Journal of Agricultural Economics;* Vol. 9, No. 2, pp. 129-140.

Deb, F.C. and Sharma, M.L. (1969), Characteristics of Adoptions of Improved Farm Practices, *Indian Journal of Extension Education,* 10(3); 204-209.

Desai, D.K. (1984), *Analysis of Rice Production and Productivity in Eastern India, Agricultural Situation in India,* 39(5), pp. 335-341.

Deshmukh, V.U., and Bajaj, S.S. (1981), *Impact of Different Information Sources on the Adoption of High Yielding Varieties of Paddy in Akola Tribal Block of Ahmednagar District.*

Dhaliwal, A.J.S. (1963), *A Study of Some Important Factors Affecting the Adoption of Few Selected Agricultural Practices by the Cultivators of Ludhiana C.D. Block,* Unpublished M.Sc. (Ag.) Thesis, Department of Extension Education; P.A.U., Ludhiana, Punjab.

Diez Patier, F. (1980), *The Relationship Between Various Socio-economic Characteristics and Adoption of Modern Techniques by Farmers of the Inter Plateau of Galicia, Sociological Agrorias,* 5: 95-108.

District Annual Plan, (1991-92), Birbhum, West Bengal.

Directorate of Economics and Statistics (1967), *Regional Difference in Crop Output Growth in Punjab* 1952-53–1964-65, Directorate of Economics and Statistics; Ministry of Food, Agriculture, Community Development and Corporation; Government of India, Nov. 1967.

Dube, S.C. (1958), *India's Changing Villages: Human Factors in Community Development in Madras,* Allied Publishers Pvt. Ltd.

Dube, S.K. (1961), Factors Influencing the Adoption of Improved Farm Practices in Berala Block, Jabalpur, M.P., *Indian Journal of Extension Education;* 32: 214.

Dubey, U.D. (1968), *Scope of Plant Protection Measures in Kshetra Samiti, Pipraich; Dist. Gorakhpur, U.P.,* Unpublished M.Sc. (Ag.) Thesis, Govt. Agriculture College, Kanpur.

Dutta, Amlan (1968), *Religion, Education and Development;* Orient Longman, Culcutta, p. 27.

Dutta, D.C. and Gogoi, K. (1973), *An Assessment of Small and Marginal Farmers Programme in Assam: A Case Study of Kharif Programme in Nowgoan District, Assam,* 1972-73, Agro-Economic Research Centre for North-East India, Assam Agricultural University, Jorhat.

Ernest, R.S. (1973), *A Study of Communication Utilization Behaviour of Small and Big Farmers and Its Implication to Communication Strategy,* Unpublished Ph.D. Thesis, Division of Agricultural Extension, I.R.R.I., New Delhi.

Fale, J.B., Thakare, G.C. and Borude, S.C. (1985), *An Economic Analysis of Yield Gap in Rice in Ratnagiri District, Maharastra, Agricultural Situation in India,* 39(12); pp. 925-929.

FAO (1980), *Information Note on Water for Agriculture, Issued at FAO Regional Office for Asia and Far East,* No.11, July 1978: 10

Fliegel, F.C. (1957), Farm Income and the Adoption of Farm Practices, *Rural Sociology,* 22: 159-162.

Fliegel, F.C. (1960), Obstacle to Change for Low Income Farmers, *Rural Sociology,* 25: 349-351.

Flit, I. (1981), *Appropriate Technology or Appropriate Handling of Technology, The Case of Agricultural Industry,* CEDEAL, Cali, Colombia.

Freeman, D.M. and Azadi, H. (1983), Education, Power Distribution and Adoption of Improved Farm Practices in Pakistan, *Community Development Journal,* 18(1) 60-67 (Ex. 5 tab: 23 reb; OC), Department of Sociology, Colorado State University, U.S.A.

Gangadharan, T.P. (1980), Impact of Credit on the Use of Modern Farm Input, *Agriculture and Agro-Industries Journal,* 13(3), pp. 15-18, N.D.R.I., Karnal.

Garg, J.S., Singh, C.N. and Prasad, V. (1976), Impact of the Increase in Input Prices on Farm Productivity: A Case Study, *Indian Journal of Agricultural Economics,* 31(3): 130-131.

Gee-Clough, D., Q. Day-Peterson, J. (1985), Technology for the Small Farmers, Agricultural Research to Help the Small Scale Farmer in Developing Countries, *Extension Bulletin,* Food and Fertilizer Technology Centre, Taiwan, No. 222, 1-61, 8-21., Division of

Agricultural and Food Engineering Asian Institute of Technology.

Gour, R.A. (1979), *Transfer of Technology: A Tool for Modernizing Agriculture,* Paper Presented at the National Workshop on Management of Transfer of Farm Technology, NIRD, Hyderabad, November 19-24.

Gill, K.S. (1982), *Post Harvest Market Technology for Cereals (paddy and wheat)—Needed Improvements (The Punjab Case) in Rural Technology, Rural Institution and Rural Poorest,* (Edited by M. Greeley and M. Howes) Comilla; Bangladesh; CIRDAP (1982), 152-165 (En, 11 tab, 11 reb, OC).

Gomez, K.A. (1977), On Farm Assessment of Yield Constraints: Methodological Problems, Constraints in HighYields on Asian Rice Farms: *An Interim Report,* IRRI, Manilla, Philippines.

Gomez, K.A.; Herdl, R.W.; Barker, R. and De Dutta, S.K. (1979), *A Methodology for Identifying Constraints to High Rice Yields in Asia;* IRRI, Los-Banos, Philippines: 24-47.

Grewal, R.S. and Singh, P.C. (1975), Prospect and Problems of Marginal and Small farmers in Haryana, *Indian Journal of Agricultural Economics,* 30(3): 257.

Gupta, D.P. (1969), *Evaluation of HYV Programme 1968-69. A Study in District of Aligarh, U.P.,* Agro-Economic Research Centre; Delhi University, Delhi (Memio).

Gupta, D.S. and Kurkkute, K.D. (1978), New Rice Technology and Small Farmers, *Eastern Economist,* 71(14), pp. 666-668.

Hanumantha Rao, C.H. (1966), Alternative Explanation of the Inverse relationship Between Size and Output Per Acre, *Indian Economic Review* 1(2): 1-12.

Henry, C.M. (1978), *Farmer Response to New Technology: An Economic Appraisal of the Case of Guyana, Report,* Institute of Agricultural Economics, University of Oxford, No.10, p. 26.

Herdt, R.W. and Mandac, A.M. (1980), *Modern Technology and Economic Efficiency of Philippines Rice Farmers, Economic Development and Cultural Change,* IRRI, Los-Banos, Philippines.

Herdt, R.W. and Wickman, T.H. (1975), Exploring the Gap Between Potential and Actual Yields in Philippines, *Food Research Institution Study.* 14: 163-181.

Hildebrand, P.E. (1980), Motivating Small Farmers, Scientists and Technicians to Accept Change, *Agricultural Administration,* Vol. 8., No. 5.

Hirsch, H.G. (1943), Crop Yield Index, *Journal of Farm Economics,* 25(3): p.583.

Hodgedon, L.L. and Harpal Singh (1966), *Adoption of Agricultural Practices in Madhya Pradesh,* N.I.R.D.

Hoffer, C.R. and Strangland, D. (1958), Farmers' Attitude and Values Relation to Adoption of Approved Practices in Crop Growing, *Rural Sociology,* 23: 112-120.

Hoque, M.Z., Ahasan, E. and Hossain, M. (1978), Constraints to High Rice Yields, Bangladesh, 1975-77, In *Farm Level Constraints to High Rice Yield in Asia,* IRRI Publications, pp. 49-85.

Huijeman, A. (1987), Choice and Uncertainty in a Semi-Subsistence Economy: *A Study of Decision Making in a Philippines Village,* Amsterdam, Netherland Konouk Instituut Uoor de Tropen (1986), 15: 335 (c.f. World Agril.: Rural Socio. Abst. 29(4): 279-280).

ICRISAT (1982), Annual Report (1981), ICRISAT; Andhra Pradesh.

IRRI (1977), Constraints to High Rice Yields on Asian Farms: *An Interim Report,* Los-Banos, Philippines.

IRRI (1978a), Research Highlights of 1977, Los-Banos, Philippines; 122.

Jaiswal, N.K. and Arya, H.P.S. (1981), *Transfer of Farm Technology in India in Management of Transfer of Farm Technology—Some Experiences (Ed.),* NIRD, Hyderabad.

Jaiswal, N.K. (1965), *A Study of Factors Associated with Low Level of Adoption of Improved Agricultural Practices,* Unpublished Ph.D. Thesis; IARI; New Delhi.

Jetly, S. (1977), Modernising Indian Peasants: A Study of Six Villages in Eastern U.P., *Asian Educational Services; India.*

Joff, A.E. (1980), *Investigation of the Spatial Diffusion of Agricultural Innovations in Sierra Leone: The Case of Swamp Rice Farming,* Dissertation Abst. International 41(2), p. 805.

Jogarathan, J., Dias, J.N.S. and Jayawardena, A. (1977), *Constraints to High Rice Yields in Sri Lanka, Farm Level Constraints to High Rice Yields in Asia: 1974-77,* IRRI, Los-Banos, Philippines.

Kalirajan, K. (1980), The Constraints of Location Specific Research to Agricultural Productivity, *Indian Journal of Agricultural Economics,* Vol. XXXV, No.4, Oct-Dec.

Khalon, A.S. and Singh, K. (1981), *Economics of Farm Management in India: Theory and Practice,* Allied Publishers Pvt. Ltd., New Delhi.

Kamphol, A. (1977), Rice Production and Relevant Agricultural Research, *16th Lal Bahadur Shastri Memorial Lecture;* IRRI, New Delhi.

Kamphol, A. and Others (1977), *Rice Production and Development in Thailand, Constraints to High Yield on Asian Rice Farms: An Interim Report,* IRRI, Philippines.

Koch, B.M. (1987), The Role of Knowledge in the Adoption of Agricultural Development Practices, *South African Journal of Extension* (1985) 14: 11-16 (c.f. World Agril. Econ. Rural Socio. Abst. 29(1): 68).

Kuada, J.B. (1984), *Agricultural Technology Development in the Third World:* Working Papers, Developemnt Research Series, Development Research Group, Aslborg University.

Kulshreshtha, J.P. (1978), Role of Operational Research in Integrated Rural Development, National Symposium on Increasing Rice Yields in Kharif, held at CRRI, Cuttack; 360.

Kuo, Y.C. and others (1977), *Rice Production in Taiwan's Agriculture Constraints to High Yields on Asian Rice Farms: An Interim Report,* IRRI, Manila; Philippines.

Lakshminarayan, V. and Rahim, K.M.B. (1983), *Some Constraints of Institutional Credit in Agriculture: A Case Study,* Paper Presented in the National Seminar on constraints in Crop Production of sub-Humid Zones, College of Agriculture, Visva-Bharati, Nov. 26-28.

Land, K.C. (1969), Principles of Path Analysis; Edgar P. Borgate (Eds.), *Sociological Methodology,* Jessey Ban. San. Fransisco, pp. 3-7.

Lees, S.C. (1979), *Choice of Technology in Irrigated Agriculture, Studies in Third World Societies* (1979) 7, 37-48; Humber College, U.S.A.

Legans, J.P. and Loomis, C.P. (1971), *Behavioural Change in Agriculture: Concepts and Strategies for Influencing Transition;* Cornell University Press, Ithca, U.S.A.

Librero, A.R. (1983), *Socio-Economic Factors in Agrotechnology Transfer in the Philippines, Research Extension Series,* College of Tropical Agriculture of Human Resources, University of Hawai (1983), No. 027, 81-85.

Lionberger, H.P. (1960), *Adoption of New Ideas and Practices: A Summary of the Research Dealing with the Acceptance of Technology Changes in Facilitating Social Change,* Ames, Iowa State University Press.

Masud, A.B. (1978), *Factors to Consider in the Transfer of Appropriate Technology to the Rural Areas, in Technology for Rural Development (Ed.),* S. Radha Krishnan and M.M. Singh; Indian Institute of Science, Bangalore.

Manshm, M. (1980), *Credit Technology: The Needs of the Small Farmers.*

Manson, M. Hode (1979), *Concept and Models for the Development of Appropriate Technology for Rural Areas in Fundamental Aspects of Appropriate Technology, (Ed.)* J.De Schulter, G. Benber, Delft University Press, Sijthet and Noordhofr, International Publication, 1975, p. 55.

Marothia, D.K. (1983), *Constraints Analysis of Farm Level Adoption of Paddy Technology in Raipur District, M.P.,* J.N. Krishi Viswa-Vidyalaya, p.11.

Matlock, W.G. (1984), Problems and Solutions in Agricultural Technology Change or Transfer, *International Journal for Development Technology* (1984) 2(2): 93-105., Irrigation and Water Management Institute, Arizona University.

Matiramani, D.P., Mishra, B.L. and Bisan, P.K. (1979), Constraint Analysis of Paddy Production in Balaghat, *Eastern Economist* (1979), 73(8), pp. 406-411.

Matiramani, D.P. and others (1979), Developing Appropriate Production Technology—A Case of Soyabeans in M.P.; *Agril. Situation in India,* 34(8), 523-528.

Mead, M, (1954), *Cultural Patterns and Technological Change,* UNESCO; 2nd Ed,: The Ijsel Press Ltd.; Deventer; Holland, pp. 209-210.

Mecoemick, S.; Macdonald, T.; Windlep, P., and Elering, C. (1984), *Issues in Technology, Agriculture and US Foreign Aid: A Technical Memorandum in Washington,* D.C., U.S.A., 1984.

Mishra, J.P.' Singh, R.I. and Singh, G.N. (1976), Impact of Increase in Input Prices on Profitability in Agriculture, *Indian Journal of Agricultural Economics,* 31(3), 131.

Misiko, D.A.M. (1976), *Incentives and Disincentives Influencing Farmers in the Adoption of Agricultural Innovation: The Case of Bangoma District, Kenya,* Dissertation Abst. International, (1977) 38(3) p.974, (En. Diss, Cornell Univ.; U.S.A.; 1976, 363 p. Order No. 77-18, 180).

Monu, E.D. (1984), Transfer of Technology to Small Farmers in Nigeria, *Eastern Africa Journal of Rural Development,* 12(1/2); pp. 237-247.

Morris, J. (1983), Small Holder Mechanization Man, Animal or Engine? *Outlook on Agriculture* (1983); 12(1), 28-33, National College of Agricultural Engineering, Siclsoe, Benford, U.K.

Mosher, A.T. (1966), *Getting Agriculture Moving: Essentials for Development and Modernization,* New York, p. 13.

Mosher, A.T. (1971), *Agricultural Development (Ed.), Behaviourial Change in Agriculture,* Cornell University Press, Ithca.

Mukherjee, D.K. (1977), *Gap Analysis—An Effective Production Increase Concept in Rice,* Summary of Lecture Delivered at the State Level Training Meeting of Rice Production, Held at Purulia, Department of Agriculture, W.B.; India (memeo).

Mukhopadhyay, S.K. (1982), *New Perspective of Agriculture and Rural Development, Everyman's Science,* April-May, 1982, pp. 54-57.

Murthy, A.S. and Singh, S.N. (1974), *Communication Behaviour of Farmers,* New Heights, Delhi.

Nadkarni, M.V. and Ghosh, P.K. (1978), Instability in Rainfall and Agricultural Yields in a Drought Prone District (Tumkur), *Indian Journal of Agricultural Economics,* (392), 32-46.

Nair, G.T. (1969), *A Multi Variate Study on Adoption of High Yielding Paddy Varieties by the Farmers of Kerala State.,* Unpublished Ph.D. Thesis , Division of Agricultural Extension, IRRI, New Delhi.

National Commission on Agriculture (1976), Ministry of Agriculture and Irrigation, Govt. of India, New Delhi.

National Council of Applied Economic Research (1979), *Impact of Indo-German Fertilizer Educational Project in W.B.: An Evaluation,* NCAER. New Delhi.

Ongkili, M.J. and Quilkey, J.J. (1986), Determinants of the Adoption of Agricultural Technology in Developing Countries-Review, *Journal Economic,* Malaysia (1983), No.8; 76 (c.f. World Agril. Eco. Rural Sicio. Abst. 28(5): 234-235.

Oram, P. (1980), Development of Appropriate Crop Technology for Irrigated Agriculture in the Mediterranean and Near East, *Agriculture and Development,* 3, pp. 45-70.

Osmania University (1962), *Seminar on Technology Transfer to Rural Areas,* Osmania University, Hyderabad.

Pal, T.K. (1974), *Changes in Rice Farming in Selected Areas of Asia* (Cuttack, Orissa), IRRI. Manila, Philippines.

Pal, T.K. (1978), *Yield Constraints in Rice,* Paper Presented at Workshop on Rice Yield Constraints. Held at Kendy, Sri Lanka.

Pandey, S.M. (1974), *Development of Marginal Farmers and Agricultural Labourers,* Sri Ram Centre, New Delhi.

Padheria, M.M. and Patel, I.C. (1975), Adoption Pattern of Recommended Farm Practices in Gujarat, *Indian Journal of Extension Education,* 11(1&2), 70.

Pandit, U. (1984), *Impact of Lab to Land Programme on the Adoption Behaviour of Farmers in Munger District of Bihar,* Unpublished M.Sc. (ag.) Thesis, Department of Extension Education, R.A.V., Pusa.

Pandya, D.N. (1981), *Transfer of Plant Protection Techniques in Management of Farm Technology—Some Experiences* (Ed.): N.I.R.D, Hyderabad.

Parthasarathy, G. (1969), Tenancy Legislation in Labour Surplus Economics and Economic Analysis—A Note, *Indian Economic Journal,* 16(3), pp. 371-374.

Parthasarathy, G. (1975), *Changes in Rice Farming in Selected Areas of Asia* (West Godavari, A.P.), IRRI, Manila, Philippines.

Parthasarathy, G. and Prasad, D.S. (1977), *Spatial Variations in Rates of Growth of Productivity in Rice: An Analysis of 'Top' and*

'Bottom' Districts, Department of Co-operatives and Applied Economics, A.P. University, Waltair, A.P., India (memeo).

Patel, I.C. (1976), *Change Agents Role in Motivating Small and Marginal Farmers for Action,* Paper Presented at National Seminar on New Agricultural Technology and Extension Strategy for Small and Marginal Farmers, Ludhiana.

Patel, M.N. (1965), *A Study of Small Farmers and Their Problems as Related to Agriculture,* Unpublished M.Sc. (Ag.) Thesis, Division of Agriculural Extension, IARI, New Delhi.

Patil, M.P. (1964), *Adoption of Improved Practices and Its Effect on Paddy Yield, Agricultural Situation in India,* 18(10), pp. 671-674.

Pearson, A.W. (1982), *Approaches to Appropriate Agricultural Technology in Egypt: A Special Case Study, AID Research and Development Abstracts* (1982), 10(1/2) 63.

Pongprayoon, C. (1979), *Determinants of Crop Choice: A Case Study of Farmers Behaviour in the Kampaeng Saen Irrigation Project,* Thailand, Dissertation Abst. International, A (1980) 40(B), p. 4744.

Ponnuswamy, K.A. (1979), *A Study on Yield Gaps in India's Crops: A Micro Analysis,* Unpublished M.Sc. (Ag.) Thesis, Divisional Agricultural Extension, IARI, New Delhi.

P.R.A.I., U.P., Lucknow (1968), *Problems of Small Cultivators in U.P.:* An Evaluation Study Report.

Prasad, S.D. (1967), *Study of Socio-Economic and Technological Changes in Some Villages in Gaon Ki Our Movement Launched at College,* Unpublished M.Sc. (AG.) Thesis, Govt. Agriculture College, Kanpur.

Prasad, C., Chaudhury, B.N. and Nayar B.B. (1987), *First Line Transfer of Technology Projects,* I.C.A.R., Krishi Anusandhan Bhavan, New Delhi.

Prenberton-Pigott, C.R. (1987), Raising Awareness: Appropriate Technology for Rural Development, *Development Southern Africa* (1987), 4(1).

Programme Evaluation Organization (1968b, and 1968c), *Evaluation Study of the HYV Programme,* Kharif 1967, First Report (memeo); Planning Commission, Govt. of India, New Delhi.

Programme Evaluation Organization (1968), *Evaluation Study of the HYV Programme*—Kharif 1967, Second Report (memeo), Planning Commission, Govt. of India, New Delhi.

Programme Evaluation Organization (1969), *Evaluation Study of the HYV Programme*—Rabi, 1968-69; Paddy and Jowar; Vol. II (memeo); Planning Commission, Govt. of India, New Delhi.

Quasem, M.A. and Hossain, M. (1979), *Fertilizer Use in Two Selected Areas of Bangladesh,* Bangladesh Development Studies, 7(4), pp. 69-86.

Radhakrishna Menon, K. and Doraiswami, K.M. (1975), Critical Analysis of the Extension Agencies Contact with Small Farmers, *The Madras Agricultural Journal,* Vol. 62911-12, pp. 645-649.

Radhakrishna Menon, K. and Knight, A.J. (1976), *Extension Strategy for Small and Marginal Farmers,* Paper Presented at National Seminar on New Agricultural Technology and Extension Strategy for Small and Marginal Farmers, Ludhiana.

Radhasyam, (1965), *A Study of Socio-Economic Factors Affecting the Adoption and Retension of Improved Agricultural Practices* in C.D. Block, Khairabad, District Sitapur, Agricultural College, Kanpur.

Raheja, S.K. and Singh, R. (1981), *Lab to Land in Garchi Randhala in Management of Transfer of Farm Technology: Some Experiences (Ed.), NIRD, Hyderabad.*

Rai, B. (1985), Strategies for Increasing the Production of Kharif Crops in Bihar, *Farmers and Parliament,* 20(2), 11-12.

Rai, R.N. (1967), Diffusion of Information and Farmers' Response to an Improved Farm Practices, *Research Extension Bulletin,* Bihar Agricultural College, Sabour, 8(9), 116-118.

Rajagopalan, V. (1975), *Changes in Rice Farming in Selected Areas of Asia* (South Arcot, Tamil Nadu), IRRI, Manila, Philippines.

Rajagopalan, V. (1981), Summaries of Group Discussion: Subject to Long Term Prospects of Agricultural Growth Viewed in the Light of Soil-climate, Technological and Institutional Constraints and Costs Involved in their Removal, *Indian Journal of Agricultural Economics,* Vol.XXXVI, No.1.

Rama Rao, B. (1969), *Impact of Agricultural Extension Programme on Small Farms of Hyderabad District,* APAV, Rajendranagar, Hyderabad.

Ramachandran, P.K. (1974), *A Multi-Variate Study on Information Source Utilization by Big, Medium and Small Farmers,* Unpublished M.Sc. (Ag.) Thesis, University of Agriculture Sciences, Dharwar.

Rao, P.V.G.K. (1969), *Economic Analysis of HYV Programme in Punjab: A Study of IR-8 Paddy in Amritsar District Kharif 1968-69,* Agro-Economic Research Centre, Delhi University, (memeo), 1970.

Rauf, A. (1984), *A Study on the Impact of T and V Extension System in Changing Communicational Behaviour of Farmers in Nepal,* Unpublished M.Sc. (Ag.) Thesis, Department of Extension Education, R.A.V., Pusa, Bihar.

Rawal, T. (1981), *An Analysis of Factors Affecting the Adoption of Modern Varieties in Eastern Nepal,* Research Paper Series, HMG-USAID-A/D/C, Project of Training Nepalese in Agricultural Research and Development Planning (1981), No. 11, p.13, Agricultural Projects Services Centre, Kathmandu, Nepal.

Reddy, A.A. (1981), *Essential Linkages for Effective Transfer of Agricultural Technology: A System Approach in Management of Transfer of Farm Technology—Some Experiences* (Ed.), NIRD, Hyderabad.

Reddy, M.S.K. (1962), *A Study on Adoption of Improved Agricultural Practices as Function of Some Socio-Economic Factors and Sources of Information,* Unpublished M.Sc. (Ag.) Thesis, Division of Agricultural Extension , IRRI, New Delhi.

Reserve Bank of India (1975), *The Small Farmers' Development Agencies (1972-73): A Field Study,* RBI, Bombay, p. 23.

Reserve Bank of India (1976), *Marginal Farmers' and Agricultural Labourers Development Agencies (1972-77): A Field Study,* RBI, Bombay.

Robertson, A. (1981), Technological Innovation and Their Social Impact, *International Social Science Journal,* Vol.33, No. 3, pp.437-440.

Rogers, E.M. and Sevenning, L. (1969), *Modernization Among Peasants: The Impact of Communication,* New York, Holt, Rinehart and Winston.

Roychowdhury, S.P. (1975), *Problems of Fertilizer Use and Crop Production,* Economic and Scientific Research Foundation, New Delhi.

Roy, P., Fliegel, F.C., and Sen, L.K. (1968), *Agricultural Innovation Among Indian Farmers,* National Institute of Community Development, Hyderabad.

Roy, R.N. (1960) Causes of Success and Failure of Improved Farm Practices, *Research Foundation Bulletin,* Bihar Agricultural College, Sabour, Bihar, 5: 35-36.

Ryan, B., and Gross, N. (1950), Acceptance and Diffusion of Hybrid Seed Corn in Two Iowa Communities, Ames; Iowa Agri. Exp. Sta. *Research Bulletin,* 372.

Ryan, J.G. and Binswanger, H.P. (1979), Socio-Economic Constraints in the Semi-Arid Tropics and ICRISAT Approach, ICRISAT Symposium, Hyderabad.

Sagar , R.L. (1983), *Study on Agro-Economic, Socio-Psychological and Extension Communication Variables Related with the Farmers' Productivity of Major Field Crops in Haringhata* Block, B.C.K.V., W.B.

Sahay, R.R. (1960), *Role of Size of Farm, Farm Income and Farming Efficiency in the Adoption of Improved Agricultural Techniques,* Unpublished M.Sc.(Ag.) Thesis, Bihar Agricultural College, Sabour, Bihar.

Saini, G.R. (1971), Holding Size, Productivity and Some Related Aspects of Indian Agriculture, *EPW;* 6(26), A/79-A/65.

Saini, J.C. (1972), *Assessment of Credit Needs and Deposits Mobilization in Union Territory of Delhi,* Unpublished M.Sc. (Ag.) Thesis, Division of Agricultural Economics, IARI, New Delhi.

Sen, D. (1975), A Suggested Paradigm of the Innovation Decision Process, Paper Presented at the National Workshop on Management of Transfer of Farm Technology at NIRD, Hyderabad, Nov. 19-24.

Sengupta, S. and Ghosh, M.G. (1968), *HYVP for Rice Performance in Bengal District,* EPW; 9(43), A. 26-A.28, 1968.

Sen, S.R. (1984), Agricultural Productivity in Eastern India (Vol. 1), Report of the Committee on Agricultural Productivity in Eastern India, RBI, Bombay.

Setty, B. (1978), *A Study of the Technological Gaps in Adoption of Fertilizer and the Constraints Involved,* Unpublished M.Sc. (Ag.) Thesis, Division of Agricultural Extension, IARI, New Delhi.

Shah, S.M. (1980), *Technology for Strengthening Rural Base, Commerce,* Vol.141, No. 3628, Annual No., pp. 21-23.

Shandilya, R.S. (1985), *A Critical Analysis of Technological Gap in HYV Paddy Culture in IRDP Village in North Bihar,* Unpublished M.Sc. (Ag.) Thesis, R.A.V., Bihar.

Sharma, S.R. and Nair, G.T. (1974), A Multi Variate Study of Adoption of HYV Paddy, *Indian Journal of Extension Education;* 10(1-2): 30-35.

Silier, O. (1980), *Some Aspect of Turkish Agricultural Structure During the 1970's,* Studes Balkaniques, No. 2.

Singh, A.I. (1974), *A Study of Adoption of HYV of Paddy and Its Associated Practices by Manipur Farmers,* Unpublished M.Sc. (Ag.) Thesis, IARI, New Delhi.

Singh, A.K. (1981), *Study of Some Agro-Economic, Socio-Psychological and Extension Communication Variables Related With the Level of Fertilizer Use of the Farmers,* Unpublished Ph.D. Thesis, Department of Agricultural Extension; B.C.K.V., W.B.

Singh, B.K. (1971), *A Study of Low Level of Agricultural Progressiveness of Small Farmers and Their Socio-Economic Behaviour,* Unpublished Ph.D Thesis, IARI, New Delhi.

Singh, D. and Srivastava, V.K. (1970), *Adoption Problems of Small Farmers in U.P.,* Research Extension Education, Edited by K.N. Singh, C.S.S. Rao and B.N. Sahay, *Indian Society of Extension Education Division of Agricultural Extension,* IARI, New Delhi.

Singh, D. *et al.* (1970), Small Scale Farmers: Technologies and Extension Implication, Paper Presented at National Seminar on New Agricultural Technology and Extension Strategy for Small and Marginal Farmers, Ludhiana.

Singh, D.N. (1963), *A Study of the Factors Associated With Adoption of Improved Agricultural Implements in the Development Block*

Kalyanpur, District Kanpur, Unpublished M.Sc. (Ag.) Thesis, Govt. Agricultural College, Kanpur.

Singh, L. and Sharma, R.K. (1986), *Rice Production System in Neck-Deep of Constraints Causing Concern of Paddy Growers,* Journal of Extension System, 2(2): 32-35.

Singh, L.S. (1984), *A Study on Profile Characteristics of Farmers in Relation to Adoption of Scientific Rice Production Practices in Valley and Hilly Regions of Manipur State,* Unpublished M.Sc. (Ag.) Thesis, R.A.V., Bihar.

Singh, N.N. (1966), Selected Factors Affecting Innovativeness of Farmers, *Review of Extension Research,* B.A.C, Sabour; Vol. 6; pp.14-17.

Singh, R., (1983), Selected Characteristics of Farmers in Relation to Adoption of Farm Mechanization, *Indian Journal of Extension Education,* 19(3&4): 16-17.

Singh, R. (1979), Appraisal of Some Selected Variables in Farm Adoption Research, *Indian Journal of Social Research,* 20(3): 203-222.

Singh, R.P. (1977), *Farmers Response Towards HYV of Paddy,* Unpublished M.Sc. (Ag.) Thesis, Ranchi Agricultural College, Kanka.

Singh, S.N. (1969), *A Study of Adoption of HYV and Investment Pattern of Additional Income by Farmers in Delhi Territory,* Unpublished Ph.D. Thesis, Department of Agricultural Extension, IARI, New Delhi.

Singh, S.N. and Singh, K.N. (1970), A Multi Variate Analysis of Adoption Behaviour of Farmers, *Indian Journal of Extension Education,* 6(3-4): 39-45.

Singh, S.N. (1968), Social Psychological Consideration in Agricultural Production, in Singh, K.N. (Ed.) *Towards a Dynamic Agriculture,* Division of Agricultural Extension, IARI, New Delhi.

Singh, T.R. (1975), *Analysis of Rationality of Decision Making in Relation to the Adoption of Innovations of Varying Nature,* Unpublished Ph.D Thesis, Division of Agricultural Extension, IARI, New Delhi.

Singh, T.R., Singh, R.I., Singh, Y.P., and Singh, R.K. (1976), Impact of Rising Prices of Fertilizers on the Level of Their Use and

Farm Productivity, *Indian Journal of Extension Economics,* 31(3):132.

Singh, U.S. and Jha, D.N. (1971), A Normative Analysis of the Impact of Capital Availability on Farm Income and Demand for Term Credit of Farms in Delhi, *Indian Journal of Agricultural Economics,* Vol. 26, No. 4; pp. 524-532.

Singh, Y.P. (1974), *Problems of Transfer of Agricultural Technology,* Occupational Papers, Department of Extension Education, H.A.V., Hissar.

Sinha, I.M. (1978), *A Study of Selected Factors Associated with Adoption of Chemical Fertilizers,* Unpublished M.Sc. (Ag.) Thesis, Govt. of Agricultural College, Kanpur.

Skromme, L.M. (1980), *Appropriate Agricultural Mechanization in the Developing Countries,* In Proceedings of the Agricultural Sector Symposia, January 7-11, 1980.

Sriballav (1964), *A Study of Factors Affecting Adoption of Improved Implements in Development Block,* Ajitmal, Etawah, Unpublished M.Sc.(Ag.) Thesis, Govt. of Agricultural College, Kanpur.

Supe, S.V. (1969), *Factors Related to Different Degrees of Rationality in Decision Making Among Farmers,* Unpublished Ph.D. Thesis, IARI, New Delhi.

Swaminathan, M.S. (1977), *Sciences and the Conquest of Hunger,* Concept Publishing Co.; New Delhi, pp.52-149.

Swaminathan, M.S. (1978), *Recent Advances in Agriculture, Science and Agriculture,* 44(1): 227.

Swanberg, K.G. (1980), *Small Farmer Technology Adoption—Reducing the Constraints Caused by the Requirements—Limitation Gap,* Department Discussion Paper, Harvard Institute for International Development, Harvard University No.88, pp. 30.

Swindale, L.O. (1979), Problems and Concepts of Agro-Technology Transfer Within the Tropics, ICRISAT Symposium.

Tandon, R. (1979), On the Relevance of Appropriate Technology for Growth and Employment, *Indian Journal of Economics* (1979), 59(234): 319-338.

Timmer, C.P. (1982), Appropriate Technology for Food Production and Rural Development, The Rural Sector from a Food Policy Prospective, in Research in Domestic and International

Agricultural Business Management, *A Research Annual,* Vol. 3 (1982).

Tripathy, A. (1977), *A Study of Technological Gap in Adoption of New Rice Technology in Coastal Orissa and the Constraints Responsible for the Same,* Unpublished Ph.D. Thesis, Division of Agricultural Extension, IARI, New Delhi.

Veda, M. (1984), *Agricultural System Efficiency: A Case Study of Japanese and Philippino Rice Farming, Dissertation Abstracts International,* A (1984) 45(2) ; 641-642 (En.Diss, Columbia University, 1983, pp. 303.

Veeraswamy, S. and Bahadur, T. (1979), Some Psychological Correlates of Adoption of Improved Rice Technology by Small Farmers of South Arcot District, *Indian Journal of Extension Education,* 15(3&4):88.

Waghmare, V.S. and Waghmare, S.K. (1985), Lab to Land Programme: A Far Crying Filip to Gujarat's Agriculture, *Journal of Extension System* 1(1): 70-71.

West Bengal District Gazette—Birbhum Annual Production Plan on Agriculture 1989-90, Birbhum.

Wilkening, E.A. (1952), Acceptance of Improved Farm Practices in Three Coastal Plain Countries, *North Carolina Agric. Expt. Sta. Tech. Bulletin;* 40: 1407-1417.

Wilkening, E.A. (1953), Adoption of Improved Farm Practices as Related to Family Factors, Wisconsin Agric. Expt. Sta. *Research Bulletin;* 183, Madison, Wisconsin.

Yojiro, H. and Ruttan, V.W. (1970), Agricultural Productivity Differences Among Countries, *The American Economic Review,* December 1970, pp. 895-911.

Zinyama, L.M. (1988), Farmers' Perception of the Constraints Against Increased Crop Production in the Subsistence Communal Farming Sectors of Zimbabwe, *Agricultural Administration and Extension:* pp. 97-107.

Index